W9-BNA-972

THE SHAMELESS CARNIVORE

The SHAMELESS Carnivore

A Manifesto for Meat Lovers

SCOTT GOLD

Broadway Books
New York

PUBLISHED BY BROADWAY BOOKS

Copyright © 2008 by Scott Gold

All Rights Reserved

Published in the United States by Broadway Books,
an imprint of The Doubleday Broadway Publishing Group,
a division of Random House, Inc., New York.
www.broadwaybooks.com

BROADWAY BOOKS and its logo, a letter B bisected on the
diagonal, are trademarks of Random House, Inc.

Excerpt from "Osso Buco" from *The Art of Drowning*, by Billy Collins, © 1995.
Reprinted by permission of the University of Pittsburgh Press.

Book design by Jennifer Ann Daddio

Library of Congress Cataloging-in-Publication Data
Gold, Scott.
    The shameless carnivore : a manifesto for meat lovers /
Scott Gold. — 1st ed.
        p. cm.
    1. Food of animal origin—United States. 2. Cookery
(Meat) 3. Food habits—United States. I. Title.
TX371.G65 2008
641.3'06—dc22

                                    2007031029

ISBN 978-0-7679-2651-5

PRINTED IN THE UNITED STATES OF AMERICA

1   3   5   7   9   10   8   6   4   2

For

Harriett Goldberg,

and the memory of

Melvin Goldberg

And for the

City of New Orleans

Wherever I am, you will always be home.

CONTENTS

PART I
All Creatures, Great and Small

PART II
The Tour de Boeuf

Some hae meat and canna eat,

And some wad eat that want it,

But we hae meat and we can eat,

And sae the Lord be thankit.

—*The Selkirk Grace*, attributed to Robert Burns (1759–1796),
Scottish national poet

Vegetarians are cool. All I eat are vegetarians—

except for the occasional mountain lion steak.

—*Kill It and Grill It*, Ted Nugent (1948-   ),
Motor City Madman

THE SHAMELESS CARNIVORE

PROLOGUE

I am the great and mighty warrior Beowulf, bravest of the Geats, a hulking, sweaty tower of muscle and masculinity feared by man and creature alike. After days locked in battle with a pair of vicious monsters—the murderous Grendel and his equally bloodthirsty mother—I have returned, weary but victorious, to Heorot, the majestic mead hall of King Hrothgar. The king himself seats me at the head of the Viking warriors' long table, so that I might lead them in a meal of exultation so vast it will become known as the feast to end all feasts.

My appetite is profound.

With a clap of the king's hands, I am beset by voluptuous serving women, their silken tresses flowing as though on currents of enchanted air, each bearing a hefty pewter tray with a different delicacy: magnificent racks of lamb and legs of mutton, dripping with fat; whole sides of slowly roasted beef, the tender meat almost falling from the bone; mas-

sive flanks of wild oxen; smoked loin of venison; suckling pigs brought right from the fiery spit; a host of broiled and roasted foul—plump and juicy turkeys, chickens, guinea hens, pheasants, and peacocks; goat and yak meat cubed and skewered; mountains of plump sausages; a dizzying variety of strange and exotic animals—snake, alligator, ostrich, even llama—all served succulent and steaming.

I devour everything, using bare hands to tear into each new, savory delight. The fragrant juices drip down the side of my face, deep into my beard and down my chest, and I smile a broad smile. The Viking warriors around me bellow lyrical odes to battles fought and friends lost, and we slake our thirst with barrel after barrel of the country's finest mead, celebrating the victory of our lives. At this moment, everything comes to a vertiginous, heady crescendo. The meat, the comradeship, the women, the drink: in all of creation, there has never been a moment finer than this.

Then I wake up.

I blink a few times, survey my surroundings, and realize that I am not, in fact, the great and mighty warrior Beowulf. I am a pale, bespectacled publishing grunt who spends most of his days inside underneath fluorescent lighting. Hell, I don't even have a beard. And my small Brooklyn studio apartment is, sadly, a far cry from a Viking mead hall (though I do have a worn folding-leaf table from Ikea). I sigh, wipe my bleary eyes, and have a nice long yawn and a stretch.

Then I go to the refrigerator in search of bacon.

Hello. My name is Scott, and I am a carnivore.

I love meat. I always have. You could plunk me down on the therapy couch and have the shrewdest analyst drill into my memories like a deranged Texas oilman, and I doubt he'd uncover a single time in my life when I haven't delighted at the thought of a perfectly grilled filet, a slab of ribs, or even just a good old-fashioned hot dog. For years, I've harbored this passion like some sort of dirty secret. It didn't keep me from enjoying the occasional half-pound hamburger or barbeque brisket platter, but these days, if you're looking to make a good impression, you'd be safer ordering a salad than a fourteen-ounce T-bone. Sadly, I can count on one hand my friends who regularly patronize a butcher shop. (Can *you* name the butcher shop nearest your home?) And no, the meat section at your local McGroceryStore doesn't count. I'm talking about an honest-to-God butcher shop, the kind of place that proudly displays slaughtered animal carcasses in the front window, where you can ask for hearts and blood and entrails and they'll answer you, straight-faced, with "What kind and how much?"

I don't get it: where at one point in American history a vegetarian would have been branded as a godless communist and advised to return forthwith to the CCCP, abstaining from the consumption of animal flesh these days is largely viewed as an enlightened life decision, even though it's not what most of us do. And to make things worse, we have to deal with the admonishments of anemic, skeletal celebrities who try to pass off the notion that it's perfectly okay to subsist on a diet of cigarettes, croutons, and energy drinks while pumping botulism toxin into their faces, so long as we don't eat the defenseless animals. I'm loath to criticize anyone for limiting their diet because of sincere religious convictions—I'm Jewish after all, though my love for pork products, cheeseburgers, and shellfish will forever trump my fidelity to the laws of kashrut—but it must be said:

The defenseless animals taste really, really good.

So this is my rallying cry. A call to arms. I believe that there's a veritable army of carnivores out there, ready and waiting for someone to come forth waving that blood-red banner high, unabashed, in true carnivorous splendor. And if, as I suspect, that army—a legion of honest, meat-loving individuals who are made to feel morally lacking simply because they consume in a way that's so natural and elemental—is longing to be vindicated, and should you, gentle reader, be among them, I'm here to say that you are not alone.

Repeat after me: I am a carnivore, and I'm damned proud of it.

Carnivorism: A Philosophy

It doesn't take a genius IQ to arrive at the realization that we are living in a nation obsessed with meat. It's not just that Americans consume 218.3 pounds of beef, chicken, turkey, and pork per person annually*; the whole *idea* of meat has invaded the public consciousness with staggering zeal. Judging by what many believe to be the cultural barometer of meat eating in America—the fast-food industry—the year I began working on this book, 2005, may well be viewed as a banner year for carnivorous excess.

There was Paris Hilton in that infamous Carl's Jr. advertisement, bikini clad and slick with suds, sexing up a Bentley while holding a cheeseburger approximately the size of her head—a direct appeal to that glorious trifecta of the American male id: sexy girls, fast cars, and,

---

* As of 2003, according to the American Meat Institute. Do the math, and it adds up to over 85 *billion* pounds total. The AMI is a national trade association representing companies that process 70 percent of U.S. meat and poultry and their suppliers throughout America.

of course, red meat (I'm still wondering why they didn't decide to show SportsCenter somewhere in the background). Burger King introduced its Meat'Normous Omelet Sandwich, a gargantuan breakfast offering filled with sausage, bacon, ham, two egg patties, and cheese. Not to be outdone by the King, Hardee's unveiled its Monster Thickburger, which manages to incorporate two third-of-a-pound slabs of Angus beef, four strips of bacon, three slices of cheese, and mayonnaise on a buttered sesame seed bun (1,420 calories and 107 grams of fat), prompting the Center for Science in the Public Interest, an advocate for nutrition and health, to coin the term "food porn." And then, in a display of the free market one-upmanship that made this country great, a humble Pennsylvania eatery called Denny's Beer Barrel Pub decided that even Hardee's had undershot the mark and unleashed unto the world the Belly Buster, a fifteen-pound cheeseburger with enough caloric content to feed thirty to forty people (a cup and a half of relish; a cup and a half each of mayonnaise, mustard, and ketchup; a head of lettuce; two onions; three tomatoes; and twenty-five slices of cheese atop ten and a half pounds of ground beef and a bun specially crafted by a local bakery)—eat it in under five hours and you get the meal for free, plus $350, a T-shirt, and your name on a wall-of-fame plaque. I'll hazard a guess that the T-shirt is of the XXXL variety.

The result of this near-orgiastic embracing of gigantic meat? Eager guys crashed the Carl's Jr. website with download requests for Paris's ad, Hardee's significantly increased its profits due to media attention, BK had so much success with the humongous omelet sandwich that it now offers a *triple* Whopper and a *quadruple* Stacker, and the Belly Buster was enthusiastically featured on the morning-show circuit, placing Denny's Beer Barrel Pub squarely on the map of America's great palaces of gluttony, alongside such institutions as the Big Texan, home of the seventy-two-ounce steak, and, naturally, Nathan's of Coney Island, proud host of the annual July Fourth hot-dog-eating contest.

Oddly, as I watched all this unfold I felt a growing sense of unease. Meat was *everywhere*. So why did I feel so, dare I say it . . . queasy?

After much introspection, an epiphany: A fifteen-pound cheese-burger might seem the perfect embodiment of what a proud carnivore wants, but despite the laudable ambition behind the Belly Buster, the burger itself is little more than a false idol. A Golden Calf, if you will. By wallowing in this sort of greasy crapulence, we meat lovers are actually falling into enemy hands without recognizing it. We've given not just militant vegetarians but the general public all the more reason to equate the joys of eating meat with unabashed gluttony, and to judge those who engage in such behavior as wholly lacking in both self-control and self-respect. Worse still, with the advent of the term "food porn," we've been labeled perverts as well, culinary deviants on par with, say, Caligula. The true meaning of carnivorism is being altered and distorted, and may even be in danger of becoming lost altogether. So it begs the question: What *does* it mean to be a carnivore?

Carnivorism 101: A Primer

First, it's important to realize that human beings are not, technically speaking, carnivores. We're omnivores, as most people know, meaning that our bodies and digestive tracts have evolved over hundreds of thousands of years to be able to process and gain nutrition from all kinds of foods, including meat. Lions are carnivores. However, if I were to follow the same diet as a lion or a python or a Tyrannosaurus rex, not only would I likely wind up suffering from malnutrition (as wonderful as meat is for the human body, meat alone does not contain everything we need to survive, and can even be downright harmful if overconsumed), I'd likely wind up spending most of my waking hours on the can, grunting like an Olympic deadlifter.

Many zealots of the vegetable cause are quick to point out the number of crucial anatomical characteristics of carnivores in the wild that humans don't share, noting that we lack their shortened digestive tracts and vicious predatory claws and elongated canines. This is true, but it hardly follows that we're not supposed to eat meat, or that it's some-how "unnatural." You know what's unnatural for human beings to eat? Grass. We don't eat like cows and other ruminants because our bodies don't have the ability to process cellulose for nutrition, which is why we're not outside munching away on the lawn. We can process meat, however, and it's good that we do, since meat is extraordinarily benefi-cial for the human body (more on this later). In fact, having meat in our diet might actually be one of the most important contributing factors to the evolution of human intelligence.

That's right: today, we have these great big brains that developed lightbulbs and airplanes, nuclear fusion, beer, and the Internet *because our ancestors ate meat.*

Or at least that's the theory of Dr. Craig Stanford, a professor of an-thropology at the University of Southern California. For years, Dr. Stanford studied apes and monkeys in Asia, Latin America, and Africa, as well as researching chimpanzee behavior alongside legendary pri-mate expert Jane Goodall. From his field studies and observations about the lives of our closest evolutionary relatives, Dr. Stanford came to theorize that eating meat is the basis of human intelligence, an idea that became the central argument of his book *The Hunting Apes: Meat Eating and the Origins of Human Behavior* (Princeton University Press, 1999). For a proud meat lover, this is incredibly fascinating and edifying stuff. So how, I asked the good doctor, does this all shake out?

He cited the widespread belief that the nutritional value of meat was good for brain evolution. "Certainly, the package of fat and protein is good for development." But his argument has more to do with the so-cial effects of meat on chimps and humans. "You have a limited com-modity, meaning meat, that would play into social behavior." He explained that meat is a limited commodity because it's both hard to obtain and nutritionally valuable due to all the animal fat. "Really the only source of animal fat at the farm, as it were . . . This made it a po-tential barter chip or commodity that would put a premium on brain complexity and intelligence . . . The intellect required to be a clever, strategic, and mindful sharer of meat is the essential recipe that led to the expansion of the human brain."

So even though meat is wonderfully nutritious, it wasn't the nutrition itself that made it so important to the development of cognition. Chimps, for example, don't even really need meat in their diet at all. "They don't need meat to survive; they're not carnivores," said Dr. Stanford. "They eat meat, but it's only a very small percentage of their diet. But they obviously love it. They relish it. They sit underneath trees for hours on end, waiting for droplets of blood [from a fresh kill] to fall down or little shards of bone, meaning they're willing to put dramatically more time and energy into hunting and getting meat than they would ever get out of it. It's really unlikely that anybody, except maybe two or three big males, would get more than just a scrap of meat after a hunt. And yet the whole community is eager to go off and try to catch a smaller animal."

So for these chimps—and, by extrapolation, our primitive forebears ("Because chimpanzees are so closely related to us and share such a high percentage of our DNA sequence," said Dr. Stanford, "it's almost an a priori given that their behavior has relevance for understanding our ancestors")—meat was the ultimate currency: hugely prized and extremely difficult to come by. If you were able to score some and keep your rivals from stealing it, you became the BMOC (or rather, BPIT: Big Primate In Tree), and you had to figure out how best to effectively share it, and with whom. This takes intelligence, and the more you have, the more successful you're likely to be. Meat was power, money—even, yes, sex. "Males will trade meat with their allies, deny it to their rivals (or snub rivals for denying *them* meat), and offer it to females they're interested in having sex with," Dr. Stanford says. Hence, the quality of intellect needed to keep up with the Chimpanzee Joneses in the big meat race steadily climbed, and primates evolved into intelligent hominids, eventually giving rise to human beings with extraordinary natural brainpower. And all because of meat. Make sure to note this research if you need a trump card when arguing with someone about the ethics of meat: "If it weren't for the importance of meat in our evolutionary ancestors' societies," you can claim, "we wouldn't be having this conversation at all. There might not even *be* humans!" Then mark the *Z* for Zorro in the air with your finger and contentedly walk away.

So aside from taste and nutrition, eating meat is really something of an evolutionary legacy, especially since, as humans, we've been doing it for about 2.5 million years, according to the fossil record (animal bones with microscopic cut marks on them indicating stone tools used for butchering). True, like those chimpanzees, we don't *need* to eat meat, but that doesn't make it any less important. Carnivorism is a philosophy, a way of life, and it has to do with a lot more than just meat consumption. As I see it, the three most important principles of carnivorism are as follows:

1. *Be Discerning.* The difference a meat eater and a carnivore is a lot like the difference between a moviegoer and a cineaste. It's not just the act of consumption; there's an account for taste and complexity that, for the true carnivore, accompanies the sheer pleasure of savoring meat, whether it's grilled bratwurst on a lazy late-summer afternoon, a perfectly done porterhouse at your favorite steak joint, or a lamb shank rubbed with rosemary and drizzled with black truffle oil. Make no mistake: this is important stuff. To be a true carnivore, it's simply not enough to stuff a couple of dirty-water hot dogs into your face as you hurry back to work from your lunch break. You should be dedicated to the cause not just of eating meat, but eating good meat, quality meat, and considering it thoughtfully and with perspicacity. If anything, a true carnivore should go out of his or her way to avoid bad meat.

   Allow me to illustrate. About an hour and a half into my flight back to New York after visiting my family in Louisiana, the flight attendant offered us poor economy-class passengers some food. I was hungry, so my first thought was "Great! I haven't gotten food on an airplane in years, with all the cost-cutting by airlines and whatnot." And when she told us that our meal offering was cheeseburgers, I was doubly excited, because, as you might well imagine, I love cheeseburgers. Then I saw the thing—a spongy gray patty, covered in a sticky white goo that I can only imagine someone was trying to pass off as cheese, placed in the midst of a very stale-looking bun-type object, all of which was quietly steaming inside a plastic bag. Did I eat it? No. And by *no*, I mean "I'd rather remove my own eyeballs with a plastic spoon." That's right: The Shameless Carnivore said no to meat. And I'll tell you why.

That sickly, artificial, alien substance so cheerily handed out to us represents everything that, in my mind, is wrong with meat in America. Set something like this before me and expect me to eat it, and you might as well be giving me a good, hard slap across the face. This stuff, which I have had the misfortune of eating in the past, only vaguely tastes like meat at all, as it's full of added hydrogenated fats, preservatives, binding agents, artificial flavorings, and other chemicals. And the meat itself is probably "mechanically recovered," meaning that the "patty" has been formed out of the little scraps of flesh that were stuck to the bones after all the more tasty, commercial cuts had been removed—after these scraps have been separated from the pulverized bone meal in a machine that is, for all intents and purposes, a super-high-pressure meat sieve. What's left over is a liquid mash known as "meat slurry," which is later combined with the vertiginous variety of additives listed above and shaped into what eventually becomes the final product. Sounds really appetizing, doesn't it?

Now, I'm all in favor of using every bit of the animal possible, and in fact I feel that doing so is important; what rankles me is all the added chemicals. If you have to treat your meat like a science experiment to get it to a point at which a person—and not a particularly discriminating one at that—would consider it palatable, something is very, very wrong with your raw material. For any true carnivore, the best meal is the one with the least interference between animal and dinner plate, i.e., a really nice cut of steak taken directly from the butcher shop and thrown soon thereafter onto a cast-iron skillet with a generous helping of salt and a dash of ground black pepper. Or better yet, a breast of wild turkey or venison tenderloin a friendly hunter who killed the animal himself might graciously offer you as a gift, and in which case you should consider yourself extraordinarily lucky. This airplane burger, on the other hand, had a whole goddamned laboratory between me and the cow. I'm not even going to get into the cheese, which for all I know was the kind that had to be labeled "pastuerized, processed cheese-type food," or maybe it was that junk they're forced to call "sandwich slices" because it doesn't actually contain enough cheese to be considered "cheese." I don't want a "-type" or "-style" or anything else hyphenated on my burger, dammit. I just want a slice of fucking cheese! You know . . . FROM A COW!

If you're alarmed by any of this, particularly that bit on mechanically separated meats, remember it every time you go into a McDonald's and get some chicken nuggets. There might be some comfort in knowing that you can get the same identical food, right down to the shapes of the individual pieces, in Portland or Jacksonville or Boston or wherever you might be, but consider this: You know what slurry-based foods also tasted really great and consistent to every person that ate them? Soylent Green and The Stuff. Good rule of thumb: If it can be compared to a foodstuff that played a central role in a horror movie, don't eat it.

You deserve better, don't you? Be a true carnivore. Be discerning.

2. *Don't Be a Glutton.* Meat has never, in the history of our great nation, been as inexpensive or bountiful as it is today, a fact we owe to tremendous advances in agricultural science since the Second World War. As a result, we're eating way more of it than we ever

have, a phenomenon readily noticeable in the national waistline, which seems to be expanding in step with the known universe. Here's the thing: you don't have to eat a seventy-two-ounce steak to be considered a carnivore. Or eat fifty-two hot dogs in an hour, or even eat meat at every meal—or every day for that matter. Gorging ourselves on meat causes us to take it for granted, something that for a true carnivore should be considered anathema. Try going a week without meat, and see how much you appreciate it afterward. I have, and it's absolutely true. The more you pay attention to the meat you eat, the less you'll want to devour it wantonly or haphazardly, without really thinking about it, and the more you'll value it. Plus, the concept of the "meat eater as glutton" gives all carnivores a bad name. We definitely don't want to give any more ammunition to the antimeat lobby than we have to. Gluttony is also not particularly good for your health—you don't need to eat an entire tub of fried chicken or a burrito the size of your leg to meet your nutritional goals and still be able to enjoy your food. Take it easy. Relax. Choose your meat wisely, and savor it languorously instead of just shoveling it in. And speaking of wanton consumption . . .

3. *Be Conscientious.* Eating meat is not only a wonderful thing to experience (and anyone who has ever had one of the majestic filets at Ruth's Chris set before them, sizzling and popping in melted butter, knows *exactly* what I'm talking about here), but it is also a very natural, instinctual, beneficial, even spiritual human act. Thus, it's vital for a carnivore to really consider his or her meat and everything about it. When you sit down for a meal, ask yourself a few questions: Where did the meat come from? Was it a family farm or a concentrated animal feeding operation (CAFO)? What was the animal fed? What were its living conditions like—did it get to amble peacefully around in a pasture, or was it imprisoned in a pen its whole life? Was it killed by a hunter, in the wild? What's the breed?

How was it slaughtered, butchered, and processed? How old was the animal? Was the meat aged and, if so, for how long? Was that aging "dry" or "wet"?

There are dozens of questions like these that you could ask, and the answer to every single one of them has a bearing on how your meat tastes. And if, per rule number one, you're going to be discerning about meat, it stands to reason that you should be actively concerned with those answers. The fun thing is, exploring all of these issues is a fantastic way to sample a great variety of different and delicious meats. Try a dry-aged steak versus a wet one, grass-fed versus corn-fed, lamb versus mutton, a Heritage turkey versus a Butterball, and so on. Keep reading; you'll see what I'm talking about.

Most important, a true carnivore does not shy away from the fact that meat comes from animals—creatures that were once mooing, clucking, slithering, hunting, crapping, and having sex with other animals, and that, unless you're eating in vitro meat, had to die so that we can have meat on our plates. The hardest part of living the carnivorous lifestyle, for many, is justifying the killing of animals for our own nourishment and pleasure. Why, the green militia goads, do we insist on slaughtering defenseless animals when we can get our nutrition elsewhere? The knee-jerk reaction is, of course, that we are at the top of the food chain and it doesn't matter, and that we eat meat simply because we *can*. Carnivores have to do better than that. We have to take it a step further and say, "I have made a conscious decision to eat the flesh of dead animals, and I'm fine with that." So long as we can accept responsibility for our actions, acknowledge exactly what we're doing, embrace it, and not cravenly distance ourselves from the reality of it by, for instance, buying prepackaged meat and ignoring the fact that it was once part of a living, breathing, and possibly happy animal, we can practice what I like to call "conscientious carnivorism." It's the reason that more and more meat eaters are drawn to companies such as Niman Ranch, which prides itself on producing natural, organic meat (sans growth hormones and other adulterations) and on treating its animals humanely until the very end, as well as Heritage Farms USA, which actually gives its customers the option of getting to know their chosen animal's daily life and personality. And if that animal is a turkey, you can even keep tabs on it via webcam to ensure that it's living the high life. It's the truth: happy animals make the tastiest meat.

The purpose of this book is to explore all of these topics and more, to get to the very essence of what being a proud, shameless carnivore is all about. This is not a screed against vegetarians, a polemic on why humans are so much better than all the other animals on the planet, or an endorsement for any meat producer or organization. It's a celebration of meat—something that, for my whole life, has been a consistent and pure source of joy and fun—as well as an attempt to appreciate its nutritional, cultural, and anthropological importance. For one year, I dedicated myself to meat, to learning everything about it that I could, from perspectives ranging from the scientific to the dietary, ethical, spiritual, and historical. In the process, I discovered a veritable galaxy of meaty knowledge and found answers to such pertinent questions as "How do Tibetan Buddhists feel about carnivorism?" "Is there really such a thing as 'deathless meat'?" "What's the deal with the 'tastes like chicken' phenomenon?" and, naturally, "What qualities should one look for in a butcher?"

But it wasn't all research and philosophy—in order to truly understand meat, to fully embrace it, I had to walk the walk, as it were. I decided that I needed to go full throttle, to become the "ultimate carnivore," by undertaking two major challenges: First, I attempted to eat no fewer than thirty-one different animals in a single month—from llama to yak, rattlesnake, turtle, birds of every feather, and each creepy, crawly critter in between—after which I went about systematically eating (and attempting to enjoy) every part, cut, and organ of a cow deemed appropriate for human consumption, everything from steaks, ribs, and roasts to heart, blood, glands, and brains, right down to the animal's "naughty bits." There were further adventures along the way—by the time my research came to a close, I'd hunted squirrels in the forests of Louisiana, attended the annual Testicle Festival in Montana, helped a family butcher their cow for the year, and, yes, I even spent an entire, painstaking week as a vegetarian. After all of this, I can only think of two words to say about the book that these adventures produced, two words to sum up my entire carnivorous philosophy:

"Dig in."

Genesis of a Carnivore

They call me Steakbomb. "Steak," for short. It is the only nickname I've ever had that stuck.

The origin of my carnivorism has much to do with the fact that I was raised in New Orleans. While many people immediately link South Louisiana cuisine to seafood—and Lord knows I adore all the creatures of the Gulf, particularly oysters, though I'll take whatever's fresh-caught, boiled, spicy, or deep-fried—few have stopped to realize the astonishing contributions the Cajun/Creole kitchen has made to the meat-loving world. Seriously, we are a people who took a dish like red beans and rice, which in itself is not just healthy but also a complete protein, and said, "No, no, no . . . *mais cher*, dis won't do at all! We need some ham hock in dere! And sausage!" The result is culinary history, and the dish of choice in New Orleans every Monday, to this day. Not even an American staple like French fries makes it through the NOLA ringer unscathed. We have to dump a boatload of roast beef gravy on them and make "boo fries." And don't even get me started on Thanksgiving—my fellow Louisianians were so staggeringly ambitious (and reckless) in their gastronomic enthusiasm that they created the deep-fried turkey and, of course, the turducken. If you don't know what a turducken is (and John Madden has been extolling its glory from the NFL commentator's booth every Turkey Day for years), I'll tell you now that it might just be the most singular affront to vegetarianism ever: a fully boned chicken, stuffed into a fully boned duck, stuffed into a fully boned turkey and baked in toto like a loaf. I think it's safe to say that, if push came to shove, a turducken would kick a tofurkey's ass and not break a moist, delectable sweat.

Yes, my countrymen are simply mad over meat, and it had an enormous impact on my upbringing. When I was ten, my parents brought me and my brothers to the annual Critter Dinner, a collaboration between local hunters and restaurateurs that took place an hour north of the city, in the middle of the dark, swampy, creature-infested Fontainbleau National Park. The sportsmen would kill whatever they could, and the chefs would gamely cook it up, whatever it was, in tasty and innovative ways. There, amid prodigious amounts of beer (Barq's root beer for us kids), bonfires, and the revelry of live zydeco, we dined on all the delicacies of the swamp, including deer, duck, squirrel, alligator sauce piquant, and, yes, nutria. With a name like that, you'd think it was some sort of eco-friendly, protein-rich meat substitute. Wrong. Quite simply, nutria is swamp rat. Imagine the "Rodents of Unusual Size" in *The Princess Bride*, three-foot-long rats, only these monsters are amphibious and have, I swear to God, *bright orange teeth*. They were imported to South Louisiana for their fur and quickly multiplied into ecologically problematic numbers, wreaking havoc on the natural wetlands so sacred to the state as a buffer against storm surges. All this nutria sex and spawning and wetland chewing eventually prompted local officials to hunt them with unfettered gusto just to control their population. During my formative years, if you happened to drive by certain canals in suburban Metairie after midnight, you might just see the Jefferson Parish police SWAT team practicing their night sniping on these beasts. So, in the interest of ecology and in the spirit of the night, and drunk as I was on the *bon temps* and tender stickiness of Louisiana autumn, I ate my nutria stew at the Critter Dinner like a good boy. And I loved it. That day, a carnivore was born.

Although I didn't realize my true nature as a carnivore until years later, when I look back on several episodes of my life, it seems as though it was a foregone conclusion. Take, for instance, the time that my older brother, Colin, brought his college sweetheart Alexandra home to New Orleans to visit our family for the first time. That first evening, the three of us and my youngest brother, Eric, all went out to a pasta restaurant. It was the kind of place where the menu was divided into sections according to what you wanted in your spaghetti, linguini, or penne, each section clearly labeled "seafood," "vegetables," or, naturally, "meat." As Eric and I caught up with Colin, chatted with Alex, and examined the pasta offerings, each one of us, independently of the other, said the exact same thing when our eyes ran across that last menu section: a sotto voce imitation of Homer Simpson's drooling voice gurgling "Mmmm . . . MEAT . . ." with dreamy, hungry reverence.

"Oh my God," said Alex, stunned. "Are you messing with me?" We didn't know what she talking about—none of us had heard the others. She registered our confusion and explained. "You all just said, 'Mmmm . . . MEAT,' one right after the other. You planned that, right? Didn't you?" My brothers and I all looked at one another and giggled, a little embarrassed. It was as though we shared the same brain, and that brain had a major fondness for meat. To this day, even though Colin is a strict vegetarian, it's all but impossible for any of us to see that word on a menu and not break into that same quote.

When I moved to New York to work in publishing, most of the delicacies I treasured in my Louisiana upbringing were lost to me. No more roast beef po-boys at my favorite hole-in-the-wall, and definitely no boudin* and cracklins,† which I'd always looked forward to eating with my dad at the Texaco station in Opelousas on our way back from visiting my grandparents in Shreveport (any true Louisiana native will tell you that you'll only get the very best boudin at filling stations and bait shops).

Even though I've moved away from Louisiana, I've done my best to stay true to my carnivorous roots, and to fervently lobby for my cause, especially when my dietary proclivities are called into question by the league of vegetable people. In a Chinese restaurant, when they groan and half gag at seeing "oxtail and tripe" on the menu, I know that I have little choice but to order up a generous helping and gleefully devour it in front of them. More and more, I've started going public with my carnivorous accounts. I wrote a short piece, published in the New Orleans *Times-Picayune*, in which I described in detail the near-divine experience of sharing an eight-pound lobster with my mother. A bright red jumbo jet of a crustacean, it tasted better than any lobster I'd eaten in my life. It took us over an hour to make our way through the thing, right down to the tiny scraps of delicate white flesh in the head and legs.

I wouldn't have it any other way.

A Brief Note About Terminology

It's critical, before we go any further, to define the word *meat*. When I use that term, I'm speaking specifically about animal flesh. Certain nuts and fruits are described as having "meat," but that simply doesn't ap-

---

* boudin (pronounced "BOO-dan"): Cajun sausage made with pork meat, liver, and rice, seasoned and stuffed inside a natural hog casing, which is most often discarded on the ground in the parking lot, where approximately 90 percent of all Louisiana boudin is consumed.

† cracklins: Fried fatback. Like pork rinds, only fattier and tender on the inside, served hot in a waxed paper bag. The end result is kind of like eating small hunks of salty, chewy, crispy bacon.

ply herein. Meat, to me, is strictly a matter of eating animals. However, as you continue with this carnivorous adventure, you'll likely notice the conspicuous absence of seafood. This is not because I don't think that fish, oysters, squid, and so forth are not meat—they absolutely are, and I absolutely love them. This is why people who are vegetarian but for the occasional sushi dinner are in no way actual vegetarians, and they probably shouldn't refer to themselves as such. As much as I adore all the "fruits of the sea," as the Italians say, for the sake of my sanity and that of my publisher (who wanted this book to come in under seven hundred pages), I had to sadly restrict myself to the meat of the air and land, as well as amphibians, despite the tempting desire to wax poetic about the deliciousness of ocean creatures. Also, I don't get into insects. Whether or not bugs should be considered "meat" is debatable; however, I didn't have the time to explore that matter further. Which might be a good thing—I really wasn't too fond of the idea of eating termites and hissing cockroaches.

Additionally, I'll note that the subject of meat is a vast one, to say the least. Mega-vast, really. So vast, in fact, that there was absolutely no feasible way for me to cover everything about it in these pages—there have been countless books written about the subjects of barbeque, smoking and curing, bones, butchering, exotic game . . . The list goes on and on. Someone could write a voluminous tome in praise of pork alone. Or the history of beef cattle in the United States. Or the cultural and culinary importance of guinea pigs to the peoples of Ecuador, Peru, and Bolivia. And so forth. So consider this less the definitive bible on absolutely everything pertaining to meat, and more of a spirited embrace of the meat-loving lifestyle, a survey covering the basics (and then some), seasoned with anecdotes, tips, and commentary and served with a generous helping of adventures both in and out of the kitchen.

So here you are. Enjoy the recipes. Enjoy the ride!

PART I

All Creatures,
Great and Small

CHAPTER 1

Becoming the Ultimate Carnivore

Entering the world of meat with hungry zeal to become an "ultimate carnivore," my first question was, of course, "How?" I was eager to explore all of the wonders provided by the animals of the globe, as well as to learn as much as I could about their anatomy, lifestyle, lore, and traditions on history's supper plates. The problem was that the subject of meat is so staggeringly vast, I had little clue where to even begin. I needed some sort of plan of attack, a strategy to help me conquer such an exhaustive (though tasty) topic. Naturally, it wouldn't suffice to consume mass quantities of only one kind of dish—nothing but burgers, say—not just since that would be unhealthy (even I have to admit this, as much as I adore a lovingly crafted, fresh-grilled hamburger) but it would get very old, very fast. People who dwell on only one dish are what I call Wimpys, after that *Popeye* character's unusual fixation. The saying "I'd gladly pay you Tuesday for a hamburger today" remains his sad but amusing legacy. Nor would it be prudent to gorge myself on steaks and chops at all hours of the day and night—again, horrible for the body, but also unnecessarily gluttonous. If anything, I'd fear that such reckless consumption would not just cork up my arteries with plaque and swell my jowls and love handles to late-career-Elvis proportions, but—God forbid—it might even sour me on the idea of eating steak. I shuddered to think about what a terrible fate that would be. No, there could be no gastronomic stagnation; as the old marine corps adage goes, I would have to adapt, improvise, overcome. I wondered, what kind of feat would it take to approach the vaunted realm of ultimate (and shameless) carnivorism?

After days of introspection, a solution arrived: I would eat the meat of thirty-one different animals in thirty-one days. Call it my Month of Meat, featuring a special list of thirty-one flavors. Mind you, this wasn't an arbitrary decision, but one that required careful deliberation, planning, and revision. My first thought was actually to eat a hundred animals in a month. I mean, just think about how many unique animals there are roaming the plains of the earth, soaring through the skies, scaling the mountains, slithering through the swamps, and quietly going about their business in the forests and jungles. I was willing to bet that more than a few of them, if conscientiously prepared, would make for great eating. I salivated at the prospect.

Biodiversity? More like *biodiversilicious*!

There are thousands upon thousands of these creatures, I figured, so how hard would it be to find a mere hundred of them that would be appropriate for the table? Pretty hard, apparently. Once you get down to it and start making a list, many of the more exotic beasts of the world are impossible to acquire in the United States because they are illegal (orangutans, bald eagles, giant pandas, Komodo dragons, etc.), or because no one is selling them with the due approval of the United States Department of Agriculture (USDA). Not that this keeps some people from selling them anyway. According to the Associated Press, in late 2006 New York State food safety inspectors discovered and confiscated an alarming array of illicit meats in the Big Apple, everything from ar-

madillos in Queens, to iguana meat and cow lungs in my home borough
of Brooklyn, to something labeled "smoked rodent," as well as plenty of
"unidentified red meat and mysterious fish paste." Oddly enough, most
of these meats would be perfectly legal to sell if only they'd come from a
USDA-inspected facility, although I imagine that iguana and armadillo
meat might prove to be something of a marketing challenge. Now, I'm
just as intrigued as the next carnivore about how these peculiar animals
might taste, but I was understandably wary: there are many things I'd
consider purchasing on the black market—I'd enjoy a home theater system that "fell off a truck" as much as the next guy—but I draw the line at
illegal mystery meats. Call me old-fashioned.

A NOTE ON USDA INSPECTION

A good thing to remember when thinking about the safety and
quality of the meat we enjoy is that all meat sold in the United
States must be inspected by the USDA, in particular, by a licensed
inspector from the Food Safety and Inspection Service (FSIS).
The only exemptions here are for hunters, farmers, and their non-
paying guests (if some shady deer killer wants to sell you some of
his venison, know that the transaction would be illegal). And how
does this inspection process work? Examining meat for quality
goes back to August 30, 1890, when the first Meat Inspection Act
was approved, but that act only applied to salt pork and bacon being sold for export. The following year, the act was amended to
cover the inspection and certification of all live cattle for export.
But it wasn't until the public outcry following the publication of

Upton Sinclair's seminal meat industry exposé, *The Jungle*, in 1905 that domestic meat inspection really took off. Sinclair urged President Theodore Roosevelt (a noted carnivore) to do something about the squalid and dangerous conditions of America's meatpacking facilities, and it didn't take long for good old Teddy to get things done. Both the Food and Drug Act and the Federal Meat Inspection Act were passed in 1906, and they are the basis of the inspection process that ensures the safety of our meat to this very day. In 1967, the Wholesome Meat Act was added to the existing Federal Meat Inspection Act, establishing the Federal-State Cooperative Inspection Programs. This is important, because the federal government leaves inspection up to the individual state governments; however, each state's inspection program must be "at least equal to" the federal standards. So you don't have to worry about the beef being any more dangerous in Arkansas than in Tennessee or anything—it's all under the same standard.

Government-employed USDA inspectors, either veterinarians or laypersons with significant meat industry experience and know-how, have a strict set of guidelines for ensuring the wholesomeness of the meat that eventually becomes our dinner. They review the plans of the slaughterhouse or processing plant (floor plans, water supply, waste disposal, lighting, etc.), make sure the place follows stringent standards of sanitation, monitor the health of the live animals for signs of illness or disease, and examine the internal organs of each slaughtered animal for indications of contamination or anything else that might make it unfit for you and me, going by the Hazard Analysis and Critical Control Point (HACCP) system. This happens *every single day* at these facilities, from a pre-op inspection before it opens through the entire workday, and again, it's mandatory, at least for "any cattle, sheep, swine, or goats," according to the Federal Meat Inspection Act.

(Poultry has a similar set of requirements, per the 1968 Wholesome Poultry Products Act.) For all nonmandated animals—rabbits, armadillos, iguanas, buffalo—the facility has to pay for government inspection if they want to sell their meaty wares, which is why they're generally more expensive than beef, pork, lamb, or goat (I've always wondered how "goat" made it in there).

If anything seems amiss, the inspectors have full authority to shut the plant down entirely until standards are restored. And when everything's going well, they'll mark their USDA stamp of approval on each animal's carcass in blue food-quality dye. If you're worried that the steak you see in the grocery store doesn't bear that mark, don't be; it's on the outside of the carcass, so most individual cuts won't carry it. And for processed foods, the meat's "identity" also needs to be confirmed to avoid misleading or false labeling—to be labeled "beef stew" for instance, the product must contain a minimum 25 percent actual beef. All in all, it's an extremely rigorous process, one that I, as a carnivore, have a good deal of faith in. I may have my suspicions about certain aspects of the U.S. government, but I'm pretty confident that the USDA is doing everything in its power to make sure we're not being poisoned by tainted beef. Case in point: your chances of eating beef contaminated with bovine spongiform encephalopathy (BSE), also known as "mad cow disease"? One in *ten billion*. Those are pretty good odds, I have to say, especially when you consider that your chances of winning the Powerball jackpot are about one in eighty million. So you're more than a hundred times more likely to strike it super rich on the lotto than run afoul of a mad cow burger. And think back to the fall of 2006—it wasn't the meat that everyone was scared of, but spinach and lettuce tainted with *E. coli* bacteria. Don't think for one minute that going vegetarian is any better, food safety-wise, than being a carnivore.

One way I could get around some of these pesky "legal food" issues would be to go jet-setting around the globe in pursuit of warthogs and elephants and ring-tailed lemur meat, but sadly, my budget limited my culinary adventures to the continental United States. So I'd have to stay here in the good old U.S. of A. and make do, but that still left me with plenty of interesting prospects. At the end of the day, I'd changed the number from a hundred to fifty, and ultimately to thirty-one different meats that I could reliably find either in specialty butcher shops or from a reputable online retailer. I felt this number had a kind of mathematical beauty to it, too; ostensibly, I'd be eating a different animal each day during this little test, which I thought added a certain mystique to the whole ultimate carnivore idea. Who knows: perhaps an animal a day would keep the doctor away.

On the subject of taboo meats, several of my friends were eager to ask if I'd be eating dogs and cats, a common practice in certain areas of the Far East. In fact, the Chinese have been cooking and eating dogs since the Confucian era, if not earlier, and the dish is still consumed regularly, although its popularity has dwindled or died in the more cosmopolitan parts of the country. Neither dogs nor cats are legal eats in this country and hence ineligible for my Month of Meat list, for which I'm grateful. I can't say that I'd look forward to the prospect of chowing down on Sautéed Snoopy or Pan-Seared Garfield. Not that I wouldn't, but I'd have to do so under particular circumstances. If, for instance, I happened to be traveling in one of the aforementioned parts of the world in which puppies and kitties are a delicacy and I was offered one or both of these meats by a gracious host who took pride in cooking and serving it to me, then yes, absolutely, I'd eat dog and cat meat. I'd just try not to think about my family's golden retriever as I forked a chunk of canine into my mouth. The same applies to horsemeat, which is also illegal in the United States, though that law applies only to domestic consumption; we export tons of the stuff every year, mostly to Europe, despite a fervent antihorsemeat lobbying effort.* An acquaintance of mine who traveled extensively in Eastern European countries like Slovenia had an opportunity to try some horse and told me it was surprisingly delicious, similar to beef but sweeter. He was quick to recommend the foal carpaccio. But some taboos exist for a reason; I don't care how adventurous I'd like to be in the world of meat, I absolutely refuse to even discuss the possibility of eating human flesh. I'm the Shameless Carnivore, not the Shameless Cannibal.

By the final tally, my list looked something like this:

cow	buffalo
pig	ostrich
chicken	guinea hen
deer (venison)	goat
duck	snail
turkey	antelope
lamb	elk
sheep (mutton)	kangaroo
boar	rabbit
reindeer/caribou	ox
yak	goose
llama	quail
rattlesnake	squab
alligator	pheasant
turtle	poussin
frog	. . . and a partridge in a pear tree.

* Despite the relative popularity of horsemeat in the rest of the world, Americans are wildly passionate about not feeding horses to the masses, even if the masses are foreigners. A bill called the American Horse Slaughter Prevention Act, restricting the export of horsemeat for consumption, was introduced in 2006 and subsequently passed by the House of Representatives. However, it did not make its way through the Senate and wasn't signed by the president, even despite the endorsement of Willie Nelson, whose heartfelt open letter to senators was signed by everyone from Keith Richards, Tippi Hedren, Clint Eastwood, and Johnny Knoxville to Chief Arvol Looking Horse, "19th generation keeper of the White Buffalo Calf Pipe Bundle" and "spiritual leader among the Lakota, Dakota and Nakota People."

The list would eventually be subject to change for a number of reasons. It turns out that lamb and sheep are the same animal, as are pig and boar (one is domestic, the other wild), although each of these is distinctly different as far as the palate goes. I'd sample them all anyway, and more. Of course, there would be a few twists and turns during my gastrological adventures, too.

With The List in hand, I made my way down to Greenwich Village, home of Ottomanelli & Sons Butchers. As much as I thought it a nice idea to take advantage of the expertise of as many New York City butchers as possible (believe you me, there are *a lot* of them), in the end I decided it was important to find one really great shop to use as a go-to for my meaty needs. This was important for a couple of reasons: First, if you happen to find a wonderful, family-owned-and-operated business that you trust and respect, you should do your best to support it and make sure it doesn't fall prey to the Great American Big Box Menace. It's not easy for the little guy to keep up a shop these days, as the purveyors of low-priced quantity and convenience (if not low quality) seem to be running them out of town at every opportunity. This has resulted in the tragic, steady decline of classic butcher shops in this country. If anything, it's worth patronizing an independent house of butchery if only to ensure that there will *be* independent houses of butchery in America's future. Their legacy is in our hands.

Second, it was vital that I establish a solid working relationship with my new butcher. Much the way a fine tailor grows to know how best to clothe his or her patrons in style and comfort, the better a well-trained meat man or woman knows what you're looking for and how you like it, the more satisfied you'll be when you ultimately chow down. If you have access to a top-shelf house of butchery and you actually care about the meat you eat, you'd be a fool not to patronize that butcher exclusively. I could write sonnets about great butchers—not only are they proud, consistent purveyors of high-quality products (most of them would rather fall on their cleavers than sell even one ounce of tainted or subpar meat), they are also important repositories of culinary knowledge and expertise, the likes of which can only be developed after years of hard work, experience, and love. (Yes, *love*. If my butcher isn't as passionately in love with beautiful steaks, lamb chops, or pork tenderloins as I am—in the epicurean sense, of course, not the erotic sense—I immediately call his expertise into question and start looking for exit signs.) Not only should any decent butcher be able to give you a lovely piece of meat and trim it to your preferred specifications, he should easily be able to rattle off how much you need according to how many people you'll be feeding, as well as to offer possible recipes, tips on preparation, cooking times, internal temperature, and so forth. Try getting this sort of detailed attention from the pimply-faced teen behind the counter at your local grocery store—you know, the one whose chief concern is more likely saving up for a new Xbox or finding a way to go home with that cute new goth chick working register seven than learning the fine and ancient craft of butchery.

What basic qualities should you look for in a butcher? According to Frank Ottomanelli, "sanitation is the first and most important thing." You'd think this goes without saying, but a quality butcher's operation should be impeccably clean. The place is filled with all kinds of raw meats, after all, food items that are extraordinarily easy to contaminate, especially ground meat. Speaking of which, do your best to stay away from prepackaged ground beef, pork, chicken, lamb, and other meats if at all possible, since they gather and hold bacteria much more efficiently than any whole cut of meat (it's a snap to grind your own at home—all you need is a steak or two and a basic food processor). If you're not up for a home grinding party, a decent butcher should be able to grind any kind of meat you like to order, yet another quality to be on the lookout for when selecting your meat purveyor: personal service and attention to detail. Also, if you see a pet in the store, exit immediately and don't go back. "I love cats," Frank told me. "They're the world's best exterminators—not that we've ever had a pest problem. But they jump all over the counter and on the cutting surfaces, and that's just not sanitary. Can't have it." Selection is nice, too, but less essential. It's amazing to be able to get everything from dry-aged strip steaks to fresh rabbit, veal sweetbreads, and everything in between on a regular basis, but it's much more important that your butcher knows what he's doing with the meat he gets. And that he knows a quality product when he sees it. "Every morning, I inspect our fresh shipments," Frank told me, and he's quick to spurn the wholesaler when the meat coming in isn't up to snuff. The best thing to do, I've learned, is to ask what your butcher just got in, and what he recommends. Chat him up, see what he has to say, form a personal relationship, even. In these times of Qwik-E-Marts and depersonalized mega-super-grocery-store chains, don't you think it would be nice to deal with one person whom you respect as a professional, whose opinion you trust, and who you know is eager to sell you a fine product?

I settled on Ottomanelli's because it exemplifies everything good and noble about the world of butchering. A family-owned-and-operated shop, it's been in business in New York for more than seventy years, providing not just high-quality steaks and other conventional fare but also fancy birds, exotic game, and other specialty foods you simply can't find in your average meat market, much less the neighborhood supermarket. It's a glorious place. Every time I walk in and take a look around in amazement at the stunning bounty on display, I can't help but feel a little bit like Charlie when he enters that first magnificent room of Wonka's chocolate factory. It's a carnivore's dream: hanging in the front window, for all to see, are sumptuous cuts of beef, pork, lamb, and game, and when you take a gander at the display case below the counter, you'll find everything from dry-aged porterhouses to Kobe beef hot dogs, quail eggs, duck sausage, whole foie gras, and pork tenderloins. Want milk-fed baby lamb or a whole suckling pig? No problem. And for the adventurous meat-thusiast, all you need to do is open the freezer case to find alligator tail fillets, elk medallions, quail (both whole and semiboneless), poussin (also known as Cornish hens or spring chickens), giant cuts of buffalo and boar . . . The list just goes on and on. For a guy who wanted to taste as many different animals as possible, this was paradise.

Again, the trouble would be knowing where to begin. I didn't know what I'd be able to find and what might prove more difficult, so all I really had was a list. Fortunately, that was all Frank Ottomanelli needed to get me started. After I explained my intentions—which didn't give him even a moment's pause; in fact, it didn't seem particularly out of the ordinary at all for him—he picked up a pencil, took hold of my list, and went to town, rattling off each animal as if he were looking at a list of auto parts I needed for a broken Chevy, ticking them off one by one:

"This I can get, this I can get . . . that's no problem, I can get this, this . . . I'll have to ask someone about this . . ." and so on, until almost every single meat I'd put down was either duly checked off or circled for further inquiry. "This we don't do," he said at one point, and when I looked at what he was pointing to, expecting it to be caribou or ostrich or something, I saw the word *cow*.

"You're telling me you don't sell cow meat here," I asked incredulously. "But look at all those steaks! Surely . . ."

"Beef, yes," he replied, "but not from cows. Not since the mad cow thing came over, anyway. All the veal and beef we get comes from steers, you know, male cattle that have been castrated. No bulls or cows." And so my education began. When I'd written *cow* on my list, I'd meant the name of the species, not the sex of the animal, but Frank wasn't messing around. I liked him immediately.

We spent some time discussing possible options for my first big exotic meat dinner, and after a while I decided to kick off the month with wild boar. I'd never had it, although I'd often read about how wonderful it tasted, especially in classic northern Italian recipes. Having made that decision, I'd next have to decide which cut to buy. Rib rack? Leg? Chops? Boar bacon? I began to salivate right there in the store as I contemplated the options. In the end, I decided on a whole leg, which I planned on simply baking in the oven and basting with its own natural juices. After getting some tips on preparation from Frank, I walked out into the sunny West Village with my purchase, which was both ungainly and heavy. The thing wasn't just six pounds of frozen meat and bone, it was an oblong, strangely weighted object that (together with some other meat I'd picked up on impulse), proved difficult to carry. Not that I really cared at that point—I was too busy fantasizing about how good it was going to taste to worry about carrying it about on various subways and buses. Plus, the thought of lugging around the whole leg of a wild beast had a distinctly manly, Paleolithic air to it.

While the leg thawed in my fridge, I took some time to learn a bit more about the animal I was about to roast and share with friends. This, I felt, was an important thing to do, and it became a kind of ritual I would carry out during the Month of Meat, with every animal I'd eat. A true carnivore should have some knowledge about the meat he or she enjoys. You don't really need to know all of the specifics about a particular animal's life—knowing the "personality" of your Thanksgiving turkey isn't going to make it taste more or less delicious. But knowing the basic history and physiology of an animal—what it eats, how it's treated, how it was bred, and so forth—does indeed lend one a higher sense of appreciation for its meat. Those with very refined palates can distinguish and even explain the difference in the taste of an animal's flesh according to its diet and lifestyle, as well as its breed. Best of all, with a little reading you'll have some interesting anecdotes you can share during dinner to make you seem all the more charming and erudite, for example, "Did you know that the boar was the personal symbol of England's King Richard III? Or that Hindus believe that a boar was the third avatar of the god Vishnu?"

In my research I discovered that a wild boar (*Sus scrofa*) is essentially the same animal as a domestic pig (*Sus scrofa domestica*). Unlike their cute, pink relative, boars have coarse, dark hair that, in males, stands at a ridged point along their spine (hence the term *razorback*), as well as sharp tusks and a considerably more aggressive disposition. Not indigenous to North America, boars were brought here around

ıe cases)* to cripple and eviscerate you with its tusks, especially
animal is protecting its young. Think of that the next time you
harlotte's Web or watch *Babe*.

:cause of their tenacious survival instincts and their habit of man-
crops, many farmers consider these boars to be a serious prob-
'he solution? Eat more wild boar meat! For my part, I was more
appy to help those poor, distraught farmers in this matter, begin-
ith the massive hind leg I'd just pulled, fully thawed, from the re-
tor. Sadly, I learned that my boar was from New Zealand and not
l in the American South (USDA approval is necessary for retail
:re, so finding boar bushmeat at Ottomanelli's wasn't an option).
dn't be cooking this beast in my own kitchen, however. This isn't
* the fact that my apartment is small and has low ceilings or that
housand times more prone to succumbing to the forces of clutter
isorder than most normal people's apartments. No, I couldn't
wild boar in my home because, very simply, I do not have an
Unless you're a millionaire, when you live in New York City you
ɔ make certain trade-offs when you find a place to live, sacrificing
amenities (space, quiet, convenient transportation, proximity to
tic Italian delicatessens) for others. The absence of an oven and
vas the trade-off I had to make for cheap rent, no roommates, and
.nt courtyard in which to have summertime barbeques. In the
he sacrifice was worth it—I'd much rather have a nicely grilled
:han a tray of muffins any day—however, it also meant that I had
all of my friends and acquaintances if they wanted to offer up
partments to be used as test kitchens for my carnivorous endeav-
s I provided free, exotic meat and often beer or wine in exchange
:ir hospitality, I was not left wanting for volunteers.

:ase, made famous by a *National Geographic* documentary in 2005, a twelve-foot, one-thousand-
ıld boar dubbed Hogzilla was killed by a farmer in Alapaha, Georgia. These measurements were
by the *Geographic* scientists, though the farmer held to his numbers, explaining that the creature
gnificantly between the time of its death and when it was exhumed for the documentary.
:ss, Hogzilla's tusks were confirmed to be eighteen inches long, which makes them fearsome
of dinosaur-like proportions. This is precisely the kind of mythological beast Hercules was deal-
although, unlike the Georgia farmer, he lacked the benefit and convenience of modern firearms.

1525 by de Soto and his crew and domesticat[...]
would bring still more wild boars over to hunt[...]
later. Those Russki boars would mate with e[...]
produce the breed most commonly found in[...]
And find them you will. They are far from be[...]
been facing an explosion in the wild boar p[...]
now, and it's become a big problem in Texas[...]
states, including my home state of Louisiana[...]
vivors; they breed prodigiously and can subsis[...]
stroying crops, wrecking agricultural projects,[...]
hunting operations (hunters attract deer and[...]
cally doling out grain, which the boars devour[...]
the destruction spreads. Most interestingly, I[...]
mestic pig escapes, an act for which they're[...]
quickly turns feral and will soon begin to resen[...]
ing the dark bristles and other features of a tru[...]
pig breeds, its offspring will be indistinguishab[...]
spite of having a domesticated parent. It's a[...]
beasts want to be wild, and it's all farmers[...]
adorable, pink, fat, and docile. No two ways ab[...]
a successful getaway from *Green Acres,* it's only[...]
he'd start looking and acting like the irritable, v[...]
rified the schoolchildren in *Lord of the Flies.*

This idea intrigued me—what was once a fi[...]
has been domesticated to the point where many[...]
as pets. The wild boar has a rich tradition in[...]
mythology. As one of his twelve labors, Hercule[...]
ture the Erymanthian boar, a creature so powerf[...]
olent that the task was deemed all but imposs[...]
course of history, the perilous nature of huntin[...]
the activity the storied reputation of being a[...]
courage. There's no doubt that a wild boar ca[...]
charging with all of its weight (up to and over e[...]

in so[...]
if the[...]
read[...]

gling[...]
lem.[...]
than[...]
ning[...]
frige[...]
hunt[...]
sale[...]
I wo[...]
due[...]
it's a[...]
and[...]
roast[...]
oven[...]
have[...]
som[...]
fanta[...]
stov[...]
a qu[...]
end,[...]
steal[...]
to a[...]
thei[...]
ors.[...]
for t[...]

* In o[...]
pound[...]
dispu[...]
shran[...]
None[...]
weapo[...]
ing wi[...]

So I'd prepare the boar at my friends Dan and Hillary's place, not far away from my own home. They shared their apartment with another couple, our friends Dan and Nicole (yes, two Dans, a constant source of fun and confusion—Nicole has taken to numbering them, Dan1 and Dan2), both of whom are long-standing vegetarians. It would be interesting to see how they felt about the gigantic hunk of meat I was rinsing off in their sink.

Now, pork may be known as "the other white meat," but this boar's leg was anything but. As I patted it dry and prepared to season it with the Lysander's spice rub I'd picked up at Ottomanelli's, I noted that in its raw state, the meat was a deep red, almost identical in hue to a fine cut of steak. Whenever I'd bought pork from a butcher in the past, mostly chops and sections of tenderloin, it had always been a distinctly pink color, so this was certainly a change. I wondered what it might look like once it was cooked through, but I had a sneaking suspicion that it would *not* be comparable to a baked chicken breast. As for preparation, I decided to make this dish as easy as humanly possible, as it was my first time either eating or preparing boar. Plus, I'd hate to brazenly attempt some ultracomplicated recipe requiring doctorate-level kitchen mastery, for fear of ruining a sixty-dollar piece of meat and leaving my dinner guests to sate themselves on side dishes. No, I'd be keeping this one simple: dry-rubbed boar's leg cooked in a baking tin, uncovered, at 350 degrees for about an hour and a half. Frank Ottomanelli advised me that one doesn't need to cook wild boar as long or at as high a heat as your standard-issue domestic pork, which is notoriously prone to drying out. So instead of looking for an internal temperature of 170 degrees, which you'd want to do with a normal pork roast, I only had to get the boar's leg to about 145 degrees, making sure to take my measurement by placing the meat thermometer in the thickest part of the thigh, away from the bone.

By the time the roast came out of the oven, the heady aroma that began to fill the room about an hour into the cooking process had quite nearly driven us crazy with anticipation. I was just hoping, when I pulled it out, that we wouldn't devolve into our primate ancestors and start tearing into the leg right there in the kitchen, grunting and fighting with each other over the tastiest scraps. It smelled that good, and looked it, too—a deep, dark red, the kind that signifies a beast has been roasted right, glistening in the kitchen light with a delicate sheen of moisture. Fortunately, we retained our civility as I removed the baking tin from the oven and placed it atop the stove while my dinner companions oohed and aahed in hungry appreciation. I sighed with relief, realizing that all my anxiety about my lack of culinary competence had turned out to be for naught. I also marveled at the sight of the thing, not out of pride or self-satisfaction, though I admit it was a good feeling to have prepared something so savory looking, but at the thought that this was, without a doubt, the entire leg of a formerly wild creature. There was no way of disguising the obvious animalistic nature of this whole enterprise. Here in the United States, unless you work at a traditional barbeque joint or an ethnic restaurant that specializes in spit-roasted animals, it's just not very common to see the entire leg of a pig on a platter like this. For some reason, despite the modern apartment we were in and all of its conveniences, I suddenly felt medieval, as though this leg of wild boar were to be carried out to the castle's banquet hall to be carved tableside for awaiting knights and squires, famished after a long day's joust. Indeed, a roasted boar was often the showpiece dish of big Christmas feasts during that era, its serving accompanied by the singing of spirited, boar-themed songs. Man, they really knew how to do meat back then.

It was at this point that Dan1 and Nicole, the resident vegetarians, passed through the kitchen on their way out of the apartment, and I made sure they got a gander at the steaming pig's leg on their kitchen counter. "Hey, guys, what do you think?" I taunted good-naturedly. "Pretty tasty-looking, huh? *Sure* you don't want some?"

"Ugh," replied Nicole, scrunching up her features to communicate her revulsion. It's the same expression you see on the mugs of *Fear Factor* contestants when they're confronted with having to eat live camel spiders or drink hundred-year-old eggnog.

"Fine then," I said to my fellow carnivores after the vegetarians had evacuated the apartment. "In the words of Marie Antoinette, 'Let them eat tofu!' " No one laughed. "Never mind," I said. "Let's eat."

I carved the leg—which proved to be more or less the same activity as carving a turkey breast, one I always enjoy for its patronly air (though ironically I don't think my own father ever carved anything in his life, especially not a turkey)—and served it in thin slices that each got a quick baste with the *jus* that had accumulated in the bottom of the baking tin. As I suspected, the meat was different in both color and flavor from its domestic equivalent, although the grain of the meat and its "mouthfeel" were essentially the same. On my first bite I discovered that the texture had the same consistency and give against the teeth as a regular pork loin or chop, but then the taste kicked in and took the experience to the next level. Not only was this boar meat darker and richer in color—light brown instead of white—it was darker and richer in flavor as well. It didn't taste altogether alien from normal pork, which is to say that it had a definite piggyness to it, but it was earthier, more pungent, more like . . . well, a wild animal. At this point I realized, with some sadness, that all domestic meats might pale in comparison to their wild brethren, as though the flavor of the animal was leached out of its flesh along with the darker color. If that was the case, and if I wanted to become a connoisseur, I was going to have to make a point of eating much more wild meat.

And what a terrifically awful assignment *that* would be.

MEAT GEEK

Ever wonder where meat gets its color? Why veal is pink, beef red, and poultry white? Or why a duck breast is so dark compared to the relative paleness of a chicken breast?

The answer, in a word, is *myoglobin*. A purplish-colored protein found fixed within animal muscle tissue, myoglobin is responsible for storing the oxygen in the muscle cells, to be drawn on constantly as a source of energy. The more active a muscle is, the more energy it needs, and hence the more myoglobin you'll find. Most red meat comes from "slow-twitch" muscles, which are used for everyday activities like standing, walking, and mooing at passing automobiles. When mixed with oxygen, it's converted to oxymyoglobin, which has the bright-red hue you'll find at the center of a rare steak. The presence of myoglobin in these muscles varies from species to species—beef, which we all know to be a rich crimson color, contains significantly more myoglobin (about 8 mg/g) than light-red lamb (6 mg/g) or pink pork (2 mg/g). Age is also a factor: the older an animal grows, the more exercise its muscles get, assuming they're not kept relatively motionless, which means the more oxygen those muscles will need, and thus more myoglobin and a deeper, redder color. This is why veal meat is considerably lighter than young beef, and why old beef is the reddest (and toughest) of the bunch.

When it comes to poultry, the same principles apply, although white meat is generally made up of "fast twitch" muscles that are mostly used for quick bursts of speed and activity. As with beef or lamb, the more a bird uses certain muscle groups, the darker the meat from that muscle will be. This is why a chicken breast is almost always white, and a duck breast is a rich brown— being migratory birds, ducks use their breasts to power their wings to fly long distances, whereas chickens generally don't, a fact much lamented by the stop-motion plasticine poultry in the film *Chicken Run*. Chickens might fly a short distance to escape the advances of a hungry neighborhood dog (or Colonel

Sanders), but they're certainly not off to Florida for the holidays, hence the dark meat in chicken thighs and legs, as opposed to the more rarely used muscles in their breasts. And as for the color of my sliced boar's leg, like most wild game it was darker because the animal was running around, foraging for sustenance, getting into fights with other animals, destroying Farmer McDonald's turnip crop, scaring schoolchildren, and so on, rather than sitting around in a pen all day.

Another interesting fact about the color of meat—you ever wonder what the deal is with that iridescent rainbowlike sheen on the surface of a steak or hunk of prosciutto you just brought home from the butcher shop? I'm never able to keep from worrying about whether or not my shiny technicolor meat is going to poison me. Fortunately, it's nothing to fret about. The scientists at the Texas A&M Meat Science Department (the Mister Wizards of the meat world) explain the phenomenon thusly:

> A natural phenomenon in cured meat (and some fresh meat) is the occurrence of iridescence or a rainbow appearance on the cut lean surface. Technically, this is referred to as birefringence. It is caused by the reflectance of light off of muscle proteins, and it is analogous to the color distribution produced by a prism. Muscle proteins are arranged in strands called myofilaments, which are bound together to form myofibrils. Myofibrils are bound together to form muscle fibers, which form together to form muscle bundles and finally whole muscles. When the myofilaments are cut at the appropriate angle, exposing a cross section of the myofilaments, the reflectance of light off the proteins produces the characteristic appearance associated with iridescence.

And if you're still worried, the ever-vigilant USDA makes a point of noting that such iridescence does not mean either decreased quality or safety. So go ahead and dig into that beautiful, rainbow-tinted side of beef, because it's going to taste just fine, assuming you don't burn it to a crisp by forgetting about it on the grill.

Speaking of which, do you know why meat turns brown as it cooks? It's pretty fascinating: meat proteins are, in a raw state, shaped like coils and held together by bonds. If you were to look at them through a high-powered microscope, the protein strands would resemble the massive tangle of Christmas lights you pull out of the box just after Thanksgiving (though the proteins do not, to the best of my knowledge, blink in rhythm to "Jingle Bells"). When you expose these proteins to heat, the bonds break down and the proteins get a chance to relax, unwinding from their natural state. This little protein vacation doesn't last long, though, as continued heating pushes out the muscle's water content and causes the proteins to coagulate, or clump together. The proteins go through several stages, depending on how hot they get: Above 140 degrees Fahrenheit, myoglobin loses an iron atom at the center of its molecule and produces a compound called hemichrome, the substance that gives medium-done meat a tan color. When the internal temperature reaches 170, the raised hemichrome levels create metymyoglobin, that tell-tale brownish-gray color betraying a steak's well-doneness. This whole process from beginning to end is called "denaturing."

So what on earth is a carnivore to do with all of this information, other than impress your culinary-nerd friends with your newfound, intricate knowledge of the meatological sciences? Here's a fun game: The next time you're in a steakhouse and your filet comes to you well done instead of medium rare, make sure to instruct the waiter to send it back to the kitchen for a replacement because "the continued denaturing of the proteins in this steak have raised the hemichrome levels to an undesirable and unappetizing level." If he has any idea what the hell you're talking about, make sure to give him a handsome tip.

CHAPTER 2

Month of Meat, Round 1

"Honey, I Barbequed the Kid!" (Notes on Goats)

After beginning my meaty month with that wild boar, the fun continued on a novel note when I was invited to a barbeque at a friend's
house out in New Jersey. Wanting to be a good guest, I felt it only prudent to bring something tasty to share. I'd just assumed that I would
pick up some nice kielbasas at the Polish butcher shop in my neighborhood, until my wanderings brought me to the farmers' market in Union
Square.

If you've never been there, let me tell you: it's an amazing place. A
classic, open-air market, it's been availing hungry, discerning New
Yorkers of a wondrous variety of local produce, cheeses, and other fare
since the inception of the city's Greenmarket program in 1976.
Producers from nearby locales like upstate New York, New Jersey, and
Pennsylvania trek into Manhattan four days a week to display their

wares—nearly always touted as "organic"—beneath canopies on dozens of card tables. Sure, there are plenty of sexy-looking vegetables, baked goods, cheeses, juices, and cider and so forth, but the market also plays host to a number of small local farmers who raise their own poultry, beef, pork, game, and other meats. Meandering through the stalls appreciating the various offerings, I serendipitously ran into the booth operated by Elly Hushour from the Patches of Star dairy, located in Nazareth, Pennsylvania. The good folks at Patches of Star are dedicated to producing high-quality goat's milk, cheese, and meat. And you can just guess which one I was interested in. I have nothing but respect and admiration for the type of endeavor personified by people like Elly: providing the hungry public with a product that has been raised and prepared conscientiously and with respect for every facet of the quality of the ingredients. The goats—which range in breed, though South African Boer goats are interbred with Saanens at Patches of Star to produce the most desirable meat—live a cushy, free-range life. They dine on pesticide-free hay and graze freely in a large paddock with plenty of nonchlorinated water to drink. The result? Kickass goat meat, which is exactly what one should expect from happy, healthy animals. How could I afford not to bring such a high-quality, locally raised foodstuff to share at the barbeque? I figured no one else would. And really, who wants to go to a goat-free party, anyway?

The prospect of grilling up some nice goat delighted me to no end, mostly because it was so new to me. I'd never eaten it before, not that this was particularly odd. Most goat meat you'll find in American restaurants is largely relegated to Caribbean and West Indian cuisines, in which curried goat has long been a popular dish. And since there were few, if any, restaurants offering these cuisines in the New Orleans of my childhood, I was simply never availed of the opportunity, a fact that I now reflect on with tremendous sadness, knowing how delicious goat meat can be. In truth, the only knowledge of goats I had growing up, outside of the petting zoo, came from the traditional Jewish Passover song "Chad Gadya," which tells of a "kid my father bought for two *zuzim*." It was years before someone informed me that the kid in question was actually a goat, and that the song had nothing to do with either child slavery or cannibalism. I still feel I had a right to be confused, though—after all, the angel of death shows up near the end of the song to slay a butcher, not to mention there being a pointed reference to dog beating, so how was I supposed to know?

Standing there at the goat stall in the market, I was left with a number of options. (Dare I buy a whole kid?) As with the boar, I chose a safe route, and purchased two pounds of cubed goat meat that I could marinate overnight and grill on bamboo skewers, kebab-style. Elly was even kind enough to suggest a Mexican-style marinade that she enjoyed herself. "The meat is extraordinarily tender, since it comes from a younger animal," she said, so it's best not to place it directly on the grill. Tinfoil works as a good intermediary between the grill and the meat because you won't have to worry about undue charring, and you also get the added benefit of having the kebabs simmer in the juices from the marinade. "And make sure you don't overcook it," she admonished. Heeding her advice, I thawed and marinated the cubes, which seemed to be on the fatty side with a fair bit of fascia (connective tissue), but oh well, I thought, better trust the goat lady. She seemed like she knew what she was talking about. Arriving at the BBQ the next day, I dutifully skewered the meat, placed it in aluminum foil on the grill, and hoped for the best.

I have to admit, I was more than a little nervous—I usually am when I'm trying out a new recipe for people—and that anxiety was multiplied by the fact that I hadn't ever eaten this kind of animal, much less prepared it myself for a bunch of hungry and increasingly inebriated partygoers. What if it turned out to be awful? I'd heard that goat meat has a distinct, sometimes even pungent, flavor. What if it ended up tasting like a sweaty jock strap? After getting so excited about the whole prospect of this dish, I would undoubtedly have to endure some horrible ridicule from my host, my friends, and a bunch of rowdy party people I'd never met before. So I did the only reasonable thing I could think to do in such a moment, which was finish my drink, fetch a fresh one, let the kebabs cook, and trust that Elly the goat lady had steered me in the right direction.

When all was said and done and I took the meat from the grill, I was rewarded for my faith: goat tastes awesome! I was hoping that it would at least be passable, if only to spare myself shame and humiliation, but when I popped that first morsel into my mouth, the flavor was so striking that my knees actually buckled a bit, and I'm fairly certain I even let out a little moan of pleasure. I've come to know this sublime moment of sheer meat-induced pleasure as "carnirvana." I can't imagine a single vegetable dish that would make me swoon this way. The marinade kept the meat juicy and tender, and most of the excess fat had either cooked away or into the meat itself . . . and, of course, everyone knows that fat makes just about everything taste better (check out the prices on the intensely marbled Wagyu beef for confirmation of this phenomenon). Also, like the boar's leg before it, the color of this meat surprised me—it came out not brown like beef or lamb, nor white like poultry, but a pale red, though ultimately the color didn't matter. It could've been neon green or solid black for all I cared . . . The taste, man! The taste!

So, thank goodness, the gods of meat smiled on me that day, and my goat was a triumph. Not that it really helped when it came to sharing, oddly enough—Americans have a very strange attitude when it comes to eating goats, it seems. Some friends and party guests leapt at the opportunity to try my kebabs, and almost all of them found, as I did, that the meat was juicy and uniquely flavorful. But others, when asked "Would you like to try some goat?" reacted with the same expression of terror and disgust they might employ had I just pulled the family dog off the grill and, grinning maniacally, offered them a steaming slice. I'll never understand people's apprehension when it comes to trying new and interesting dishes, as though they're horrified they might actually enjoy it. Picky eaters have no place in my carnivorous empire. They can go and eat a chemical burger and some chemical fries at a miserable fast-food joint for all I care. More goat for me.

Nevertheless, I can't help but be disappointed by such attitudes, and my disappointment applies not just to the squeamish party guests who refused my kebabs but also to the American palate in general. With meat this tender and satisfying, I'm shocked (shocked!) that it has never really caught on in the United States. This is not just one man's opinion—the *Food Lover's Companion*, the chef's go-to bible of culinary terms and references, says under the entry for goat that "it has never really caught on in the United States," despite its long-standing and continued popularity in Mediterranean, Latin American, and southern European cultures. Roasting a whole goat on a spit is an act of celebration in Greek tradition, often used to mark joyous occasions such as weddings and births. But as far as I'm concerned, the roasting of a whole goat is a joyous occasion in and of itself. Even today, when we're starting to see animals like rabbit and wild boar turn up more often on the menus of notable restaurants, you'd be hard pressed to find a great goat dish. Maybe it's that most Americans see goat as a swarthy peasant meat, the kind of food they rely on in impoverished nations, though, as far as the palate goes, the meat of a fresh young kid can easily be as delectable as a nice cut of lamb, which is largely considered a luxury meat. This, to me, is almost masochistically absurd—why would you deny yourself the pleasure of such a wonderful ingredient? We're quick to enjoy goat's-milk cheese such as chèvre, so why not meat, too? There's a big, shiny gold star in my book just waiting for that intrepid and inventive chef who manages to bring goat meat to its rightful popularity and abundance. The American people would be indebted to you.

Finally, here's one more truly wonderful thing about cooking goat: the best goat meat comes from young goats (normally less than six months old), also known as "kids." Now, the kebabs I cooked tasted outstanding, but the whole experience was made infinitely more enjoyable by the amount of riffing we did on this simple accident of nomenclature. Case in point: My friends and I decided to take in a movie the night before the big barbeque. Armed with the knowledge that two pounds of cubed goat meat were slowly marinating in my refrigerator, my buddy Bobert and I took endless pleasure in pursuing conversations, at very loud volume in the lobby of the theater, that sounded something like this:

"Hey, you ever eat a kid before?"

"No, but I hear eating kids is both nutritious and tasty!"

"It's true—kids have less fat than chicken, and are way low in cholesterol."

"Really? That makes me want to go out and get a whole bunch of kids, chop them up, and throw them into the fire right now!"

"You said it, man . . . There's really nothing like roasting a young kid! Just wait until you sink your teeth into the kid I have marinating in my fridge at home right now!" And so on, much to the disconcerted glances—and sometimes genuine alarm—of the theatergoers around us.

See—meat can be fun, even when you're not eating it.

Marinated Goat Kebabs

2 POUNDS FRESH OR FROZEN CUBED GOAT MEAT	1 TEASPOON GROUND CUMIN
¾ CUP VEGETABLE OIL	1 TEASPOON SALT
JUICE OF 3 LARGE LIMES	1 TEASPOON CHILI POWDER
½ CUP FINELY CHOPPED FRESH CILANTRO	5 TO 10 BAMBOO SKEWERS ALUMINUM FOIL

Thaw the meat if necessary in cold water or preferably overnight in the refrigerator. Place marinade ingredients into a medium bowl and whisk together until combined. Add additional seasoning to taste. Place the meat in a large zip-lock freezer bag and pour in the marinade, making sure all of the meat is covered, and refrigerate overnight.

When ready to cook, light the grill. Skewer the meat and place the kebabs on a sheet of aluminum foil. Place the foil over a medium-hot fire and cover the grill. Cook 5 to 7 minutes, until the meat is a light reddish brown. Turn the kebabs over and cook another 6 minutes.

Serves 4 as an entrée, 8 as an appetizer

Where Chicken Comes First

After the dual successes of my roasted boar and grilled goat, I thought it would be nice to take a break from the kitchen and let someone else do the cooking for a change, so I made plans with a couple of friends to have a nice dinner out. And what would be on the menu for the Shameless Carnivore as he explores the wide world of exotic meats—lizard, okapi, possibly a nice bat ragout? No, this night would be all about something far less unusual: chicken. While it might seem boring, chicken was quite probably the most important animal on my entire list of different meats. Humans have been keeping the humble *Gallus gallus domesticus* for their meat and eggs for so long that its first domestication predates all recorded history. Today, it might be the most prevalently consumed meat in the entire world, spanning nearly all continents and cultures (though it is largely agreed that modern chickens are derived from the wild fowl of primeval Asian jungles). In the United States alone we eat approximately eighty pounds of chicken per capita each year, twenty pounds more than beef, believe it or not. There are seemingly endless ways to cook a chicken—the most famous recipes alone make up an extensive list: chicken Kiev, chicken à la king, chicken potpie, buffalo chicken wings, chicken cordon bleu, chicken salad, barbequed chicken, chicken noodle soup, tandoori chicken, chicken enchiladas, chicken pizza . . . Once you start saying these aloud, you begin to sound something like Forrest Gump's friend Bubba, though I reckon the chicken list would easily surpass Bubba's inventory of shrimp preparations by an order of magnitude.

With all of this amazing variety, why does chicken have a reputation for being so, well . . . *dull*? You'll find chicken on almost every menu in the country, even in the haughtiest of fine dining establishments, though more often than not it seems like chefs put it there so that people can have a safe bet, a dish that anxious, picky eaters can fall back on in case the more interesting offerings are a little too scary. Even in most sushi restaurants I know that my father, a man appalled by the thought of ingesting raw fish, can rely on the presence of chicken teriyaki. For some reason, chicken has become synonymous with the lackluster and the uninspired. Yet most great chefs, and indeed most people I know who consider themselves gourmets, will agree that a simply seasoned, roasted chicken is a thing of honest beauty, one of life's truly reliable pleasure. So what gives? Why the poultry paradox?

There are a number of reasons for the contemporary concept of the boring chicken, but the primary one is a matter of taste. Many people feel that chicken, as a meat, simply doesn't have much flavor to it. This is both true and false: chicken does, of course, have its own distinct flavor, and it's a wonderful one at that; however, the natural chicken essence isn't as prevalent in modern domestic chickens because of the way most of them are bred and raised. Like the difference between wild boar and domestic pig, a wild chicken, or even a free-range chicken, is going to taste distinctly more "chickeny" than a bird raised on a factory farm. On the other hand, that essential chicken flavor is a mild and delicate thing to begin with, easily lost or unappreciated. Why is this? Again, it all goes back to science. The flavor in meat comes mainly from two places: the fat and the concentration of glutamate. An animal's diet is directly reflected in the flavor of its fat, which is one reason that wild animals, which eat more varied foods than domestic critters, are generally tastier. Then there's glutamate (the amino acid found in all foods containing protein—everything from milk to fish to mushrooms and tomatoes), which is responsible for the so-called "fifth flavor," traditionally referred to as *savory* in English (the others of course being sweet, sour, bitter, and salty) and widely known today by the name *umami*, derived from Japanese. If you've ever wondered what monosodium glutamate is or why it's used, here's the answer: MSG is the synthetic salt form of glutamate added to foods as a "flavor enhancer" that serves basically the same function as naturally occurring glutamate. Your body can't tell the difference between regular glutamate and MSG, so it's added to bring forth the natural savory flavor of your Kung Pao chicken. And no, it's not particularly dangerous, according to numerous scientific studies. While there's still some debate about a small percentage of the population that claims various side effects from consuming the stuff, it's largely agreed that eating MSG isn't going to make your head explode like that guy in *Scanners*.

Since chicken meat is relatively low in glutamate to begin with, it's not going to have a particularly strong flavor, as opposed to, say, a mature lamb or a goat. Add to this the fact that many people remove the skin and fat from their chicken to make the meal more healthful, and voilà—welcome to meat dullsville. And because, without these seminal flavor agents, chicken doesn't really taste like anything in particular, most undistinguished, flavorless meats are said to "taste like chicken." When I'm cooking a chicken, I make it a point to never remove the skin or trim off too much fat, for fear of succumbing to what I call "boring chicken syndrome." If you want flavor, especially with chicken, you gotta have the fat. In fact, the very best traditional recipes for latkes (potato pancakes) employ rendered chicken fat, known in Yiddish as *schmaltz*, instead of cooking oil. If you've ever had schmaltz-fried latkes, you'll know them to be infinitely superior to the oil-fried alternatives.

Another factor contributing to the poultry paradox is the sheer ubiquity of chicken. From the haute-est of haute cuisine restaurants to precooked rotisserie chickens at the grocery store and every fast-food chain restaurant in the world, chicken is everywhere, to the point where its joys are often and easily overlooked. This was not always the case. In fact, chicken was a fairly expensive food before modern agricultural practices turned it into the economical meat we have today.

Until the period of American prosperity following the Second World War, most people considered chicken a luxury dish—if you had a chicken to cook for your family, your family was doing pretty darned well. "Oh my, look at the Joneses," the neighbors might say, "eating chicken on a Tuesday. Aren't *they* well-to-do!" When addressing the country's poverty issues during the Great Depression, Franklin Delano Roosevelt famously paraphrased France's King Henry IV's coronation address by speaking of a glorious future in which there would be "a chicken in every pot." If you're not of that generation, can you imagine a time in which you would just *dream* about the prospect of eating chicken? I wanted to get back to that. As the Shameless Carnivore, I felt an obligation to reclaim the delights of chickendom.

When it came time for me to finally go forth and chicken it up to the max, I was confronted with hundreds of options, but none that I felt truly embraced all the flavors a chicken has to offer. I wanted a place that really worshipped chicken and didn't treat it as a mundane fallback dish. But where to find such a place? I posed this question to a number of friends, and all of them were left scratching their heads, minus one—a Japanese colleague named Timeo.

"Have you heard of yakitori?" she asked. I confessed that I hadn't. For the most part my familiarity with Japanese food was limited to sushi joints, noodle shops, teriyaki and tempura bento box lunch specials, and the carnivalesque theatrics of Benihana's knife-flipping stir-fry chefs. "It's chicken on a stick," she said.

Chicken on a stick? I wondered about this. Was she talking about a whole chicken roasted on a stick, like a spit? Or something like an Asian-flavored chicken corn dog, maybe? That seemed like a strange concept, but who knows—certain elements of Japanese cuisine can be pretty weird to us *gaijin*. Timeo saw the look of puzzlement on my face and explained. "Like shish kebab," she told me, "but all parts of the chicken."

"All parts? Really?" I imagined a kebab loaded with feathers, beaks, and coxcombs.

"Oh yes," she said. "Hearts, liver, skin, tail . . . everything." As she rattled off the various types of grilled offal found in the yakitori stalls on the streets of Tokyo, a look came over her that I recognized instantly: it was the dreamy, hungry, slightly wistful expression of a true carnivore remembering her favorite meats. That was all I needed as an endorsement.

When asked for a recommendation, Timeo was quick to tell of her fondness for a restaurant in midtown Manhattan called Yakitori Totto, a darkly elegant little place prized by Japanese businessfolk and expats for its authentic tastes of home. The restaurant occupies a small space on the second floor of a building, a counterintuitive real-estate position for a Manhattan restaurant, as you have to climb a long, narrow staircase to enter, almost as though the place wanted to be hidden. If this is the case, it's for good reason—the food is so miraculously good, the establishment might be best suited away from the beaten path for fear of being overwhelmed by hungry throngs. As it was, the few tables it does offer, as well as a couple of small private booths and several seats at the bar, are highly coveted, particularly by Japanese, who seemed to make up the lion's share of its clientele.* My two dinner guests and I had to wait over an hour before being seated at a small banquette table in the corner. To say that it was well worth the wait is a gross understatement—many repeat visits later, Yakitori Totto has easily become one of my favorite restaurants in all of New York City, perhaps even the world.

My adoration for this restaurant derives from various sources—including food quality, preparation, presentation, variety, atmosphere, and service—but mostly I love the fact that it has a single concept, superlatively executed: chicken. Sure, the oversized laminated menus (complete with photographs of each item, of course) offer a smattering of fish and pork dishes, but here chicken rules the roost. The word *yakitori* literally means "grilled bird," and like most styles of Japanese cui-

---

* This is *always* a good sign—when the majority of people dining in a restaurant are of the same ethnicity as the establishment's cuisine, you know you've found the right spot.

sine it has a long and storied history. According to the information provided at the table in amusingly fractured English:

> In Japan, the chicken has been kept for many years, and since its
> egg has the precious source of nutrition, it has been dealt with as
> a kind of property. It is said that the "yakitori" as a cooking name
> has appeared since the time in the middle of the Edo period. The
> cooking document "Goruinichiyoryorisho" of Edo can be started
> in the cooking method of yakitori. It seems that "bird was put in
> the skewer, sprinkled and burned with salt, and dipped into the
> soy sauce which added alcohol, and taken out to the drawing
> room." Moreover, the yakitori called one of the prototypes of
> today's yakitori was currently sold at the approach (and entrance
> path to a Shinto shrine) in Kyoto Fushimi Inari as a noted prod-
> uct. The sparrow which becomes the hindrance of rice cultiva-
> tion was taken and it was made yakitori on the approach to the
> Inari shrine which prays a good harvest. In such a place with
> much traffic, it is said that it is sold with the skewer so that it may
> be stood and eaten at a worship going way back then. Public ya-
> kitori can be enjoyed now by the spread of the chicken for meat
> called broiler in Showa 40 and afterwards. However, while it be-
> came popular as a public dish, the stores opened as a high-class
> dish before and after World War II also increased in number. The
> skewer of a good part of chicken, the skewer of vegetables, the
> skewer of decent seasoning, etc., that was not for the former style,
> appeared, and became the present form of yakitori.

I didn't find it at all surprising that yakitori has something of a holy
background, as I felt almost like the restaurant itself is a sanctuary devoted to the worship of chicken (in a gustatory sense, not as an actual
deity, of course). Even climbing those stairs was somewhat akin to scaling the stone steps leading up to a mountain temple or ziggurat, though
on a considerably smaller scale.

The protocol with yakitori is similar to what you'd find at a Spanish tapas restaurant. Most of the dishes are both modest in portion and price (anywhere between two and five dollars per serving), making it easy to take advantage of the dozens of available items, most of which are simply seasoned and grilled over charcoal on bamboo skewers, in plain view of diners. As we sipped at the house drink, iced sake with lime, my friends Brad and Katie and I decided to go to town and, between the three of us, order one of almost everything. I've long noticed that many people are protective of their food in restaurants, hesitating to share more than a single taste of the dish they ordered, which is ludicrous. I love sharing food, especially when your dining experience necessitates a large number of small dishes. And this was precisely one of those situations.

After placing our initial order (many more would follow, once we got into the addictive rhythm of the place), we nursed our drinks and tried not to go insane with hunger at the pervasive aroma of grilling chicken, which filled the dining room like an intoxicating fog. To amuse ourselves until the first wave of our order arrived, we turned our attention to chicken trivia and philosophy, things like "Who would win in an epic battle between the armies of Colonel Sanders and General Tso?" Both are famous military figures in the poultry world (sorry, Frank Perdue, you're going to have to be knighted or something to join this club), but who would win out? we wondered. Tso does outrank Sanders—Harland David Sanders was merely an army private serving in Cuba and was only later awarded the honorary title of Kentucky Colonel by the state's then governor, Ruby Laffoon. In contrast, General Tso was a distinguished military commander who showed his tactical genius in the Taiping Rebellion, one of the bloodiest conflicts in history. However, it is historically documented that the Colonel did indeed cook and serve fried chicken; few can confirm the same of the General. Plus, the man behind KFC has his secret blend of eleven herbs and spices, so who's to say he doesn't have some more tricky maneuvers up his sleeve? In the end, we agreed that victory would inevitably go to General Tso—like those partaking of his eponymous dish, his soldiers would undoubtedly be ready for more after only a couple of hours, as opposed to Sanders's chicken, which sticks with you for what seems like days.

Soon enough our own chicken arrived, our table now crowded with various grilled delights. The restaurant prides itself on serving only organic chicken—no steroid- and antibiotic-fueled megabirds for these chefs—and the difference was easy to discern in the flavor of the dishes we enjoyed with that first round of skewered morsels. First came *mune*, or small cubes of skinless breast meat, served plain with wasabi on the side, and we could tell by its texture that the wasabi was freshly grated, perhaps with an *oroshigane*, the traditional sharkskin grater (easily one of the coolest kitchen implements ever), instead of the inferior, toothpaste-consistency green glop you see in most Japanese restaurants in the United States. It was a perfect complement to the chicken breast, which, while juicy and tender, wasn't particularly flavorful by itself because of the whole glutamate/fat issue. We much preferred the crunchy *tebasaki* (wing), the silky *reba* (livers), and, my favorite thus far, *hatsu*, or heart. I'd never eaten chicken hearts before, presumably because every time we had chicken during my formative years my mother would, in the process of cleaning the bird, casually toss the small package of giblets into the trash. This, I now realize, was a tremendous mistake—chicken hearts have a surprisingly beefy taste and texture. It feels strangely voodoo-ish to say it, but I *love* sinking my teeth into the heart of a fresh hen. Brad was quick to share my enthusiasm. "When I was a kid having dinner at my grandmother's house," he said, "I loved the hearts so much that she would get extra from the butcher shop, just for me." Now that is the kind of love only a grandmother can provide: one that comes with extra chicken hearts.

More meat arrived, then still more. "I forgot I'd asked for an extra order of these," said Brad, joyously surprised to have a second helping of *reba* set in front of him. "I love this waitress. The way she keeps bringing us gifts like this . . . she's like the Japanese Mrs. Claus!" This second wave brought more exotic specialties. We eagerly took to the *kawa*, crispy chicken skin, wrapped around the skewer, that had all the fat (and hence all the decadence) missing from our helping of *mune*. Then came *shishito tsukune*, a "chicken meatball" stuffed into slender boats made of Japanese green peppers and garnished with a wedge of lemon, as well as *aspara maki* (chicken asparagus roll) and *sunagimo*, the bird's gizzard. I have to confess that this was a slight down note in an otherwise stellar dining experience. I've never particularly cared for gizzards, the muscular, specialized stomach that birds use to grind up their food, and that I've always found to be unappetizingly gristly. These gizzards were no exception, but I will say that, among all the gizzards I've eaten in my life, these were certainly the best. But my disappointment didn't last long; next we dug into *tsukune tare*, a chicken meatball with a brown sauce, complemented by a raw quail's egg, floating placidly in a small dish, in which to dip the meat. The richness of the egg yolk combined with the spiced ground chicken to produce a powerfully savory taste. No MSG needed here—this had all the natural umami we needed. Then came the most interesting flavor combination of the night: *sasami shisomaki*, light breast meat wrapped roulade-style around shiso leaf, otherwise known as "Japanese mint," and drizzled with a thick red plum sauce. We all found the presentation delightful— three little morsels of spiraled meat and mint on a stick with the playful zigzag of sauce traipsing across them, making them look more like something out of the Lollipop Guild than a dish fresh off a Japanese hibachi. The combination of the delicate meat and the coolness of the shiso was lovely, but it was the plum sauce, with a tanginess that pistolwhips you right in your sour receptors, that made the dish explode. It wasn't just good—it was a pairing of flavors that was completely new to me in the most exhilarating way. This is the type of rare, bittersweet moment that makes you smack your head and pound your fists on the table, exasperated by regret at not having discovered this dish sooner.

There's nothing you can do but wish for a time machine so you can go back and throttle your younger self for such an egregious oversight.

But oh, we weren't done yet; there was still more chicken to come. Our night would be capped off by dining on parts of the animal that most people wouldn't even feed to a stray dog, much less shell out hard-earned cash for, but that here were offered as a specialty of the house. There were chicken tails (*bonchiri*), meaty little nuggets with a crackly, satisfying crunch to them, as well as *hiza nankotsu*, the soft cartilage from the birds' knees, and—get this—*nankotsu*, or "soft bone." I never would have pictured these last two on a menu anywhere but the most desperate restaurants, and I certainly never envisioned myself eating them, but they turned out to be, like many of the other yakitori we'd feasted on that evening, surprisingly enjoyable. I've long delighted in cleaning all the meat from chicken bones at the end of a meal, but I'd never actually consumed the bones themselves. I didn't even know a person *could* eat chicken bones, much less that doing so could be considered a special treat. I was learning a lot about my own ignorance that night. Neither cartilage nor bone had the same savory flavors as some of the other yakitori, lacking as they were in actual meat; what you got instead was a deep, smoky taste of the grill as you carefully worked the ingredients between your teeth. It's a little scary at first, putting small, sharp-looking wedges of bone into your mouth—having the word *asphyxiation* paired with *chicken bone* on your obituary would have something less than a noble air to it—but it's ultimately worth it. It took some faith and a little effort to initially grind the material with my molars, but just before I could begin to worry that I'd gotten in over my head with this dish, the bones simply melted in my mouth, as if by magic. Who would've known?

When all was said and done, and the three of us sat back in our chairs fully sated and a little dizzy from the hours of eating and the many glasses of sake and beer we'd consumed with each new round of skewers, we all agreed with utmost conviction that none of us would ever, for the rest of our lives, think of chicken as boring again.

Wabbit Season (The Cuteness Factor)

Of all the meats I enjoy, there is one that, when I bring it up in conversations about food, tends to make certain people's faces drop in abject horror, an expression usually accompanied by the words *Oh noooo!*

I am talking, of course, about rabbit—though judging by that expression I might as well have been extolling the delights of devouring braised human infants. There's something about eating rabbit—"bunnies" in the parlance of the sensitive set—that scares people off. The reason, I've gathered, is that rabbits are cute, and people don't want to eat cute things. Hell, I know some people who won't eat the smiley-faced pancake breakfast at IHOP because they can't stand it looking at them with those big fried-egg eyes. This is absurd, for the simple, incontrovertible reason that *rabbit tastes great.* That's right, I said it. Those adorable little balls of warm, happy fuzziness you had in your kindergarten classroom are absolutely delicious, not to mention healthful and easy to prepare.

The biggest problem with eating rabbit that I've encountered is that in most parts of the country it's fairly difficult to find, and when you do find it, it's pricey. Why is this? I mean, it's not like rabbits are an endangered species or anything, nor do they have panda-like difficulties getting busy. Anyone who's made the mistake of pairing a male and a female in the same cage can attest to that (cue Barry White's "Can't Get Enough of Your Love, Babe"). So why, I ask again, do we not have beautiful sections of plump, pink rabbit shrink-wrapped in the meat section of every chain grocery store across the country?

In the meat world, rabbit (*Oryctolagus cuniculus*) has what marketing executives might refer to as an "image problem." The first reason is the cute factor, an immediate turnoff for many. I have one word to say about that, a word commonly employed by the English, which is this: *bollocks!*

If you aren't eating meat because the animal it comes from is cuddly and precious, you shouldn't be eating meat at all. Cuteness holds no sway for the true carnivore. Shunning the meat of cuter animals while continuing to enjoy the less adorable ones reeks to high heaven of hypocrisy—what does it matter how an animal looks, so long as it's pleasing to the palate? If you don't have any moral qualms eating a cow, why get all teary-eyed and choked up over a rabbit? True, it's more likely that you've had a rabbit as a pet than a cow, but this still doesn't mean that the rabbit's life is worth more, and should therefore be spared. It would be one thing to forgo broiled bunnies if you didn't care for the taste, but claiming some sort of ethical high ground based on an animal's preciousness is an expression of profound idiocy. Several years ago, one particularly evil genius capitalized on bunny sensitivities by founding a website called Save Toby, in which he described his pet, a rabbit named Toby whom he'd found bleeding near his home, apparently from a run-in with some feral cats. Like any decent human being, he'd nursed the poor, victimized animal back to full health. Then, on the Web (and in charmingly blunt language), he declared that while he loved Toby, he was planning on killing and cooking him unless he received $50,000 in PayPal donations and Save Toby merchandise sales by a certain date in the very near future. He even made sure to include a slideshow featuring adorable photos of Toby in a stockpot, in addition to a number of classic rabbit recipes he might put to use. It didn't take long before the enterprise incited a big brouhaha featuring a cavalcade of do-gooding hippie types, some of whom even tried to file lawsuits, although nothing could really be done to him legally, since he hadn't done, nor was he planning to do, anything against the law. It's perfectly within your rights, as an American citizen, to kill and cook a rabbit. Eventually, some unnamed advertiser paid an undisclosed sum to Toby's owner, and the rabbit lived. As a shameless carnivore, all the site did for me was to confirm the crazy power of the cuteness factor, and then make me hungry for braised rabbit.

And hey, what about fish? Decidedly uncute. And yet even some people who pass on all other animals continue to dig into sushi with no moral apprehension whatsoever. You don't think a two-hundred-pound tuna feels pain when a fisherman tears through the walls of its mouth with his hook, then bashes in the writhing, suffocating creature's head on the deck of his boat? In the ironic words of the late Kurt Cobain: "It's okay to eat fish, 'cause they don't have any feelings." In fact, some of the best-tasting meat in the world comes from the most lovable little critters, especially rabbit. Puffin, a colorfully billed relative of the penguin, is a prized delicacy in Iceland (though killing one is illegal throughout much of the world, maybe because of its cuteness). Think of that the next time you rent *Happy Feet* or *March of the Penguins*. Most people identify with the penguins . . . Me, I'm rooting for the leopard seal. I think my carnivorous muse, Ted Nugent, said it best: "The cuter the animal, the sweeter the meat." If this dictum holds true, I'd love to get my hands on some nice baby panda.

Others might see rabbit as a "poverty meat," like raccoon or possum. Or, conversely, they might think it too effete and, in the words of my crimson-collared brethren, "too Frenchy-sounding." Doesn't it strike you as bizarre that the same animal can simultaneously conjure up images of backward hillbillies scooping up skid-marked roadkill with a snow shovel (rabbits are related to rodents, after all) and snooty, white-gloved European gastronomes picking at a precious delicacy with expensive silverware? This is both perplexing and weird, but true nonetheless.

The scarcity of rabbit meat on the market is also caused by the fact that Congress doesn't mandate its inspection. And since most stores won't sell non-USDA-approved meat for fear of being busted by the feds, they simply won't put rabbit on their shelves. Those who are still bent on selling their rabbity wares (God bless them) have to pony up extra dough for a voluntary inspection, which doesn't come cheap, and as a consequence both producer and retailer have to jack up their prices to cover their costs. As a shameless carnivore, I think this is a scandal, a *shonda*, a crying shame! I'm looking to start a petition going around to endorse rabbit meat for USDA inspection and approval. Especially in these times of avian flu, when some people are a bit anxious about the chicken salad, rabbit would make a wonderful alternative. Just think, if everyone shared this opinion, we could have rabbit nuggets, rabbit salad sandwiches, rabbit caesar wraps, rabbit penne with pesto sauce, rabbit cordon bleu, rabbit Francese, buffalo rabbit tenders, rabbit Kiev . . . The list goes on and on.

I learned to love rabbit at one of my very favorite restaurants in the world, Brigtsen's, on Dante Street in New Orleans. Chef Frank always manages to have rabbit on the menu, and I love the man for it. Whether it's the classic New Orleans dish I devoured lo those many years ago—panéed rabbit tenderloin with Creole mustard sauce, collard greens, and grits—or his current rabbit special, this is a place that does rabbit right, and consistently. It makes me feel a little homesick (not to mention peckish) every time I think about it, so I was more than happy when the time came during my Month of Meat to cook some up.

If you've never cooked rabbit, you're in serious luck—it is every bit as easy to prepare as chicken and just as healthful and tasty, though I've always found rabbit meat, on the whole, to be slightly more savory than chicken breast. You can cook it any way you'd do a sectioned chicken, since the texture and the flavor are so similar, so feel free to bread and deep-fry it, make it into a stew or a soup (I love a good rabbit chili), pan-sauté it, or, one of my favorites, throw it in the slow cooker with a few vegetables and some braising liquid. I like white wine, but you can just as easily use chicken stock or even beer. I have a deep love for my Crock-Pot—it's one of the easiest, most reliable ways to prepare a big, satisfying meal. You can throw in your ingredients in the morning, set the pot to cook on low, spend the day at work or running around town, and eight or nine hours later you get to return to a house filled with the aroma of your slow-braised meat and vegetables, hot and ready to enjoy. For a lazy person (not to mention ovenless), it's a godsend. Make a Crock-Pot dinner for a friend or date, and they'll even think you're a whiz in the kitchen, wholly unaware that all you did was chuck a bunch of stuff in a pot and run away.

This is exactly what I did with my rabbit, a lovely cottontail happily provided by Frank Ottomanelli, who was keen to let me know as soon as he had some freshly in stock, and was, like the fine butcher he is, more than accommodating in saving me the work of cleaning and sectioning it. All I needed to do was take it home, rinse the meat and pat it dry, add a little salt and pepper, then toss it into the pot with some coarsely cut vegetables and a little chicken stock. Six hours later, Bugs was a tender dinner for two, with leftovers to spare.

Crock-Pot Rabbit

1 RABBIT (FRYER), CUT INTO SERVING PIECES
SALT AND PEPPER
½ CUP COARSELY CHOPPED CELERY
½ CUP PEELED AND COARSELY CUT CARROTS
½ LARGE ONION, COARSELY CHOPPED

2 CUPS SLICED WHITE BUTTON MUSHROOMS
2 CUPS CHICKEN STOCK
¼ CUP MARSALA WINE
1 TABLESPOON CORNSTARCH
1 TABLESPOON BUTTER

Lightly season the rabbit pieces with salt and pepper. Place all ingredients except Marsala, cornstarch, and butter in a Crock-Pot and cook on low for 6 hours. While it cooks, go out and do something fun . . . a nice afternoon shopping, perhaps? Remove the rabbit from the pot. In a separate bowl, combine the Marsala and cornstarch. Pour the mixture into the Crock-Pot to thicken the sauce; add butter and stir. Return the rabbit to the Crock-Pot and coat with the sauce.

Serves 3 to 4

CHAPTER 3

Meat and You

How Carnivorism Can Help You Lose Weight, Feel Great, and Keep Your Children from Having to Repeat the Third Grade

Amid my carnivorous explorations, when I tell people about all the new and interesting animals and organs I'm enjoying, they react in alarm, as though I'd told them that I savor a nice fat pipe stuffed with crack on my afternoons off. "My God," they say, "you're going to kill yourself! All that meat, it's got to be terrible for your body." For some reason, the notion of enjoying meat has now become synonymous with unhealthy living. I don't know whether to credit this phenomenon to vegetarian propaganda or American gluttony (probably a combination of the two), but something has gone terribly, terribly amiss. When did meat become the enemy? This shouldn't be a shocking revelation by any means, but here it is, just in case you didn't already know it: *Meat is good for you.* Very good for you, in fact. Today, vegetarianism is often seen as a much more healthful alternative to carnivorism, but the truth is that while a vegetarian diet can be a healthy way to live, it can also be worse for you than a diet that contains animal flesh. Conversely, filling your days with meat can also lead to health problems, which many health professionals were quick to point out when the Atkins "restricted carbohydrate" diet craze swept the nation, leading some people to consume huge quantities of meat and little else, which is a dangerously unhealthy way to live, even if you are losing weight. Hell, if you're a diabetic, you can lose weight by avoiding your insulin injections—no doctor's going to recommend that, either. But here's the good news—you can absolutely stay true to the carnivorous cause and be a perfectly healthy, robust person. It's all a matter of balance. And when you're balancing your diet, as the government says you should with its long-standing, annually updated food pyramid (go to www.mypyramid.gov if you want to see what they're recommending these days—and yes, meat is still very much on the menu), it's a good thing to keep meat in the picture.

Consider the nutritional content of beef, for example. "Oh dear," you might say, "I thought steaks, chops, and ground beef were insidiously designed to clog my arteries, raise my blood pressure, and send me to an early grave," and you might be right, if you eat way too much of them (of course you could be wrong, too, but I'll get to that in a bit). "Meat is absolutely good for you," says Kathleen Zelman, a nutritionist and dietitian who for twelve years was the national spokesperson for the American Dietetic Association. "It's rich in all sorts of nutritional elements that are great for your health. The problem is that when people think of meat being bad for you, they're thinking of those Texas steakhouse portions—and if you're going to eat a twenty-six-ounce steak, they're probably right. But if you have instead a four-ounce filet trimmed of excess fat, it's just as nutritious and as good for you as the same quantity of any other lean protein." You heard it here—the meat you love loves you right back. So what, exactly, are the good things that a sizzling filet has to offer your body?

Easily the most important thing meat has to offer a person is protein, without which your body would basically run out of battery power. According to Mary Young, the executive director of nutrition for the National Cattlemen's Beef Association, "The protein in beef is complete and high quality, like all animal protein. This means beef supplies all of the essential amino acids (protein building blocks) the body needs to build, maintain, and repair body tissue and muscle, form hormones and enzymes, and increase resistance to infection and disease. Research suggests higher amounts of protein may be needed for optimal health and protein may enhance the benefits of exercise and help boost muscle development." Of course, it's possible to get your protein from other sources, but the plain fact is that not all protein is created equal, a dirty little secret that "go-veg" proselytizers are rarely quick to share. Soybeans are chock full of the stuff, sure, but you still need to carefully combine your proteins if you want to get the same benefits that meat offers up alone. That complete protein has tremendously beneficial effects on your body—one study, published in the *Journal of Nutrition*, showed that combining plenty of dietary protein with exercise has "additive effects on body composition during weight loss in adult women." A protein-rich diet, along with exercise and reduced carbohydrate intake, not only improved the study participants' body composition as they lost weight but also "reduced triglyceride levels and maintained higher HDL (good) cholesterol levels." That's right, ladies: if you're on a fitness kick and losing weight, eating meat will not just keep you healthy, it will actually make you *look better*. How scary does meat seem now, eh?

Another crucial component of meat is iron, which is essential to the proper functioning of a human body. Many meats are loaded with the stuff, and good that they are. According to Ms. Young,

Beef is the third most abundant food source of iron (behind fortified cereals and yeast breads) and is the best source of readily available iron. Iron plays an important role in cognitive health throughout life and helps red blood cells carry oxygen to body tissues, and as a good source of iron, beef can help protect against iron deficiency anemia—the most prevalent nutritional deficiency in the United States. Iron deficiency anemia during pregnancy increases the risk of preterm delivery and low birth weight babies. Some research has suggested that low birth weight babies are at increased risk for certain diseases later in life, including cardiovascular disease, gestational diabetes, and obesity, as well as possible educational disadvantages.

If you ever wondered why parents were once told to feed their children plenty of red meat, there you go. And as studies on iron continue, still more interesting, even shocking, revelations arise about its importance to growing kids. "There is a significant body of evidence linking alteration in neurological and cognitive function to iron deficiency and iron deficiency anemia in children," continues Ms. Young. "These children were more likely to have repeated a grade, been referred for special services, and experienced anxiety or depression problems, social problems, and attention problems." The subtext is pretty clear: feed your kids beef, folks, because it will help keep them from being depressed misfits with ADHD who spend two years in the third grade and wind up in juvie.

And it's not just protein and iron—beef also contains plenty of B vitamins that maintain normal functioning of body cells and the nervous system; it's the most abundant food source of zinc, an essential mineral that helps build muscles and heal wounds; niacin, which promotes healthy skin and nerves and helps digestion; riboflavin (good vision); selenium, which works as an antioxidant with vitamin E to protect from heart disease and other health problems; and phosphorus, an element that helps regulate metabolism, among other things. Now, it's of course true that you can get all of these nutrients in other ways—by studiously and regularly combining other foods that contribute the same amount, or by taking supplements. However, it's undeniable that simply eating beef is the easiest (and of course tastiest) way to go about it, not to mention that most health professionals advise a "food first" approach, which entails getting most if not all of your essential nutrients from your diet rather than popping pills. If you want, you can go ahead and rigorously plot out your dietary intake on a series of graphs and spreadsheets—me, I'd rather just have a roast beef sandwich and call it a day.

So once again, meat is really good for your body, provided you make a reasonable attempt to balance your diet. Do you know what's bad for you? Veganism. Well, at least if you're a baby, in which case it can even be deadly. In recent years, there's been a tragic rash of infant deaths at the hands of their idiotic vegan parents. Take, for instance, the case of poor little six-week-old Crown Shakur, whose parents were convicted by an Atlanta court in 2007 for malice murder, felony murder, involuntary manslaughter, and cruelty to children and sentenced to life in prison following the newborn's death. With all of those heinous charges, what on earth could they have done to that innocent child? Did they beat him? Shake him? Throw him in a Dumpster? Not quite. They fed him a diet based on what they perceived as appropriate according to their beliefs as vegans—mostly soy milk and apple juice—and the boy basically starved to death. "No matter how many times they want to say, 'We're vegans, we're vegetarians,' that's not the issue in this case," said prosecutor Chuck Boring in an Associated Press story. "The child died because he was not fed. Period." If the parents had been responsible carnivores, or even vegetarians who consumed enough animal protein (milk, eggs, cheese), there's little doubt young Crown would be alive and well today. I'm sure I'm not the only person who found a heartbreaking irony in the fact that in an attempt to be either healthy or ethical to animals, these people killed their son, a human being. Humans need all those wonderful nutrients found in animal products—this is why, no matter how hard you look, you won't find *any* indigenous vegan societies. Without the benefit of supplements, most vegans would probably be undernourished at best, and at worst have very serious health problems. Aside from having a more difficult time getting enough protein and iron, they'd have little real access to vitamin B_{12}, which is only found in animal products—B_{12} deficiency can lead to pernicious anemia and even permanent nerve damage. Pregnant women should be particularly concerned. Ms. Young told me that "according to a *Journal of Nutrition* study, pregnant women who followed a vegetarian diet that included eggs and dairy products, but no meat, had an increased risk of vitamin B_{12} deficiency, which is a risk factor for neural tube defects. In addition, breast-fed infants of a vitamin B_{12}-deficient mother are at greater risk for developmental abnormalities, impaired growth, and anemia." So if you're with child, getting some meat in your diet can be an especially good thing. Ultimately, though, if you're an adult and you want to be a vegan, go ahead and make that choice. This is America, after all, home of the free, and you're welcome to feed yourself (or not feed yourself) whatever you want, whatever your beliefs are. But when you inflict malnutrition and starvation on an innocent child, that, my friends, is criminal. Literally.

Okay, so now that you know meat is your friend, it's probably important to note that eating a thirty-ounce porterhouse for two every day does not mean you're being twice as healthy. Indeed, too much meat can in fact be a bad thing, especially if it's particularly fatty meat. But there are plenty of lean meats to add to a healthy diet, and I'm not just talking about skinless (flavorless) chicken breasts here. There are a whopping twenty-nine cuts of beef that meet the government guidelines for "lean" (less than 10 grams of total fat, 4.5 grams or less of saturated fat, and less than 95 milligrams of cholesterol per three-ounce serving), including, astonishingly enough, a T-bone steak. The first important thing to take into account, if you want to get the full spectrum of health benefits of carnivorism without causing your blood pressure and cholesterol levels to skyrocket, is portion size. How much meat is a good thing? It doesn't take much. Ms. Zelman agrees with the USDA's assessment in its 2005 *Dietary Guidelines for Americans*, which says that you should eat about five ounces of lean protein every day, on average. In addition, a review published in the September 2006 issue of the *American Journal of Clinical Nutrition* suggests that at least 15 grams of essential amino acids, or four ounces of high-quality protein, like beef, *at each meal*, can enhance quality of life and prevent disease by helping build and maintain adequate levels of muscle mass. How does that translate to a serving on your plate? "In terms of meat," Zelman says, "think of the size of your palm, no bigger than that." Naturally, I was quick to imagine a hamburger patty as wide as my palm and three inches high, but I'm sure that's not what she was talking about. "Portionwise, we've begun to really rethink how much meat is necessary and beneficial," she continues. "Instead of seeing meat as the star on your plate, with everything else relegated to side-dish status, think of meat as the bonus of the meal, focusing mostly on eating lots of whole grains and as many vegetables as you like." I have to admit that, as a shameless carnivore, it's unlikely that I'll ever see meat on my plate as anything other than the star attraction, but I took heed from her advice on portion size. It's well known and documented that the satiety center in the human brain is a little lazy—it takes us a while to feel like we're completely filled up, and as we wait for that to happen we're prone to keep forking more food into our mouths. So by the time our brain tells us we're full, we've eaten way more than we should have, and now we're loosening our belts and looking around for the Alka-Seltzer. Some scientists now suggest an evolutionary advantage to this: since high-quality protein was so difficult to come by back in the cave days, and our forebears' mealtimes were anything but regular or pre-dictable (you rarely knew where, when, or what your next dinner would be), stuffing yourself silly when you had the opportunity would help keep your body filled with nutrients for longer periods, keeping you alive until someone else managed to bring home a huge woolly mammoth sirloin. These days, though, that's hardly necessary for most of us. I did a little experiment, then, to see if these recommended allotments of lean protein would do the trick. Lo and behold, the government was actually right about something: you can eat a satisfying meal that contains all appropriate food groups and is still appealing. As advised by the USDA's MyPyramid website, I had a turkey sandwich with cheese, lettuce, tomato, and mustard (even a little mayonnaise!) on whole-grain toast, and it was fantastic—more evidence for my theory that the turkey sandwich is the world's perfect food.

But say you don't want to eat only turkey sandwiches. Say it's just gotten warm outside and, after a winter's worth of yearning, you're dying to fire up that sweet grill you have in the backyard and cook up some steaks. Wouldn't that be verboten by all those nutrition gurus? Good news, carnivores—the answer is a resounding no. Again, portion size is critical, and you should probably trim away any excess fat if you want to stay on the healthy side of things, but there are other important factors to consider. Many people were alarmed by studies showing that that black, charred stuff on grilled meats is a carcinogenic agent, so they started shunning those backyard barbeques altogether to keep from getting cancer. This, you should know, is an overreaction—all you have to do to avoid any problems is simply pay close and careful attention to the meat you're cooking, which you should be concerned with in the first place. If you cook meat too fast over heat that's too high, you'll wind up inadvertently causing your protein to create harmful heterocyclic amines (HCAs), as well as polycyclic aromatic hydrocarbons (PAHs), which form when the fat from your meat drips down into the hot coals and flares up. You know—like what happens when you absentmindedly poke that burger you're grilling so that all the juices run into the fire and fill your yard with smoke. For the sake of your health—and your burger (you don't want to lose those precious juices!)—don't do that. The best thing to do, as both a cook and a health-conscious carnivore, is to cook your meat over medium heat until it's nice and brown, but not black. Browning is good, charring is not. Browning is the product of something called the "Maillard reaction," a chemical process that is, in fact, the whole basis of the flavor industry.

This occurs somewhere north of 300 degrees Fahrenheit, when the denatured proteins on the surface of the meat recombine with its sugars, leaving the most intense flavors on the surface of the meat (which is why most people consider the skin of the chicken the tastiest part—well, that and the fact that it's filled with delicious fats). According to the National Cattlemen's Beef Association, "Beef's tender, juicy texture is optimum when cooked to medium rare (145°F) to medium (160°F) doneness. Burgers and anything with ground meat should be cooked to medium (160°F) doneness, until no longer pink in center and juices show no pink color, turning occasionally. [As for chicken, look for an internal temperature of 165.] Overcooking meat, poultry or fish is not recommended." Amen to that—who wants a big black hunk of charred nastiness when you can have a beautifully browned burger or steak?

"Great," you say. "Now I know how to cook my meat so that those blackened bits won't give me cancer. But what about the meat itself? Wasn't there some sort of study showing that eating too much beef might give me cancer?" Yes, there was, I'm afraid. Research published by the American Cancer Society aimed to illustrate how diets containing an abundant amount of red meat could be linked to increased risk of colorectal cancer, and it was yet another thing that scared once-proud beef-loving folks straight into shunning their beloved steaks and chops. *Too risky*, they thought. *I love my meat, but I'll stay away from colon cancer, thank you very much.* First, it should be noted that even the researchers conducting the study were quick to say they weren't condemning red meat, but rather advising people not to make it the mainstay of their diet. So even if you accept their findings, you can still enjoy the occasional strip steak, pot roast, or taco, as long as it's a limited affair.

But there's now growing evidence that maybe you don't need to be so restrictive after all. A number of physicians and statisticians consider the conclusions reached in that study to be suspect, and indications are that the literature on the subject might be in for a change. First, the study clearly stated that obesity, smoking, heavy alcohol consumption, and physical inactivity are significantly riskier than just eating red meat. According to an article by George Mason University's Statistical Assessment Service (STATS), a nonprofit, nonpartisan organization aimed at correcting scientific misinformation in the media resulting from bad science, political bias, or a simple lack of information or knowledge, "if you look at the study itself, red meat is not quite the red flag claimed by the media. Even comparing those who consume the most meat with those who consume the least, the authors found varying results, some of which were conclusive and many of which were not." Basically, when you take out all those environmental factors, only 1 percent of long-term carnivores have a somewhat increased risk of colorectal cancer in their lifetime. Says STATS, "That may be too high a risk for some people, but it shouldn't lead you to avoid eating red meat." Me, I'm not worried. After all, I do love red meat, but I love a varied diet, too. All the more reason to fill my meals with all kinds of different meats!

And what about cholesterol? Will eating steaks and chops today inevitably lead to heart problems down the road? Maybe, maybe not. According to Dr. Rian Tannenbaum, a gastroenterologist, eating meat might be the last thing to worry about when it comes to treating your body right. "The bottom line is that the most important thing about someone's health is their family makeup, where they come from. If you're born at the top of the genetic ladder, so to speak, who cares what you eat? You're genetically blessed to be able to process certain foods and not have any trouble accumulating bad (LDL) cholesterol. And if your entire family has problems with cholesterol and coronary artery disease, changing your diet is not going to make a huge difference. It'll help, sure, but not that much." He was quick to note that he wasn't speaking in purely theoretical terms:

> I worked with an ER doctor who was the ideal portrait of healthy living. He kept to a strict vegetarian diet, never even *touched* meat, ran marathons, you name it. He looked great, was lean and mus-

cular like a professional athlete. Then one day he just started feeling terrible. He got a workup from his physician and it turns out that despite everything he did to live a healthy lifestyle, he had uncontrollable high blood pressure because of renal artery stenosis. His outrageous cholesterol had caused plaques to build up in his arteries, and he ended up needing to get a stent in his heart. I remember him being absolutely shaken to the core—after all he did for his health, he *still* runs into these problems!

"So what's the lesson here?" I asked Dr. Tannenbaum. "Is it that if you have a genetic cholesterol problem, you're damned if you do and damned if you don't, so you might as well eat meat and enjoy it?"

"I have four words for you," he replied. " 'Better living through chemistry.' " He continued:

It used to be that if you had a problem, you had to radically alter your diet, and even then there might be little change in your condition. Now there are these statin drugs like Lipitor that can help your body process the cholesterol, letting the good cholesterol [HDL] do its thing untouched while helping eliminate the negative effects of the bad [LDL] cholesterol. And there are other medications, like Zetia, that you can take to keep your body from absorbing the LDL in your digestive system. So here's the thing: if you have less than favorable genetics, you can take these medications, lower your bad cholesterol up to 35 percent, and *still* eat plenty of meat. The ER doctor I mentioned? Now he's on statins, and get this—he now eats meat. He figured, "What the hell, being a vegetarian wasn't doing me much good anyway, so I might as well enjoy some meat now that I have my cholesterol under control."

Better living through chemistry, indeed! While staying active, not smoking, and enjoying a balanced diet are certainly great ideas, if you're interested in trying to live something close to a long, healthy life, it's good to know that should you be somewhat less than blessed in the cholesterol department, medical science has your carnivorous needs covered.

That, dear reader, is progress.

CHAPTER 4

Month of Meat, Round 2

Really Slow Food

A "delicacy," says the *Oxford English Dictionary*, is "something that gratifies the palate, a choice or dainty item of food" and "a luxury; a sensual pleasure." How exactly *Helix aspersa*—the slimy little lump of hermaphroditic mollusk that feeds on dirt and decayed plants, a creature more widely known as the common brown garden snail—ever became associated with either of these definitions (much less food), is something only the French can explain. History doesn't tell precisely how they managed to convince their peers that these creatures would be not just palatable but tasty, but I love imagining how it might have happened. My two best theories:

1) A Parisian criminal, wrongly convicted à la Jean Valjean, is thrown into a dank dungeon cell in the Bastille and left to rot. His minders,

lazy and cruel, often don't get around to feeding the poor wretch his daily ration of moldy black bread and muddy water, so our guy has to find his sustenance on his own, or else starve to death. Longing for vindication, the bedraggled man wills himself to live on anything he can find, though unfortunately there isn't much to be found in his cell. One day, though, he spies a slippery little animal making its way up the stone wall. With steely fortitude, he snatches the thing, rips it from its shell, and bolts it down. Since snails enjoy moist, dirty places—and his cell is certainly that—the man has no trouble sustaining himself on them in the ensuing years, as he dreams of daylight, fine cuisine, and justice. "One day," he tells himself, "they will pay. One day, *they* will be the ones eating these disgusting things!"

A couple of decades and a revolution later, the man is released from his imprisonment, and he uses his newfound freedom (and an assumed name) to study the culinary arts. His prowess in the kitchen and formidable work ethic are unsurpassed, and it's not long before our hero is feted as the most innovative and exquisite chef in all of Paris. His signature dish, of course: escargots. The Parisian elite devour his buttery snails by the dozen, and with each plate he sends to the dining room to be slurped down by the very people who forgot him in the deep recesses of the Bastille, the man laughs to himself, reveling in his comeuppance. "Justice," he chuckles, "has been served."

2) There is a modest country restaurant in Provence, known throughout the whole of Europe for its divine garlic butter. People travel hundreds of miles from the surrounding regions and countries to experience this incomparable substance. And though hundreds of chefs attempt to replicate the recipe, none succeed; it is the finest in the land.

"We have ze best garlic butter!" says François to his fellow chef over a snifter of cognac. A hard evening's work at the restaurant, which was spilling over with patrons as usual, has finally concluded, and he's had a snootful.

"Indeed, we do," replies René, also into his cups. "Ze people, zey simply can't get enough of eet."

"*C'est vrai, René, c'est vrai.*" The two men toast each other merrily and take another swallow of the fine brandy.

"Hey, François . . . I bet we could put anything in zat garlic butter, and ze people, zey will eat it still!"

"Like what?"

"Oh, eet could be anything, François, anything!" Glancing out into the garden, René has an idea . . .

One extraordinarily successful month later: "*Mon dieu,* François . . . more snails!"

Truth be told, eating snails goes back a long way in the history books, and though we currently view the French as the world's premier snail aficionados, it's thought that the practice of eating the "slippery little suckers"* goes back to ancient Rome. This isn't a big surprise— all it takes is a cursory look into the dietary habits of ancient Romans to find truly mind-boggling forays into gastronomic excess. They all but pioneered the practice of stuffing various animals into other animals (the historic forebear of the modern turducken) and were known to devour just about any critter they could conceivably bake, broil, grill, or sauté, not to mention their famous habit of ritual bulimia during daylong feasts in order to keep gorging themselves on every new delicacy presented at the table. Talk about shameless carnivorism! They did very much enjoy their snails, too, as excavations of certain ancient towns in Italy reveal that the Romans kept special vineyards in which to feed and fatten the animals. At some point, most likely between the Dark Ages and the Renaissance, the practice of eating snails was adopted by the French, and while I'd love to say "the rest is history," that's simply not the case. Over the centuries, the eating of snails

---

* Remember when Julia Roberts inadvertently launched one across the restaurant in *Pretty Woman*? I love the nonchalant expression on the waiter's face after he catches it and deftly hides it in his white-gloved hands.

in French culture went in and out of fashion numerous times, though that fact shouldn't be particularly shocking when you recall what snails look like both living and cooked. You'll find food writers during these periods alternately praising the animals for their flavor and nutrition, and disdaining them as being unconscionably repugnant—either way, they've always felt strongly about the subject. Since about the early 1900s, however, escargots have been consistently enjoyed by the French and by enthusiasts of French cuisine, although I still occasionally wonder when I order them if the chef isn't really snickering at me back there in the kitchen.

With snails on my list, I had little choice but to head out to a French brasserie looking for some fine escargots, because there was no way I was going to cook them myself. As noted above, I think it's crazily bizarre that people eat these things, and even more so that these people include me. I mean they're *snails*, for God's sake! Just look at them, with those googly eye stalks and that viscous slime oozing out from underneath that stumpy "foot" of theirs—they're like creatures from another galaxy, and not particularly delicious-looking ones at that. You'd have to be a hundred ways out of your skull to see one of these animals in its natural state and imagine it might make for a nice lunch. But when they come to your table sizzling in their own individual Jacuzzis of heavenly garlic butter, resistance is useless. Plus, I have a childlike fondness for any food that requires its own specialized dish and utensils.

There are plenty of people out there who don't eat escargots, and I can't blame them for being squeamish. But René was right: you could drown just about anything in garlic butter this good, and it will be absolutely delectable, as were the snails I enjoyed on my little foray into mollusk meat that afternoon. The best part, of course, is that when the snails are gone, you get to sop up the rest of that magnificent goo with a crusty baguette, and the hot, intensely flavored goodness is enough to make you half faint out of sheer pleasure. It's difficult to eat this stuff with your eyes open—mine tend to reflexively close, perhaps to make sure that anything I might see in the meantime won't distract me from the glories of warm bread and hot garlic butter. The only thing in the world that comes close to surpassing this experience are the char-broiled oysters at Drago's in Metairie, Louisiana, which are, naturally, soaked in the same divine substance as my snails, only they also have a little parmesan cheese sprinkled on top for good measure. It's the stuff dreams are made of.

As a meat, the snail itself is basically unremarkable; I haven't no-ticed a whole lot of natural flavor to them, although that might be be-cause every time I've eaten them, they have been thoroughly inundated with garlic butter. Which is a wonderful thing, of course. (Who wants to say, "Wow, you can really taste the snail!"?) It's worth noting that snails are directly related to abalone, which are prized throughout the world as one of the most sought-after seafoods in existence. Most countries either ban or restrict fishing for them, although this hasn't hindered the thriving international black market in abalone meat. In New Zealand, for instance, each citizen is allowed by law to gather no more than ten abalone a day; in California you need to have an abalone license, not to mention a good set of lungs, since gathering these mol-lusks with scuba gear is strictly verboten—skin diving only. So who knows? Perhaps if you prepared Burgundy snails or French *petit gris* (two of the most notable types of *Helix*) in the same manner as abalone, they'd be just as delectable.

I'm perfectly happy with the garlic butter, though.

Gobble Gobble

Now that I'd begun to make some headway on my list with a number of exotic new meats, both wild and domestic, and fancy French delica-cies, I decided that it was about time to enjoy one dish that, as far back as I can remember, has been my meal of choice, my own personal comfort food, simple fare that I've enjoyed almost my entire life and that in my mind will never get old.

I wanted a turkey sandwich.

I have a love of turkey sandwiches that is deep, abiding, and complete. There is a game that some people play—one of those Big Book of Questions–style thought experiments—in which they're forced to decide, if they were stranded on a desert island and could eat only one food for the rest of their lives, what they'd choose as their eternal meal. It's ridiculous, of course, trying to imagine a little atoll somewhere in the South Pacific with a limitless supply of seared foie gras, Cobb salad, or spaghetti marinara, but the game's purpose is to force people into thinking about what food they do not just enjoy, but would never get sick of if they had no option but to subsist on it and nothing more. For me, it never takes long to decide—I'm a turkey sandwich guy all the way. It is the perfect meal, so long as you have fresh ingredients, and no, I never tire of them. I eat one almost every day, in fact. It has all of your basic recommended food groups—meat, cheese, vegetables (I like lettuce, tomato, onions, pickles, and occasionally sliced pepperoncini), and grains in the bread—giving you everything a healthy body needs in one simple, convenient package, and without the necessity of silverware. Plus, within the limitations of the basic turkey sandwich concept, you're also afforded plenty of variety to keep things interesting. There are, for instance, many different types of turkey to choose from; I lean toward smoked, thinly sliced deli turkey, since that's what I grew up with, but I'd be just as pleased with Salsalito turkey, pepper turkey, oven-roasted turkey, turkey ham, or turkey bacon (which, technically, is still turkey, though that might be considered stretching the rules a little), and, of course, the very best turkey in the world: thick slices of cold, leftover Thanksgiving turkey, preferably served on multigrain toast piled high with leftover dressing and cranberry sauce. You can also keep boredom at bay by varying your condiments. There are literally hundreds of types of mustard out there, everything from garlic to horseradish to chipotle pepper varieties, as well as a few different types of mayonnaise (try blending some freshly chopped cilantro into your mayo for a refreshing change of pace). The possible combinations limitless. In this case, I had a nice smoked turkey on rye with Lacy Swiss, lettuce, tomato, and mayo at my neighborhood deli, and it was just as fresh and filling as one would expect from a mom-and-pop Brooklyn delicatessen. Forget the high rents, tiny spaces, crowded streets, and cacophany of a busy metropolis—this is one of the top reasons I find it difficult to think about leaving New York. It's all about the sandwiches.

I wanted to include the turkey sandwich as part of my official Month of Meat for a number of reasons, primarily because I love turkey—a distinctly American bird, one that saved the lives of the starving Jamestown settlers in 1609, that was a noted dish at the second Thanksgiving feast in 1621, and that Benjamin Franklin was convinced would make a better national symbol than the bald eagle—but also because I love sandwiches. Putting a filling between two pieces of bread is seriously important stuff in the history of food, and hence seriously important to any serious carnivore. No one knows exactly when the sandwich was invented, but there are some historical clues. From years of Sunday school I learned that my ancestors, the ancient Hebrews (outstanding carnivores, by the way, even in spite of the kashrut prohibitions against pork and other notable meats), would make a kind of sandwich during the Passover seder by placing a filling of *charoset*—a mixture of fruits such as apples, figs, or raisins, as well as nuts, wine, and honey—with a little bit of *maror* (horseradish, referred to as "the bitter herb," meant to symbolize the bitterness of slavery) between two pieces of matzo. We continue this tradition today, though I've always thought the combination a little unsatisfying—it's much better if you throw in a little of that paschal lamb for good measure, even though we're supposed to shy away from the symbolic lamb shank on the seder plate, something to do with avoiding animal sacrifice since the fall of the First Temple. I don't much care, to tell you the truth—I loves me a good lamb-wich.

The most popular historical account holds that the modern sandwich owes its notoriety to John Montagu, the Fourth Earl of Sandwich (1718–1792). Few know of Montagu's most notable achievements as a member of the royal family—that, for instance, he helped negotiate the Treaty of Aix-la-Chapelle; that he was a secretary of state and postmaster general; that he orchestrated the prosecution of radical journalist John Wilkes for obscene treason; or that the explorer James Cook named Hawaii (formerly known to the British as the "Sandwich Islands") after the Earl, who helped fund Cook's expedition. No, I think it's safe to say that if people know anything about Montagu, it's due to stories that he was an inveterate gambler (cribbage was his game of choice) who instructed a servant to bring his dinner meat between two slices of bread, to be eaten with one hand so that he wouldn't have to slow or halt his gaming. While I love the notion that one of the world's most enduring dishes was created out of pure, unfettered vice, many historians believe that story to be apocryphal. Either way, John Montagu loved his meat, and because the sandwich bears his name, I feel that he's earned a rightful place on the list of history's most notable carnivores.

While we're on the subject of sandwiches, I'd be remiss if I didn't mention my fondness for leftover sandwiches. No, not neglected sandwiches that have gone all soggy in the fridge, but rather sandwiches utilizing the leftover meat of whatever animal you've cooked the night before. As I dutifully made my way down the list, I of course wound up with plenty of leftovers, and a thousand shames on the person who leaves great meat to sit in the back of a refrigerator melancholically gathering mold. Making my Day-After Sandwich has been, on many occasions, just as enjoyable and fulfilling as preparing the dish in the first place. When I was faced with a freezer bag filled with roasted wild boar meat, for instance, I knew exactly what I wanted to do—I chopped the meat short, placed it in a bowl with a little BBQ sauce, heated it up in the microwave, and, after a quick stir, put it on a toasted Portuguese roll to make a barbeque wild boar sandwich. Because of the wild flavor of the meat, it was a new, special take on traditional BBQ pork. I'll bet if you added a little fancy coleslaw on top you could sell that dish for seventeen bucks in an upscale bistro. When it came time for me to make use of my leftover slow-cooked rabbit, the sandwich was just as simple and gratifying—all I had to do was pick the meat from the bones, set it on some nice rye with a dab of Dijon mustard and melt a slice of smoked gouda over it, and there you go: a gourmet open-faced rabbit melt.

I do have to confess that not *all* meats make for such excellent second-day meals, however. It's a good thing I didn't have any leftover escargots; I can't imagine they'd make a very memorable sandwich (at least memorable in a good way).

Snail Monte Cristo, anyone?

Skippy, Big Bird, and Mmmm . . . Doggies

It being summer, I thought it best to invite some friends over for a nice, late-afternoon barbeque to share some of the new meats I'd acquired over at the butcher shop. This would be my first real attempt at grilling for friends in my own backyard (or "courtyard," rather) since I'd begun my Month of Meat, and I wanted to make it special, so I went for a kind of Australian theme—we'd be dining on kangaroo and ostrich fillets, as well as some Wagyu beef hot dogs that I picked up as an impulse buy upon checkout. It wasn't until later that I realized that, once again, I was showing my ignorance: Emu was the large, flightless bird indigenous to Australia, not ostrich, which is native to Africa. Whoops. And then there's the fact that Wagyu beef is from Japan, so I was really all over the map here. I decided to scrap the Australia idea and instead market this opportunity to my friends as a chance to eat "three different meats from three different continents."

My best bet, according to Frank Ottomanelli, was to marinate the ostrich and 'roo steaks, both of which have a tendency to be tough and gamey if not prepared correctly, as each of these animals is low in fat.

"Do *not* overcook them, either," he admonished, "or they'll be too tough. Medium rare to rare is good, so keep a close watch." Clearly, this would involve a little more effort and vigilance than simply shaking on a little salt and pepper and tossing the meat on the grill. Enter marination. For an enthusiast of all things meat, knowing how to marinade correctly is often the most important part of the cooking process, especially if you're into game. Both ostrich and kangaroo meats are low in fat and cholesterol while high in protein and iron, the latter of which (along with a healthy amount of myoglobin) gives them a deep red color. Kangaroo meat also boasts significant levels of "conjugated linoleic acid," a naturally occurring trans fat that is beneficial to the body. Given all these attributes, kangaroo and ostrich are both often touted as healthy alternatives to beef. Marination gives additional flavors to the meat and balances out the wildness, as well as tenderizing it. Any marinade containing acids—vinegar or citrus juice, for instance—will help break down the muscle fibers and make them more supple, and since the meat absorbs a fair amount of liquid through the process of osmosis, the marinade also keeps it from drying out when you throw it on a hot grill.

For the kangaroo, I used my tried-and-true marinade—what I like to call The Best Meat Marinade in the World. It has almost a dozen ingredients (see recipe, p. 93) and takes about half an hour and a little work to prepare—particularly extracting the fresh citrus juices—and it makes a bit of a mess of your kitchen, but the end result is well worth the time and effort: extremely tender steaks with the perfect balance of each of the five flavors. I didn't want both of these meats to taste identical, however, so to change things up a bit I used a new marinade recipe for the ostrich, one using balsamic vinegar as its acid. By the end of the day, I had about three pounds of kangaroo and ostrich steaks in my fridge, soaking up more juice and flavor with every passing hour.

After cleaning up the kitchen, I took some time to find out a little more about the exotic animals I'd be grilling up the following afternoon. Members of the marsupial family, kangaroos have long been enjoyed by aboriginal Australians, who for centuries have used them as an important part of their diet and culture. Today, they've come to be a kind of national symbol for all Australians, which produces strangely conflicting feelings when it comes to the subject of eating them. Some see their consumption as a form of patriotism; others can't bear to eat such an important (and, it must be said, totally adorable) source of Australian pride. The animal appears on the country's coat of arms, and citizens have even bequeathed the creatures a collective sobriquet: Skippy, named after the lovable kangaroo star of an old television program. The to-eat-or-not-to-eat dilemma has caused so much consternation, in fact, that a Sydney-based magazine launched a contest in 2005 to rename kangaroo meat—ostensibly so that squeamish or sentimental Aussies could enjoy it without being reminded of where it came from—as a boon for the Australian kangaroo meat industry. According to a BBC report, the winning entry was "australus," though some of the runners-up were truly hilarious: marsupan, jumpmeat, kangasaurus, kangarly, maroo, and MOM (meat of marsupials).

Ultimately, the Kangaroo Industry Association of Australia decided against an official renaming, and Aussies everywhere returned to being prudish about eating good ole Skippy. Not that their attitude has any ill effects on the kangaroo meat industry, which does walloping good business in Europe and is worth somewhere in the range of A$200 million annually. Also worth noting is the way we get kangaroo meat in the first place: the Australian government, along with the Royal Society for the Prevention of Cruelty to Animals (RSPCA), carefully monitors the native kangaroo population in each state and, when the surveys are all in, the herds are carefully culled to ensure both the animals' health and minimal impact on the surrounding environment (overpopulation would result in extensive damage to the ecosystem, not to mention the needless starvation and death of countless kangaroos). None of the kangaroos that provide meat in Australia come from farms; they are free to hop across the outback as they please. Talk about free-range!

Then there's the ostrich, a bizarre-looking animal if there ever was one. They are, in fact, the largest birds in the world, growing up to seven feet tall and 250 pounds. That, my friends, is a big bird. But unlike the friendly yellow fella on *Sesame Street*, these big birds, given their propensity for aggressive behavior and territoriality, have been officially classified as a dangerous animal in a number of countries, including the United States. Yes, it is possible to be killed by an ostrich, which does occasionally happen, and has to be one of the most unique ways to go I've ever heard of. Ostriches used to be mainly prized for their feathers, eggs, and skin (ostrich leather is notoriously durable), but there has been a resurgence in recent decades in the popularity of ostrich meat, not just due to the health benefits mentioned above but also because these animals are fairly cheap and easy to raise (so long as you don't get kicked by one, of course). They have one of the most desirable feed-to-weight ratios of any animal in the world, more than double that of cows. But enough history and science—I was ready to eat. The following afternoon, my friends arrived with cold drinks and snacks, and we got to the serious business of carnivorism.

"Can I poke your meat?" asked Kimi, gesturing at the marinated ostrich fillet browning on the grill. Normally I'd approach such a request with a little trepidation (if not a giggle or two), but it seemed harmless enough coming from Kimi, a young woman who I learned lived in the boiler room of my friend Terri's apartment building. People in New York will do just about anything to save on rent. Kimi, a budding line cook at a restaurant in Manhattan, was eager to test her newfound ability to determine the doneness of a piece of meat by poking it with a finger to feel how firm it is. This, she told me, was the "hand test," and is one of the most simple and useful culinary practices I've ever learned. "If it feels like this," Kimi said, touching her forefinger to her thumb like the "A-okay" sign, then jabbing at the soft flesh below the thumb with her other index finger, "that's a rare steak. Like this, it's medium rare," she continued, now touching the end of her thumb to her middle finger. Then she moved one over, pressing the thumb against her ring finger. "Here's medium," she said, "and here's well done." Kimi concluded with her thumb and pinkie pressed against one another. At this point, the little lump of hand flesh was quite firm, almost hard. "That's all you need, really. No meat thermometers necessary."

"Just make sure to have a clean finger," I said.

"Well, of course," she said, laughing.

Taking Frank's advice and following Kimi's lead with the finger test, I made sure to take the 'roo medallions off the grill just before I thought they were perfectly done—it would be far better to "err toward the rare" than to kill the meat by overcooking it—and then let them rest for a few minutes before carving them into slices.* Once I'd gone around the courtyard and given everyone a chance to have a taste, the verdict was in: the kangaroo was outstanding. I attribute its tastiness to the marinade—it did most of the work, after all. It was perfectly medium rare, thanks to Kimi's dutiful poking, and turned out to taste much like a lean beef tenderloin, though slightly firmer in texture. My carnivorous guests were so enthusiastic about the kangaroo, I was even able to get two of my *vegetarian* friends to try it, which in itself was a triumph—I felt like I'd just scored a touchdown in the Super Bowl or dunked on Shaq—and even they had to concede that it tasted great, although Vegetarian Sarah did complain of massive indigestion for days following the barbeque. "Well," I told her, "that's what you get when your body forgets how to digest meat properly. Don't worry—keep eating meat, and you won't have that problem for long, I swear." She was less than thrilled with that response.

The ostrich fillets, sadly, weren't nearly as good. Again, I blame the marinade. In contrast to the more balanced flavors of the kangaroo, this meat—while ideal in its medium rareness—was overpowered by the balsamic vinaigrette. It was all you could taste, really, even though there

---

* "Resting" is one of my favorite bits of culinary terminology, by the way. Your meat's been working up a sweat on the grill, in the pan, or under the broiler, so make sure you give it a nice little siesta before serving it, since it continues to cook as it cools down, much as you'd continue to perspire for a while after you finished a long jog. As most grilling devotees know, if you cut into a piece of meat before it's had a chance to nap, you'll lose a good portion of its natural juices, and hence its flavor.

were plenty of fresh herbs in the marinade. It wasn't bad, mind you, just underwhelming, which had me a little bummed. Like anyone who enjoys entertaining friends and family with food, I was disappointed that what I'd provided didn't quite live up to expectations. Not that the evening was a bust—there were still the Wagyu hot dogs to enjoy.

Most people know Wagyu beef as Kobe beef, although that's simply a matter of nomenclature, much like the difference between brandy and cognac, or sparkling wine and champagne. *Kobe beef* is a regional term; *Wagyu* refers to the breed of cattle, the ones famously known for their fancy beer diet and extensive massaging, as well as for their extremely high fat content, which produces intensely marbled and therefore highly flavorful steaks. Kobe beef is a specific breed of Wagyu cattle raised in the Hyogo Prefecture region of Japan, of which the city of Kobe is the capital. Technically, you can't buy bona fide Kobe beef in the United States, although some Wagyu cattle have been imported and are bred in small numbers across the country. I saw my purchase of the Wagyu hot dogs as not only a way to cross beef off my list (Lord knows, I'd be eating plenty of it in the near future), but also as a nice "East-meets-West," moment, a bridging of two cultures.

Now, the hot dog is about as American as any food can get, which is to say that it was invented by someone else—there's significant debate and speculation about whose genius was first responsible for placing a hot sausage on a roll—then refined, perfected, and popularized by the masses. According to the *Oxford Encyclopedia of Food and Drink in America*:

> From the end of the nineteenth century and well into the second half of the next, the hot dog was America's chief iconic food item. Originally an ethnic food, it may have been America's first industrially produced, portion-controlled, and mass-marketed meat product. Widely sold in public venues such as ballparks, boardwalks, and fairs to consumers from every social and economic strata, its mythic attributes might be best summed up in the phrase, "America's great democratic food."

Today, the hamburger rivals the hot dog for the status of ultimate American food icon (just look at the proliferation of McDonald's restaurants across the globe—and most likely, along with Starbucks and Wal-Mart, eventually throughout the galaxy), but it's impossible to deny that the hot dog is one of the most important meat dishes in American history. Technically, a hot dog sausage should be made up of meat—usually beef and/or pork, though sometimes dog makers use offal meats as well, hence the "lips, snouts, and assholes" rumor of just what's inside your street-corner frank—as well as water, seasonings, and fat, which should make up about 30 percent of the total sausage. Fat equals flavor, remember. The key to the hot dog's texture is the fact that, in contrast to most sausages, the contents are fully emulsified, that is, chopped and blended so heavily that they basically become a paste, which is then forced into a casing, then smoked until firm, resulting in a completely cooked sausage that keeps for long periods under refrigeration and doesn't need to be cooked further. Yes, there does exist a small segment of the population that enjoys cold hot dogs, a practice that just thinking about gives me the willies. I prefer to grill mine, though you could just as well pan-fry, microwave, or boil them; roast them over an open flame;* or deep-fry them until the sausage splits open, as is common practice in certain parts of New Jersey, where they refer to the semi-exploded franks as "rippers." These days there are seemingly thousands of ways to serve a dog, each region of the country claiming its own style: New York's dirty-water dogs with spicy mustard and that thick red sauce of sweet Sabrett's onions; Rochester's white hots; the southwestern flavors of dogs found in Arizona and New Mexico (salsa, chili juice, refried beans, etc.); Seattle-style hot dogs featuring heaps of onions and, I swear, cream cheese; and countless others.

---

* If you never did this, you missed out on one of the quintessential components of the American childhood: the horror of accidentally dropping your charred wiener into the fire pit, then desperately trying to retrieve the ruined, ash-encrusted thing before realizing that the poor guy is lost, and that you have to start again from scratch, which you then do with all the anxiety and diligence of a nuclear physicist handling the enriched plutonium core of an atomic bomb.

There are also numerous gourmet interpretations of the classic dog, featuring sausages stuffed with everything from fine seafoods to duck meat, even topped with foie gras. Mostly, though, the sausage is the one consistent factor shared among hot dogs, the main difference between regional variations arising from which ingredients are piled on top of the dog. Of all the different varieties I've had in my day, one of my favorites is the Chicago-style hot dog, which sports a Vienna Beef Co. all-beef wiener stuffed into a natural casing and topped with neon-green relish, wedge-cut tomatoes, hot peppers, a pickle spear, and plenty of chopped onions, all served on a toasted poppy seed bun. I don't know what it is about these doggies that gets me salivating, but I suspect it has something to do with the quality of the sausage (that natural casing is key), as well as the fact that it's topped with what appears to be an entire vegetable garden—which not only tastes good but also makes you feel considerably less guilty about eating hot dogs, which, it must be said, are not the healthiest food items on the market.

At my backyard Skippy, Big Bird, and Hot Dog Cookout, the Wagyu dogs easily regained the ground I'd lost on the vinegary ostrich steaks. Like the Vienna Co. sausages, they had a natural casing, which many hot dog connoisseurs see as an essential element. These casings, usually made from sheep or pig intestines, provide "snap," that incomparable experience when your incisors break the sausage open with a softly audible *crack*, after which the hot, sealed-in juices spill into your mouth in a gush of fatty, beefy deliciousness, which is precisely what occurred when we bit into the quarter-pound Wagyu dinner franks.* The meat inside was a deep red, and though none of us could really discern that the beef came from beer-fed, massaged, and otherwise pampered cattle, all agreed that the beef flavor was considerably more intense than most run-of-the-mill hot dogs. I love naturally cased dogs, though I have to admit my frankfurther of choice comes from the

---

* A note on hot dog terminology: the two now interchangeable terms for hot dog sausages reflects their origins—"frank" was used to describe the spicier, beefier sausages of Frankfurt, whereas "wiener" referred to the lighter-colored and lighter-flavored veal sausages native to Vienna.

Hebrew National Company, which has been producing high-quality kosher, all-beef sausages since its founding by German immigrants on the Lower East Side of New York at the turn of the twentieth century. Because they're kosher, Hebrew National can't rightly make use of natural casings, which are verboten under the laws of kashrut; instead, they, like many other hot dog producers, stuff their sausage contents into a cellophane casing, which they remove before the packaging process. If you want to know whether or not your wiener has a natural casing or not, there's one quick way to find out: check for a thin line running down the length of the dog, which is where a mechanized blade cut open the artificial casing to expose the now solidified sausage contents. And why would I prefer these to a naturally cased dog, especially knowing my appreciation of good "snap"? I think it has to do partially with the great New York immigrant story (these were the same dogs most likely purchased by my own Eastern European Jewish immigrant ancestors), but mainly with the quality of the meat—no fillers—as well as the best slogan of any hot dog in the world, a playful take on the kosher nature of their product: "We Answer to a Higher Authority."

Hey, if these dogs are good enough for God, they're good enough for me.

The Best Meat Marinade in the World

1 ½ CUPS VEGETABLE OIL

¾ CUP SOY SAUCE

¼ CUP WORCESTERSHIRE SAUCE

2 TABLESPOONS DRY MUSTARD

2 ½ TEASPOONS SALT

1 TABLESPOON CRACKED BLACK PEPPER

2 TEASPOONS CHOPPED FRESH PARSELY

½ CUP RED WINE VINEGAR

3 GARLIC CLOVES, CRUSHED

⅓ CUP FRESH LEMON JUICE

1 TABLESPOON FRESH LIME JUICE

Combine all of the ingredients in a medium saucepan and place over low heat until simmering lightly (not foaming!), then cool completely. Place meat in a zip-lock freezer bag, pour in the marinade, then seal tightly. Let sit in the refrigerator at least 4 hours, although overnight is best for tougher cuts or game.

Makes about 3⅓ cups

Mo Momos, Yo!

Now that I'd tested my exotic animal cooking abilities on rabbit, kangaroo, ostrich, and goat meat and was well into the groove of my Month of Meat, I thought I'd put myself up to the task of cooking something a little more involved. In my freezer I had two animals whose meat I'd ordered from ExoticMeats.com—yak and llama—which I thought might be a gamble, as I'd never used their services before and the meat had to be shipped all the way from Seattle to New York in a heavily sealed package containing dry ice to keep it frozen during its long journey. Fortunately, the frozen carbon dioxide did its job and the meat arrived fresh and solid as a brick. Seriously, you could inflict grievous bodily injury on a person with these meats, though I'd be more partial to thawing and eating them. The tricky part would be finding something special I could do with this stuff. It was ground meat, which means that I could easily substitute it for ground beef in just about any recipe—my first thoughts were to make spaghetti with yak ragout, "yakos" (yak tacos), or maybe even "enchillamas" (llama enchiladas),* but doing so with both of these seemed like the easy way out. On the other hand, finding and testing out traditional or complicated recipes for both of

---

* My friend Martin desperately wanted me to make "chinchilladas," using chinchilla meat, though try as I might, I couldn't find the stuff anywhere. If you've ever seen one of these animals, you might know why—talk about the cuteness factor!

these would almost definitely put me in over my head, and I had no desire to disappoint any of my friends as I had with the ostrich. So I decided to split the difference; I'd try out one traditional recipe and do
something new and fun (not to mention easy) with the other meat, so if
I happened to screw up the more complex dish by, say, setting it on fire
or something, we'd at least have something edible to fall back on. After
due research, I chose my two dishes for the evening: yak momos, the
meaty dumplings found in Tibetan cuisine, and my own invention—
"jamballama," a basic Louisiana jambalaya, only this time made with
ground llama meat instead of beef, chicken, sausage, or seafood.

The jambalaya would be easy enough, seeing as I was making it
from a box. When I was growing up, my mother cooked up a wide array of Louisiana specialities for our family—seafood gumbo, red beans
and rice, BBQ shrimp, crawfish étouffée, grillades and grits—all of
which she proudly made from scratch. But when it came time for jambalaya, there was no intensive, multiday preparation: it was always
chicken and sausage jambalaya made from a prepackaged dinner kit
from the Luzianne Company, which took all of about thirty minutes to
prepare and, in all honesty, is usually just as good as the from-scratch
stuff. I knew that little green box like I knew my own name, so I was
confident the only way my jamballama would be terrible was if the meat
itself was bad, which I had no control over. So, if worse came to worst, I
should be able to prepare at least one edible dish between the two. I
was keeping my fingers crossed, just in case.

The simplicity of the jamballama would contrast with the relative
complexity of the momos. I'd gotten a recipe from a list of Tibetan delicacies, and at the outset it didn't seem particularly complicated. Aside
from the yak meat, there was little about these dumplings that was different from the ones I'd always enjoyed at the ridiculously cheap,
ridiculously filling, and therefore ridiculously crowded Chinese joints
in downtown Manhattan, or even the pierogis in my neighborhood's
myriad little Polish grocery stores. How difficult could it really be to

mix together some spices and a couple of chopped vegetables with ground meat, put the filling inside a little bit of dough, then let them steam to juicy perfection? Simple, right?

Once again, I would soon be astonished at the sheer breadth of my own ignorance and incompetence. Making the filling was easy enough—by the time I'd chopped up the onions, cabbage, ginger, and cilantro and mixed them in a bowl with some spices and the now-thawed (and hence ineligible for use as a bludgeon) ground yak meat, things were starting to look and smell delicious. I could barely wait. My big problem—and it was a very big problem—was the wrappers. Ignoramus that I am, I thought it'd be a good idea to make the wrappers from scratch instead of buying prefabricated dumpling wrappers from an Asian market. There is a reason that these convenient prefab wrappers exist, I was quick to learn: the two main ingredients in dough—white flour and water—are as simple as they come, but infuriatingly temperamental. As soon as I tried my hand at making the dumpling wrappers, the pot boiling away on the stove in anticipation of steaming some momos, everything went to hell. First there wasn't enough flour, then not enough water, then not enough flour again. Then, when I finally attempted to roll out a sheet of dough, it was too thick, then too thin, and when the thickness was just perfect, I was horrified to discover that I hadn't dusted the countertop with enough extra flour, and the whole mass of dough was now nearly glued in place, one big, gloppy, difficult mess. Had I been in my own house, I probably would've let loose with a torrent of my finest, top-shelf, grade-A profanity, but seeing as I was in my friend Katie's kitchen, I'd have to keep my temper in check and try to figure out some way to salvage the situation.

Standing there, covered in flour, my fingers nearly cemented together by raw dough, I don't think I could have felt more like a child. When it came to roasting, braising, slow-cooking, pan-frying, broiling, or grilling, I had no problems. Given just a little flour and water to deal with, though, you could almost watch me transmogrify into a drooling village imbecile. Before I knew it, the kitchen looked like something out of a Three Stooges episode, flour and dough *everywhere.*

It was fortune that saved me. And by *fortune*, I mean a young woman named Julia whom I'd never met, and who had arrived with our mutual friend Marigny just as I was about to fully surrender control of the kitchen to the ever-growing blob of sticky dough. "Need any help?" was all she had to say. I leapt at the chance for someone to bail me out.

"You know anything about dough? Because I'm making these yak dumplings and, well, as you can see . . ." I gestured toward the white monstrosity I'd created on the countertop.

"Oh dear," Julia said in matronly pity, the kind you'd see on the face of a kindergarten teacher when one of her pupils just wet his pants or spilled fingerpaint all over the classroom. Wasting no time, she slipped on one of Katie's kitchen aprons and took over like a pro. Julia wasn't actually a professional cook, but she'd been baking for years and had thus developed as much of a facility with the intricacies of flour and water as I had with grilling steaks and roasting chickens. Soon enough we were in business, alternately cutting out circles of dough with the top of an empty glass jar, packing them with the momo filling, then pinching the wrappers shut and placing them gently into the steamer to cook. Meantime, I took it upon myself to make the jamba-llama, which was approximately as difficult as making tacos using one of those kits you can get at the grocery store—you know, the ones they sell next to the salsa. It's not exactly molecular gastronomy—all I had to do was brown the meat in a pan, boil some water and a little bit of oil, add the meat and contents of the box, and take it down to a simmer for twenty minutes. This is how we make jambalaya in my family.

When we plated all the dishes together, all agreed that it looked and smelled great, but the combination was bizarre: Tibetan-style yak momos, jamballama paired with creamed spinach, and Marigny's "slap yo' mama" corn bread. When asked why she used this particular appellation, Marigny explained, "It's so good, it'll make you want to slap your mama!" We had to admit, it was tremendous, mainly because her recipe used buckets of heavy cream, as well as eggs, butter, and cheese, making it so rich that it was almost more corn cake than corn bread. I can't say that it inspired any of us to slap anybody, but it was hellaciously good. As for the momos, most of them came out splendidly, thanks to Julia's care and attention. A few of them got squashed, disintegrated, or dried out before we could get them into the steamer (mostly the ones I was working with), but we had more than enough for everyone to try a few. If we were graced by the company of a real Tibetan, I don't know whether he or she would have said that our momos were as good as the ones back home, but they were hot, meaty, flavorful, and juicy—the most important part of the momo experience. (If the dumpling isn't sealed properly before being cooked, you lose all of that wonderful liquid and get only a disappointing lump of dried-out meat and dough. D'oh!)

Most Tibetan exiles and expatriates tend to make their momos with beef or lamb, as they're cheaper and considerably easier to find than yak meat, and there's little flavor difference.* I was proud to be eating real yak momos, just like I imagined I might enjoy in a quaint Himalayan village or the Barkhor market in the holy city of Lhasa. Momos, like much of Tibetan cuisine, are high in protein and carbohydrates, both of which are essential if you're living at some of the highest altitudes on the planet. Tibetans have been making use of the yak (*Bos grunniens*)—sometimes known as "Himalayan beef"—for centuries. They're strange creatures, looking as they do like the gargantuan, humpbacked offspring of a buffalo and a Texas longhorn, but they make excellent beasts of burden, great for everything from plowing to transportation. In nearby Mongolia, the government has even endorsed the new sport of yak polo—yes, the game polo on yak-back—in order to generate interest in Mongolian tourism. Yaks also provide

---

* There are recipes for vegetarian momos, filled with mushrooms or other vegetables, since many Buddhists forgo meat (though many don't—more on that later). I've been told that certain carnivorous monks and nuns jokingly refer to these meatless dumplings as "faux-mos."

nourishing meat, milk, and a hard chewing cheese that Nepalese call *churpi*. While it's true that yak meat is similar in taste and texture to beef, it's considered sweeter, and is markedly lower in both fat and cholesterol, so not only will it give you plenty of energy for trudging up and down the highest mountains in the world, it'll also keep that spare tire in check. It felt a little strange eating these high-altitude delicacies in the middle of August, but all that went out the window with my first bite. The flavors came together during the cooking process (the filling is raw when placed in the wrapper and cooks through as the dumplings steam), and the fresh ginger, cilantro, garlic, and cabbage gave them an exotic taste I wasn't expecting. Try it—you'll see what I'm talking about (recipe follows).

Meanwhile, the jamballama came out just as I expected, with all the ricey, spicy Cajun goodness I've enjoyed for decades. The big surprise was the taste of the llama meat, which, even though it had soaked up all the jambalaya flavors, proved to be the single most divisive meat of any I'd try during my carnivorous explorations. Llama, like mature goat or mutton, has a strong, heady flavor to it that is simultaneously sweet and gamey. I loved it immediately, but it was all some of my friends could do not to spit it right back out on their plates in disgust. There was no middle of the road here; either you loved the llama or you despised it. I wasn't prepared to accept that something I found so uniquely flavorful could be so polarizing, so I repeated the experiment some months later for my younger brother and his friends, for whom I grilled up a bevy of exotic meats. The goat burgers and wild boar sausage were both big hits, but once again, when it came to llama, some of us devoured it and others nearly gagged. It couldn't have been the way I prepared it—I'd done it two different ways (grilled as burgers and simmered in a pot with jambalaya), and the reactions were the same. I've searched for answers to this carnivorous conundrum, but have so far found none. My guess is that perhaps the meat of a young llama would have less of a pungent taste, but then again I love that pungency, so why go through the trouble of finding ways to avoid it?

I suppose this is the reason we're not likely to find llama on main-stream menus anytime soon—too controversial!

Jamballama

Buy the green Luzianne Jambalaya Dinner Kit. Follow the in-structions on the box, replacing ground beef with ground llama.

Tibetan Yak Momos

1 POUND GROUND YAK MEAT

1 MEDIUM ONION, FINELY CHOPPED

ONE 2-INCH PIECE GINGER, PEELED AND FINELY GRATED

3 GARLIC CLOVES, MINCED

1 BUNCH FRESH CILANTRO LEAVES, MINCED

½ POUND CABBAGE, FINELY CHOPPED

2 TABLESPOONS SOY SAUCE

2 TEASPOONS WORCESTERSHIRE SAUCE

1 TEASPOON CHILI POWDER

1 PACKAGE ROUND DUMPLING (GYOZA) WRAPPERS

Combine all of the ingredients except the dumpling wrappers in a large mixing bowl. (Make sure that all of the produce is finely chopped—you don't want big hunks of onion or cabbage poking through your dumpling.) Mix everything thoroughly by hand.

Place a small amount of the filling onto a dumpling wrapper, no more than a tablespoon or so. Wet the outside edges of the wrapper with water (or egg white, if you prefer), and fold in half around the filling, making the classic half-moon shape. If you want to get fancy, you can take this a step further by folding this half moon into a circle, joining the pointy ends, so that you have a round, tortellini-shaped dumpling (these are good because they're smaller, and you can fit more into the steamer at a time).

Place the dumplings on an oiled steamer rack so that they're not touching each other. Bring to a boil a small amount of water in a large, lidded pot with the steamer attachment inside. Steam for ten minutes, until the wrappers crinkle up around the filling. Remove them to a serving dish and allow them to cool for a couple of minutes since the filling will be extremely hot. Serve them with soy sauce or hot sauce for dipping.

Makes about 50 dumplings

CHAPTER 5

On Being Shameless: The Ethics of Carnivorism

(Or "If I Eat Meat, Will I Be Reincarnated as a Cockroach?")

As you might well imagine, telling people that I am a Shameless Carnivore often evokes in them a need for spirited (sometimes pointed, sometimes downright fuming) discussion about the ethics of eating meat. First, I should probably explain how I employ the word *shameless*. I use it to mean, literally, "lacking shame," since I don't feel that eating meat, in and of itself, is anything to be ashamed of. Still, synonyms for *shameless* include *hardened*, *impudent*, and, worst of all, *unprincipled*. And according to the *American Heritage Dictionary of the English Language* (Fourth Edition): "*Shameless* implies a lack of modesty, sense of decency, or regard for others' rights or feelings: *a shameless liar; a shameless accusation*." Here's where I beg to differ. Having read this far, you'll know that I believe the precise opposite when it comes to carnivorism. Although eating meat isn't something you should feel ashamed of, it still should be afforded prudence, discrimination, and earnest, rational thought.

Matters of nomenclature notwithstanding, it shouldn't be too surprising to note that there are a lot of folks out there who believe that killing and eating an animal is wrong. Among this group, some individuals simply abstain from meat altogether (ethical or religious vegetarians), others continue to eat meat but feel conflicted about it (shameful carnivores), and still others eat meat and feel conflicted about it but either dismiss or refuse to acknowledge that conflict, alternately moralizing about the wrongness of meat and singing its praises (cowardly, hypocritical carnivores). Of these, I have the most respect for the vegetarians—they discover what they perceive to be an ethical dilemma, and instead of ignoring it decide to alter their lifestyle to reflect their beliefs as best they can. There's a lot to be said for that; it takes guts and discipline, especially if they're well aware of just how delicious meat is. For the others, there's a certain cognitive dissonance, a "carnivore's dilemma," to wit: I love eating meat, but I don't favor the idea of killing animals or the thought that the way we get most of our meat has a deleterious effect on our environment. How can I reconcile these two concepts without seeming like a hypocrite? Is it possible? How do I break through the cognitive dissonance so that I can enjoy my meat with impunity?

The answer to that question is not an easy one to come by. In fact, the whole concept of ethics and meat eating is a wicked philosophical labyrinth that's extraordinarily easy to get lost in and that, if you dwell on it, will eventually give you a searing headache. Now, I'm quick to note that I am not an expert when it comes to these matters, far from it. I am not a professional ethicist, a philosopher, or an authority on the effects of agriculture on global ecology. That said, some of the people who feel that eating meat is wrong are keen to ask me how I can rationalize or justify my behavior. If you're going to frame their argument using deductive logic, it might look something like this:

Premise #1: You eat meat.
Premise #2: Meat comes from animals, which have to be killed
to produce it.

Premise #3: Killing animals to produce meat is wrong.

Conclusion: Eating meat is wrong.

Conclusion #2: You are wrong to eat meat, so quit it already.

(Insert smug, self-righteous grin and/or the words "So there!")

I'm the first to say that this is, in fact, a valid argument. In philosophical terms *validity* means that the conclusion of an argument follows logically from the premises, which these conclusions do. The problem here is that it is not a "sound" argument—in order for an argument to really work, not only does the conclusion need to logically follow from the premises, but *the premises must also be true*. In these dicey philosophical waters, only a sound argument will stay afloat. For instance, I can argue that "all vegans are perverts; Moby is a vegan; ergo, Moby is a pervert. QED." That would also be a valid argument, but not a sound one, since that first premise is untrue (to the best of my knowledge). Moby is a vegan, and he might be a pervert, but if he is, it has nothing to do with this argument. So back to our vegetarian's line of reasoning above: The first two premises are correct and difficult to dispute. However, I feel that it's ultimately unsound because the third premise simply isn't true.

That's right: I don't believe that eating meat is inherently wrong.

This is where things get tricky. There are a number of ways you can reason here. First, many people derive their ethical systems—which is to say how they judge what is right and what is wrong—from religious doctrine. If you're a devout Christian, Muslim, or Jew, you can argue that God says eating meat is not wrong, and God is the ultimate, just good. You can yell your head off telling a Hasidic Jew that eating meat is wrong, until you're blue in the face and foaming at the mouth, and he'll simply brush you off, because the Torah, in the eleventh chapter of Leviticus, very clearly lists the animals that carry God's definitive "you shall eat" stamp of divine approval. It begins with "Now the Lord spoke to Moses and Aaron, saying to them, 'Speak to the children of Israel, saying, "These are the animals which you may eat among all the animals that are on the earth" ' " and continues with a comprehensive tally of clean animals to chow down upon and unclean animals to steer clear of. Cloven-hoofed animals that chew their cud (cows, sheep, etc.) are good to go, as are birds, sea creatures with fins and scales, and, I was surprised to learn, locusts and grasshoppers. Then you have horses, reptiles, catfish, oysters, lobsters, "creeping things," pigs (of course), and all the other nonkosher fare. God said what was okay and what wasn't okay, and that's the end of that. Case closed, now let's go have a nice brisket and a beer.

As noted earlier, I do not keep kosher. I adore just about all of the beasts that Leviticus 11 says I, a Jew, should avoid, especially pigs and shellfish. Hell, by the time I finished writing this book, I'd willfully broken pretty much every dietary law listed in that passage—which is to say that I can't rightly claim this as my moral defense of shameless carnivorism, and so I don't. But if not from the word of God, then where do I derive my system of ethics?

My problem with Premise #3 is the fact that it is an absolute, and I don't cotton to absolutes, at least not in ethical matters. I'm a "moral relativist," meaning that I believe that right and wrong should be decided after careful consideration on a case-by-case basis, according to the situation and its surrounding circumstances. In my experience, life is too complicated to rely on absolutes. I'm simply unable to concede that there are inherently right actions and wrong actions, right or wrong thoughts or deeds. For me, the world is just filled with too many gray areas for that to be the case, although for their own satisfaction and ease in making sense of things, many people gravitate toward this sense of strict moral dichotomy. For them, killing is wrong, no matter what. But what about killing one to save many? The old thought experiment of killing a homicidal dictator to prevent genocide springs to mind. Would that be wrong? In the case of meat eating, would slaughtering your only cow so that your family can survive the long, cold winter be wrong? Culling a herd to keep it from cannibalizing itself and destroying its own environment, possibly resulting in the eventual death of its entire population—wrong?

As I said, this is fantastically complex stuff when you get into it deeply, ultimately requiring a person to define the terms *right* and *wrong* (especially people trying to argue Premise #3). I'm not going to say that eating meat is wrong, because then I'd have to say that *all* meat eating is wrong, and I simply don't believe that. Philosophers have been mulling these matters over for thousands of years. Many belief systems had no problems with eating flesh, while others, like the Orphics and the Pythagoreans, much like Buddhists and Hindus, believed that animals were reincarnated human souls, and thus strictly prohibited killing them. Then again, many ancient vegetarians also believed that eating *beans* was also wrong. According to Eric Brown, a professor of philosophy at Washington University in St. Louis, "One memorable fragment of Empedocles (not a Pythagorean, but perhaps sharing some culinary beliefs with Pythagoreans) says, 'Wretches, utter wretches, keep your hands off beans!' " So there you have it: meat is wrong, beans are wrong . . . Dear Lord, what in the world could be *right*?

This "meat is wrong" argument—especially when shouted accusingly at carnivores—usually comes from people for whom vegetarianism's greatest attribute is the accompanying sense of moral superiority. There are a lot of these people, and you can't blame them for adopting this attitude. It's empowering to feel that you have a one-up on others, that the way you conduct your life is better than the way they conduct theirs. This isn't conjecture, either. I have former vegetarian and vegan friends who are quick to note that this sense of righteous indignation was one of the biggest selling points of the lifestyle (they weren't roped in by the delicious recipes, that's for certain), and they're not too proud to admit it, now that they've returned to being carnivores. The problem is that, as far as ethical issues go, even if the "meat is wrong" argument were sound (which it's not), are its proponents really morally superior? Many of these folks probably rarely consider their own culpability in the deaths of hundreds of thousands of animals in the service of their vegetarian or vegan diets—farmers have to destroy millions of insects by using pesticides; many of them also destroy whole colonies of field mice, rabbits, voles, gophers, and other critters who find the crops just as tasty as human vegetarians do. That celery stick you're munching on? Maybe an adorable family of bunnies had to die to make sure the farmer could get it to you. Is there that much moral difference between that and, say, me eating those bunnies? You can't have it both ways. Unless people can attest to the fact that everything they eat is 100 percent free and clear of any and all animal suffering and death—something that is very, very difficult to ensure (though possible, and I commend those farmers out there hard core enough to see their convictions through by shunning pesticides and employing humane pest traps)—saying "Killing an animal so that one might eat is wrong" is a big steamy load of hypocrisy. If you're going to have the cojones to condemn people's actions as wrong, you'd best bring a rock-solid argument and back it up with your own actions.

Another reason some people decry carnivorism is the environmental factor. Again, I'm no expert in agriculture or ecology, but given everything I've read about the effects our current livestock production practices have on the environment, it's hard to argue that we're operating on a sustainable trajectory. Vegetarians are eager to claim that should everyone all of a sudden go "cold turkey," we'd be doing a huge service to Mother Earth. Is this true? Probably yes. Is it going to happen? Not a chance. I hate to sound cynical, but we'd be most likely to wipe out the human race with global thermonuclear war before we arrived at a planet full of vegetarians. And even then, I'm obligated to ask: Would I even want to live in such a world, one without the pleasures of slow-cooked suckling pig and lamb chops and the hot roast beef poboy at R&O's restaurant in New Orleans? Is it worth it?

The fact is, there's no need to be so radical to induce change—we can have our meat and eat it, too. The environmental argument in favor of vegetarianism isn't actually attacking meat eating as a human behavior, or even an ethical behavior, but rather it's an indictment of the environmentally hazardous effects of industrialized agriculture. I don't think anyone is going to claim that a small family farm with residents living off the animals on their land is catastrophic for Mama Nature—people have been doing that for eons. The world didn't have our current environmental woes until relatively recently, when we turned what was once purely pastoral into something almost wholly industrial. It's perfectly reasonable to say that we could scale down and "green up" our current meat-producing ways, but no one's rushing to do that either, since it would inevitably entail giving up what we have now, which is cheap, plentiful meat. Not to mention that the jobs of thousands of meat industry workers would be jeopardized. Also, we'd have to eat less and pay more for it, and if there's one thing that could actually carry with it the possibility of a full-scale mutiny on the part of the American people, it would be the government telling them that they now have to pay more for less meat, and oh, by the way, people are going to lose their jobs, too. The country might just tear itself apart. On the other hand, if you're really concerned about these issues, take it upon yourself to be responsible for what you eat. Go vegetarian if you must, if it matters that much to you, but you could make a difference simply by eating organic meat from a local farm, and eating less of it. Encourage your friends to do the same. You might have to spend a bit more for your food and eat a lot of vegetarian alternatives, but think of it this way—when you do eat meat, it will be high quality and delicious, and not taking it for granted will make you appreciate it that much more. Then you can sleep easy knowing you're not destroying the environment (or destroying it a little less, depending on the state of your gasoline habit), enjoy some lovely meat, and help out a local farm. Doesn't sound too bad when you put it that way, does it?

I've thought a lot about what it means to be conscientious about meat, in terms of both environmental and personal ethics. What I've found truly fascinating, when it comes to taking responsibility for the death of an animal to feed yourself, is the attitude of Tibetan Buddhists.

Now, most Chinese and Japanese Buddhists are adamant that eating animal flesh is a purely negative thing, so they're almost entirely vegetarian. Tibetans, not so much. Despite the fact that Tibet is an overwhelmingly Buddhist nation, and that Buddhists believe in practicing compassion for all living beings, most Tibetans eat meat. They love their meat, in fact, and many of the country's most famous dishes contain either yak or lamb. Culturally, many of them consider salad as "rabbit food." So how on earth does this work?

I spoke about these matters at length with my older brother, Colin, who is both a Buddhist and a vegetarian. He even spent three and half years at a monastery in the Hudson valley as a member of the traditional Tibetan Buddhist meditation retreat, cloistered in a small house with his fellow retreatants the entire time with no contact with the outside world apart from the letters we'd write each other. "True, most Tibetans do eat meat," he told me, "even His Holiness, the Dalai Lama." He went on to explain that traditionally, being a vegetarian in Tibet was simply not a viable way to survive. Given its position in the Himalayas, the land is notoriously difficult to farm, so most Tibetans "have" to incorporate meat into their diet to meet all their nutritional needs. On the other hand, it's widely acknowledged in Buddhist circles that because it's the end result of an animal's death, eating meat can be viewed as a way of accumulating negative karma. For Buddhists, there aren't any absolute rights or wrongs, but rather positive and negative actions that, through karma (the principle of cause and effect), have positive and negative effects on your life, death, and rebirth. Will killing lots of animals ensure you're reborn as a cockroach in your next life? Maybe, but that also depends on all of your life's actions and previously accumulated karma. From a Buddhist perspective, it's certainly not good. "The most important thing," Colin told me, "is to be cognizant of all your actions and intentions, and to try to limit any suffering you might directly or indirectly cause in the world. But don't take it from me—you should ask Lama."

Colin was referring to the very venerable Lama Norlha Rinpoche, the abbot of Kagyu Thubten Chöling, a man whom many believe to be the incarnation of a Buddhist master. His life's story is as compelling as a movie—he grew up in Tibet before the Chinese occupation and was interned in a prison camp when the Communists moved in. He escaped in 1960, climbing across the Himalayas and into India. Eventually, on the suggestion of his teachers, he made his way to New York, where he now resides and teaches, although he also oversees two monasteries in Tibet and a number of dharma centers around the globe, in places as varied as India, China, and Peru. Though revered throughout the world for his mastery of Buddhist practices and his wisdom (I was told that when he visits his homeland, people travel hundreds of miles to meet him and receive his blessing), Lama Norlha is an unbelievably humble and funny individual. "Rinpoche has the smallest room in the entire monastery," Colin said. "He's a truly amazing person." And yes, he does eat meat (yak and lamb, and apparently he makes some wickedly delicious dumplings), and I was eager to ask him about that. Fortunately, I'd get my chance. Alhough the Lama is a very busy person, as you might imagine, he was happy to answer my questions by way of his interpreter, a nun named Ani Jamdron, who relayed his comments as follows:

> There is probably more than one Tibetan Buddhist attitude toward eating meat. Of course it is generally considered bad karma to kill animals to eat their meat. If the animal dies naturally, then it is not bad karma to eat it. In old Tibet, due to the climate and lack of other food choices, people generally had to eat some meat to survive. They did not always have meat (maybe [going] several months without it), but they tried to have dried meat ready for the winter.
>
> According to Mahayana Buddhism, all sentient beings have been one's mother in a previous life, and it is considered negative to eat meat. And in some countries (such as China) eating meat means eating lots of different kinds of sentient beings that are

killed on the spot for you, so that makes it worse. Buying meat from a store is not as negative as arranging to have an animal killed for your consumption. The person eating the meat can say prayers and mantras for the animal and make a positive connection that can benefit that being in future lives.

Advanced, realized Tantric practitioners whose minds are free of confusion do not incur negative karma from eating meat. For the rest of us, we do incur negative karma from eating meat. But it is also important to point out that being vegetarian does *not* mean one will not incur negative karma from eating vegetarian food! The processing of many, if not all, foods involves the loss of life of sentient beings. Growing and harvesting rice and other grains and vegetables kills countless insects. However, it is less negative to eat a vegetarian diet. But not everyone's health allows a meat-free diet.

I found this approach remarkable, especially the way that Tibetan Buddhists have certain rules and provisions for meat eating. First, not actively killing an animal or having an animal killed specifically for you is paramount. That means no picking your live lobster out in the tank at the seafood restaurant, sadly, and certainly no raw oysters, which are often still alive when you eat them. But if it's already dead, it's not as bad, a principle that allows Tibetan Buddhists to buy meat in a grocery store. Also, Jamdron noted, if you're going to eat meat, it's best to eat meat from larger animals, such as cows or sheep or, the popular choice in Tibet, yak. The reasoning there is that doing so gets the most nourishment for the most people with the least amount of animal suffering and death. Still, there's that karma to deal with. "We reduce the negative karma by praying for the sentient being we are eating, praying it has a fortunate rebirth," she told me. "The power of our prayer combines with the power of the Buddha's blessing, and because of the empty interdependence of all phenomena, the prayers can help the being."

That's some pretty heavy stuff. I asked Colin about this, and he confirmed that there are actually special prayers and mantras they say before a meal if they're going to be eating meat. "When you eat meat," he said, "you're forming a connection, or association, with that animal, even though it's dead. Praying benefits the animal's mind—whether it's in the bardo (the intermediate stage between incarnations) or already reborn, reciting the mantra *with compassion for that being* will help it find its way to a good rebirth." And what is this special mantra? My brother was more than happy to teach it to me, knowing how much meat I'd be eating while writing this book. It goes something like this:

།ཨོཾ་ཨ་བྷི་ར་ཧཱུཾ་ཁེ་ཚར་མོ་སྭཱ་ཧཱ།

OM AH BHI RA HUNG KAY TSAR MAM SO HA

According to the *pecha*, the prayer sheet that this mantra was written on, "Because the Buddha taught that, when eating meat, having applied this, the negativity is diminished and those sentient beings are liberated from the lower realms, it is very important to do at least this much each time."

"Say this mantra seven times before you eat," Colin told me. "It's a very beneficial thing to do if you're eating meat—not only will it help purify your own negative karma, it will benefit the animal whose life was lost to provide the meat you're dining on."

And it's not just all praying and saying mantras. For Buddhists, it's just as important to actively try to relieve any possible suffering. This is why they participate in a number of ceremonies focused on compassion for animals, notably something called "fish liberation," in which they'll go down to Ye Ole Fishin' Hole, buy up a bunch of bait fish, then set them free in the pond. Where once they were destined to be speared with a hook and fed to a larger fish (which would also die), now they are free to swim around and get up to their fishy shenanigans. On a larger scale, Lama Norlha occasionally gathers sponsors to free yaks in Tibet—once the animal is purchased, a red cloth marker is placed on its body, signifying that no one is to kill this animal, that it's to live out the rest of its life in peace. Isn't that a nice thought? Kind of like a Buddhist version of the annual presidential Thanksgiving turkey pardon, only with a much bigger beast.

Now, I'm not a Buddhist, but I have actually taken to saying the mantra above. At the very least, it keeps me mindful and conscious of where my meat came from, which I think every carnivore should consider important. At best, perhaps the rabbit from my stew or the cow from my tenderloin will go on to be reborn as a person, and maybe even one day find enlightenment. If not, at least I'm acknowledging the animal's life (and death) and doing my best to be compassionate. That, I firmly believe, is a very good thing, one I'd learn up close and personal later in my adventures, when the realities of the relationship between death and meat would become all too evident.

Hear me, then, carnivores: You don't have to be ashamed of eating meat, but you don't have to be willfully ignorant about it, either. Have some compassion, do some good in this world, help a few people and animals out when you have a chance. Then enjoy your dinner, and be happy.

CHAPTER 6

Month of Meat, Round 3

Yes, Virginia, They Do Eat Guinea Pigs

About halfway through the Month of Meat, I got an e-mail from a friend alerting me to an Ecuadorian restaurant in Brooklyn that specializes in serving guinea pig.

Yes, guinea pig.

Even more so than rabbit, the notion of eating guinea pigs elicits from most Americans a loathing and disgust they'd normally reserve for, say, devoted followers of the Church of Satan, or those perverts nabbed red-handed by Chris Hansen on *Dateline*'s "To Catch a Predator." They may not say it outright (well, some do), but most people, when I tell them I've eaten guinea pig, are quick to see me as some kind of sick deviant. They employ the cuteness defense, which I rebut with enthusiasm, but it rarely does any good. Rabbit they've seen on menus, even if they don't order it, so at least they have an inkling that some people eat them, but guinea pigs? Those . . . *pets?* The rodents used in scientific experiments? Who would possibly want to eat such a thing?

Millions of people, as a matter of fact. Guinea pigs, also known as *cuy* or *cuye*—are a prized delicacy in the mountainous regions of Ecuador. It's a dish enjoyed with great passion and fervor at every special occasion, from weddings to births, christenings, birthdays, and anniversaries. And in the Andes, it's less a celebratory treat than a dietary staple—Peruvians consume an estimated sixty-five million of the furry little guys every year. The eating of *cuy* is such an important aspect of their culture and heritage, there is even a cathedral in Cuzco in which you'll find a re-creation of da Vinci's *The Last Supper*, with one notable difference from the original: directly in the center of the painting, lying placidly on a serving platter directly in front of the Christ figure, you can clearly see the image of a roasted guinea pig. If meat could be so integral to a people's culture that they depict it as being enjoyed by the son of God on the evening before he sacrifices himself to save mankind from its sins, I just *had* to try it.

The popularity of *cuy* in that part of the world should come as no surprise when you consider the animal itself: guinea pigs are small but meaty, similar in size and nutritional value to rabbits, and just as easy to breed. If you're relatively poor, which many people in Peru, Ecuador, and Bolivia are, breeding guinea pigs is an economical source of consistently renewable protein, and it takes much less space and effort than keeping cattle, pigs, or poultry. It makes such perfect sense, and when you think about it, it's hard to believe that more people and cultures around the world aren't enjoying *cuy* as much as our Andean friends. True, some might get turned off by the cute factor, or the pet factor, or the rodent factor (guinea pigs, being members of the order Rodentia, are cousins to rats and squirrels as well as rabbits), but their popularity as a food source isn't solely based on economics. It's not just a poverty food—these people love their *cuy* with the same ardent passion with which we Louisianians love our crawfish and oysters, Italians from Parma adore their prosciutto, and Kansas City natives worship BBQ ribs. I was once in a cab on the way to the airport when I got to talking with the driver, who it turned out was originally from Ecuador. Naturally, it didn't take long for the conversation to turn to food, and then to *cuy*. The man immediately began to wax rhapsodic about his adoration for guinea pigs, rolling his head at the memories of feasts in his past (which, I admit, worried me a little, as we were on the Brooklyn-Queens Expressway, not known for the forgiving nature of its traffic). "Oh man," he told me, "I love the *cuy*. Love! And if you don't love the *cuy* . . . you are *not* from Ecuador!" With that, I was sold.

Even in New York City, where you can get just about anything if you look with a little effort, guinea pigs are hard to come by. At least as dinner. But luckily enough one of my carnivorous compatriots discovered an Ecuadorian restaurant in Brooklyn that claimed to serve *cuy*, hence that fateful e-mail. It was expensive, though (thirty bucks a pop, believe it or not), and you had to give the restaurant advance notice so they could get in touch with their supplier, but still, it seemed to be worth the trouble and expense, given the tales of untold taste sensations my Ecuadorian cabbie was eager to share with me. So I gave them a call.

"We no have them now," the restaurant man explained in heavily accented English. I asked if he could get some by Saturday. "Is maybe," he said. "I see . . . you call back Saturday, I tell you if we get the *cuy*." I agreed, and set about gathering a group of adventurous friends who might be eager to taste a storied South American delicacy. Some were revolted (naturally), others intrigued by the idea and willing to find out what the fuss was all about, though they had no desire to eat any *cuy* themselves, for which I declared them cowardly fuddy-duddies, but I was happy for the company. A few others, including my friends Brad and Katie, who'd shared yakitori, yak, and llama with me, were quick to join in, as was my friend Nina, who'd actually traveled to Peru but timidly passed on the *cuy* while there, which she felt in retrospect to be a real error. She was keen to redeem herself, though, and I was more than pleased to offer her the opportunity. By the weekend, I'd gathered a group of six, four of whom were exited to get our guinea pig on, including myself. The anticipation was killing me.

Problem was, I had no idea whether or not the restaurant would be able to get our *cuy* on the day we'd all planned to go, which, it turns out, they weren't. I was crestfallen. No guinea pigs? "Well," said Vegetarian Sarah (the one who'd tried my marinated kangaroo), "why don't you just go to the pet store?"

"You're kidding, right?"

"Well, why not?" she asked matter-of-factly. To her, it seemed perfectly sensible to go down to the local pet shop, pick out a nice, tender guinea pig, kill and clean it, then roast it up in my backyard. I was genuinely shocked by this idea, mainly because it had been put forth by a vegetarian (what had that kangaroo *done* to her?), but I also had to ask myself—was it really that unreasonable? When you think about it, how different is that from what your basic Peruvian might do, and after all, I was supposed to be the Shameless Carnivore and everything. I considered the prospect for a moment, thoughtfully weighing the respective pros and cons. Then I decided against it, because doing so would be crazy, and I told Sarah as much.

"Those guinea pigs are for petting, not for eating," I explained. "Who knows, maybe they have all sorts of genetic deficiencies and health problems," a reasonable assumption, given the guinea pig's inclination toward inbreeding, even cannibalism. I thought back to my high school biology lab, which featured a terrarium filled with the most screwed-up guinea pigs I've ever seen in my life. They'd gone absolutely batshit from generations of incest. One day, our instructor, Dr. Leslie, couldn't find one of the young boars (male guinea pigs are "boars," females "sows"), until it turned up underneath the wood chips, rendered little more than a skeleton by its lunatic cannibal relatives. "Oh no!" I remember him exclaiming. "He went and ate his uncle-daddy!" This was not the type of creature I wanted on my supper plate.

I still did want to eat some good *cuy*, though (and I prayed that this Ecuadorian eatery didn't specialize in the mutant, inbred sort), but it seemed like we'd all have to wait. In the meantime, as fortune would have it, I got a text message from Katie telling me about a South African restaurant she'd found that featured something she described to me as "monkey glands."

"Monkey glands?" I inquired, skeptical.

"That's what the menu said." To the best of my knowledge, monkeys were illegal eats in the United States, but who knows? Maybe this restaurant got some sort of special exemption—stranger things have happened in New York, that's for sure, and hey, I was actually about to go out and eat a guinea pig, so maybe they did serve monkeys. Plus, Katie also mentioned that the place served stiff cocktails in large mason jars, which was all we needed to know. I called for a reservation.

It would turn out to be our second disappointment of the day. True to Katie's word, the menu did feature something called "monkey gland sauce," which had my imagination spinning overtime. What could it possibly taste like? Where do they get their glands, and which glands are they? Do they taste anything like sweetbreads? And Lord, what happens to the rest of the monkey? Tragically, the first words out of our waitress's mouth were: "You may see the words 'monkey gland sauce' on your menus, but I want you to rest assured that it has nothing to do with either monkeys or glands." We let out a collective sigh of disappointment, quite possibly the first group of diners to be genuinely saddened by what our server obviously thought to be a comforting explanation.

"Well," I asked, sulking, "is it a sauce?" She confirmed this. "At least you got that part right." She was amused at our melancholy over the missing monkey glands but oddly wasn't able to provide us with any information on why it was called "monkey gland sauce" when it was obviously nothing of the sort. "They just call it that," she explained, telling us that it was a dark-brown concoction primarily used to accompany meat, kind of like a South African A1, only thinner, like a Worcestershire sauce, which is usually used in traditional recipes, along with port wine, garlic, pepper, soy sauce, tomatoes, and other unnamed, non-monkey-gland-containing ingredients.

It wasn't hard to bounce back from our disenchantment at the missing menu monkeys—this place had plenty of interesting South African meat dishes that were wholly new to us. We started with an ostrich carpaccio, which was tremendously more enjoyable than my failed balsamic-marinated ostrich steak, richly meaty but delicate and not heavy in the least. You haven't had ostrich until you've had it raw, sliced almost transparently thin, drizzled with olive oil and topped with marinated peppers. Then there were chicken livers (Brad again), and still another confusingly titled dish, Bunny Chow—which, of course, had nothing to do with bunnies, much to my chagrin (it's a curry dish served inside a hollowed-out bread bowl), although it did come with mutton, which is exceedingly difficult to find on American menus. The tough, strongly flavored meat of an adult sheep, mutton has long been enjoyed in certain parts of Africa and Europe—particularly Scotland, sheep central—but is almost always spurned by American diners in favor of the tender (and vastly more expensive) meat from young lambs. You'd think, with lamb being so pricey, it would be no sweat to find some good mutton, but that's simply not the case, so I relished the opportunity to try it. Yes, it was tougher than a rack of milk-fed baby lamb, and yes, it did have a huskier taste to it, but it was perfectly counterbalanced by the sweetness of the monkey gland sauce. So, even though we missed out on guinea pigs and monkeys and bunnies that night, we weren't at a loss for carnivorous pleasures.

We didn't have to wait long to get our *cuy* fix. I called the Ecuadorian place the following Monday, and it turns out that they had just gotten a fresh order of *cuy* in from their supplier. I hastily reassembled our guinea pig crew and set off to Brooklyn's Park Slope neighborhood, eager and excited to finally try this prized South American dish.

I can't quite say what I expected from a restaurant that specializes in rodents, but as we entered we saw little more than a neighborhood joint: brightly lit, tile floors, inflatable Corona marketing decorations (an airplane, a giant beer bottle), jukebox in the corner filled with Latin music, which played softly over speakers as we took our seats. The only thing that hinted at the place's theme was a hand-woven tapestry with an Inca design and the word *Ecuador* hanging above the bar. Well, that and the food. As with the yakitori restaurant, the menu here was both laminated and filled with meat dishes and English translations of their original names, many of which were comical: *bistec regular* translated as "regular steak" (we couldn't find "irregular steak" anywhere—maybe it would be a great deal, like buying an irregular shirt), and *bistec Ecuatoriano* became "steak in Ecuadorian steak." Steak *in* steak? Could it really be? We surmised that it was a typo, that the restaurant's owners had intended to label it "steak in Ecuadorian *sauce*," though I couldn't help but daydream about the implications of stuffing one steak into another. God, that would be brilliant. Just to make sure, my friend Liz agreed to order it, as she'd already declared that she would be wimping out on the *patates con cuy*, or "potatoes with *cuy*," which four of us eagerly ordered up as soon as we could get our waitress's attention.

I'd done a little bit of research about how this *cuy* thing was supposed to go down, and I gathered two very important slices of information about what to expect: 1) the guinea pig is served whole, like a tiny suckling pig—minus most of the inner organs—and the entire animal is there waiting to be devoured, head, claws, you name it; 2) speaking of devouring, you're actually supposed to eat everything, so that by the time you've finished, there should be nothing left on the plate but bones. I knew all of this, and I thought I'd fully warmed to the idea of eating a whole guinea pig—I'd made sure to bring a healthy attitude and appetite, both of which were enhanced by the first couple of beers I sucked down as we anxiously waited for the main course to arrive— but nothing, I mean nothing, can prepare you for the moment of truth, when a smiling server sets a bright-orange animal down on a plate in front of you.

We burst into laughter, because that's what terrified people do in situations like this—it would probably be seen as impolite to start hollering your head off right there at the table. It's a horrifying thing, seeing a roasted rodent for the first time like this, placed simply on a serving dish over a bed of potatoes, a thick tomato slice, and a halved hard-boiled egg. It wasn't just that lying belly-down like that, it looked like it had been actively trying to run away at the time of its demise, much like those poor Pompeiian people immortalized in volcanic ash two thousand years ago, nor was it that I could plainly see its little claws, teeth, whiskers (yes, whiskers!), and the tongue hanging out of its mouth. No—what alarmed me most was the expression on the creatures' face:

It looked *pissed*.

It had every right to be, of course: you'd be more than a little miffed if some cheery Ecuadorian turned you into a meal, and this guinea pig showed it, displaying every ounce of fury and disdain for its untimely fate. With its jaws agape and empty eye sockets squinting like Clint Eastwood's unnamed cowboy just before a gunfight,* my *cuy*'s face seemed locked in an anguished, permanent, silent scream. It's not an easy thing to confront your meal's accusatory facial expression as you stick a fork in him—Vegetarian Sarah, who for God knows what reason had decided to join us, found herself needing to place a napkin over the head of Katie's guinea pig, which she claimed "was staring at her"— but I was hungry, and he was dinner. So we dug in.

When you get past the initial shock and focus on the taste, *cuy*

---

* Well, not entirely empty—the eyeballs liquefy inside the orbits during the cooking process, which *cuy* enthusiasts make sure to cherish, sucking the boiled ocular fluid right out of the head. Yum!

turns out to be intriguingly delicious. The animal has been slow-cooked in toto and, like a suckling pig, should emerge from the oven with a deep orange, crackly skin on the outside and tender, succulent meat within. In this case, the skin was more chewy than crispy, so I mostly forwent it in favor of picking hot scraps of meat from the delicate bones. Gourmands often compare *cuy* to quail, even though the two animals have little in common biologically, because both have darkly colored meat and a fine bone structure; however, the meat from my guinea pig was on the oily side, most likely from subcutaneous fat that had been rendered during the roasting, leaving my fingers covered in flavorful grease, which I naturally licked off. After about forty-five minutes of working our way through the entire animal, some interesting options presented themselves.

"Hey," said Nina, clearly pleased by her decision to make up for her past *cuy* cowardice. "Why don't you eat one of the ears?" That's right, I thought, you *are* supposed to eat everything . . . so I picked up the animal's head, now barely attached to the body by a thin sheaf of skin, placed the cranium to my mouth and tore away one of the little triangular ears with my teeth, then thoughtfully chewed away. It was crunchy and a little meaty, remarkably similar to a tiny pork cracklin. "It's good," I declared. "You should try it!" Then came the kidneys, the liver, the bits of flesh in the cheeks and jowls, the neck, the tongue . . . I lost myself a little then, going into a wordless, rhythmic trance state as I enthusiastically disposed of each new morsel until all that remained was a pile of bones and a little skin. By the time I'd finished and was downing the rest of my beer, it dawned on me why *cuy* has been considered such a special, prized meal by South Americans for centuries. It's a ritual as much as a food, with each part of the whole animal bringing a different texture, taste, and pleasure. Yes, it's safe to say that devouring a whole animal in this way is about as joyfully barbaric as carnivorism gets.

It was marvelous.

Oh, Give Me a Home . . .

After our big *cuy* night, I found myself craving something a bit more familiar. It's fun and adventurous and all to eat dozens of strange new animals, but after a while, I thought it was time to have a little comfort food. Hence: buffaloaf.

I never had meatloaf in my own home growing up. Not that I don't like it—I love it, and so do my brothers and my father—but my mom, the only one of us eager and willing to cook for the family, has always despised it. She spent years learning the finer points of preparing classic French, Creole, and Cajun cuisines, and the thought of a bright-red, tomato-sauce-topped meatloaf has for her always smacked of crappy school cafeteria lunches and grade D mystery meat, and so she simply refused to prepare it. Once I was out on my own, though, it wasn't long before I learned to appreciate the heartening warmth of a meatloaf meal, especially when served with heaps of mashed potatoes and green vegetables, which have preferably been sautéed with cream (particularly spinach) or loads of butter.

Cooking buffaloaf is a great way for any carnivore to prepare something new and interesting without needing any special culinary expertise, since it's just as easy to cook as any meatloaf—which is about as easy as it gets—and considerably more flavorful and even healthy. Buffalo meat, like ostrich, is often touted as a heart-friendly alternative to beef, since it's about 30 percent lower in cholesterol and has half the fat and calories. Because of the low fat content, one might worry that it would also be correspondingly lower in flavor; however, the opposite is true. As similar as buffalo are to domestic cattle, buffalo meat has a sweeter, earthier taste to it. On the downside, good buffalo meat is going to be more costly than regular beef, but when you taste it you'll know exactly where that money went.

As I combined my ground buffalo meat in a large bowl with the eggs, breadcrumbs, herbs, and other ingredients, I thought about how much of a miracle it was that we were able to eat buffalo meat at all. Buffalo—more appropriately known as the American bison—are relatively new to this continent, having migrated here from Eurasia by crossing the Bering Strait (what a journey that must've been—talk about a hardy animal!), and of course have always been crucial to the lives of Native Americans in the Plains states, who used every part of the animal for food, clothing, shelter, and tools. Come the nineteenth century, however, American settlers wantonly killed buffalo in such vast numbers that the animal became all but extinct. I've seen pictures from around this time, one of them a famously horrifying sepia image of a mountain of buffalo skulls—just the skulls—that rose about five times as high as a man. Today, after years of strict conservation efforts, buffalo numbers are back on the rise, though it's likely they'll never again come near to the tens of millions that roamed the prairies in their heyday. About a quarter million of today's buffalo are raised for meat, with due approval by the USDA, and thus we're afforded the excellent pleasure, enjoyed throughout our country's history (and long before our country *was* a country), of dining on buffalo meat.

At the outset, there was nothing seemingly remarkable about my buffaloaf—it looked and smelled identical to your average meatloaf—but the taste was distinctly different, far superior to those mild-mannered, lunch-counter loafs. The meat was the same color and texture as beef, but the flavor was headier and more intense, though not gamey in the least. With only ten minutes to prep, this one's a no-brainer for a carnivore looking for a night of easy, meaty pleasure. Plus, if you have leftovers, buffaloaf makes an extraordinary Day-After Sandwich, especially if you melt some good provolone over it and serve on a toasted roll.

Buffaloaf

2 POUNDS GROUND BUFFALO

2 TEASPOONS SALT

¼ TEASPOON GROUND
BLACK PEPPER

2 EGGS, LIGHTLY BEATEN

½ CUP SOFT BREAD
CRUMBS

½ CUP MILK

1 TEASPOON
WORCESTERSHIRE SAUCE

¼ CUP FINELY CHOPPED
ONION

¼ TEASPOON DRIED THYME,
CRUMBLED

¼ TEASPOON CHOPPED,
FRESH ROSEMARY

ONE 8-OUNCE CAN TOMATO
SAUCE

5 DASHES TABASCO SAUCE

Preheat the oven to 350°F. Mix together all of the ingredients except the tomato sauce and Tabasco sauce. Pack the mixture into a lightly greased loaf pan. Mix the tomato sauce with the Tabasco and spread over the top of the loaf. Bake uncovered for 1 hour. Remove the loaf from the oven and let rest for 5 minutes. Drain the grease, if any. Slice, serve, and enjoy.

Serves 5 to 6

Swamp Things

During my college days, every year I would take a group of friends down to stay with my family in New Orleans during spring break, mostly those of us who couldn't afford a cruise through the Bahamas or a flight to Jamaica. It was perfect: without the need to pay for lodging or food (Mom made sure to keep us stuffed to the gills by preparing military-industrial-sized vats of gumbo, étouffée, jambalaya, and red beans), we'd be able to save our money for booze and mischief down in the French Quarter. One year, though, we decided to stay with our friend John Cazayoux down in Houma (an hour southwest of New Orleans) on our first night down, affording us the opportunity to really get a dose of southern Louisiana's natural beauty. For the guys from Chicago, Philadelphia, Colorado, and Indiana, even a relatively tame swamp tour was an adventure into a bizarrely fascinating and scary new world. Afterward, one of them mentioned that he thought he'd just landed in Jurassic Park, and spent a fair chunk of the tour searching the skies overhead and waiting for a pterodactyl to fly by, which he claimed would have seemed entirely normal, given the surroundings. Some of the fellas were a little freaked out by our tour guide's singing to the alligators ("C'mon baby!" he half hollered, half sang as our boat slid dreamily through the cypress knees. "Bayyyyyyyyybeeeeeee!"), hoping to draw them out of their early spring slumber. One or two were more alarmed—on the verge of anxiety attacks, even—by the fact that there were alligators in those brackish waters to begin with; as far as they knew, they were only a quick capsize away from being lunch for a prehistoric reptile. But for me and John it was fairly humdrum, because we knew that if anything, those swimming, slithering, snarling beasties out in the swamp were more likely to end up in our bellies than the other way around. Amid our friends' nervous shifting in their seats on that boat, both of us looked out into the swamp, teeming with a vast array of every kind of life, and had the reaction most typical to those from South Louisiana:

We got hungry.

Eating alligators goes back a long way in Louisiana history, mostly due to the Cajuns, who were quick to appreciate the natural bounty provided by the swamps they inhabited. And by *appreciate* I of course mean roast, stew, boil, or grill. While once almost hunted into extinction like the American bison, today alligator is a legal game meat in Louisiana,* and there are more than a few "farms" capitalizing on the high market prices of the gators' skins and the growing popularity of their meat (though it's mostly seen as a novelty outside of the state). Me, I love eating alligator meat not just because it brings back memo-

---

* The season starts in September—who's with me?

ries of home, but because it's a rare treat to eat a creature that, given the opportunity, would leap at you with shocking swiftness, clamp down on your arm, leg, or torso with those industrial-strength vise-grip jaws—rending flesh and pulverizing bones in the process—drag you to the bottom of the swamp bed, roll you over and over like a sock monkey until you drowned, and then make a leisurely afternoon snack out of your ragged, bloody remains. No cute factor here. Quite the opposite: gators are terrifying, cold-blooded murder machines whose dragonlike appearance is rendered even more chilling by their creepy stillness—if they're not actively swimming or hunting, they lie motionless in the sun looking like plastic toys. At the gator exhibits at the Audubon Zoo or the Aquarium of the Americas, it's common to see children leap three feet straight into the air, then desperately clutch at a parent's leg for safety when the alligator they've been staring at moves or blinks, forcing the kid to realize that these things are *real.*

Like any adjustment you have to make when you leave your hometown, it took me some time to adjust to the fact that most Americans do not eat alligators and turtles and frogs. In fact, most of them would think you were crazy or joking if you even suggested it. In my experience, Cajun cookery is the only type of American regional cuisine that causes those unfamiliar with it to think its devotees insane. Even in New York, a city filled with so many people who adore food, I'd get queasy looks and skeptical questions from my friends and coworkers when I would, for instance, use the company potluck as an excuse to cook up a big pot of alligator jambalaya. Sample conversation:

"What's that? It smells delicious!"

"Alligator jambalaya."

"Which means . . ."

"It's jambalaya, basically a Cajun version of paella, with alligator tail meat and alligator sausage."

"It doesn't have real alligator in it, though, right?"

"Um . . . yes. That's what makes it 'alligator' jambalaya."

"No!"

"Yes."

"Where did you even *get* alligator?"

"I get mine from Louisiana, frozen and shipped in dry ice. Where do you get yours? You don't happen to know somewhere local, do you? Because shipping costs are killing me here."

So naturally, when my Month of Meat came calling, I was near ecstatic to prepare some typical down-home dishes for my carnivorous fellows in New York, most of whom had never before been afforded the pleasures of dining on swamp critters.

First came alligator, which I was pleasantly surprised to find in the freezer at Ottomanelli's. I'd had to special-order it in the past, so I was grateful to find a local source for alligator tail fillets, the most commonly eaten part of the animal—in this case, the tenderloin is the mild, white center section of the reptile's massive tail. The question was what to do with them. Usually, when you find fried alligator strips on Cajun menus, for all intents and purposes they're mostly indistinguishable from boneless chicken tenders, and I was hoping to prepare something with a little more jazz. I ultimately landed on a recipe for alligator sauce piquant, a dish that has the meat stewed in a spicy red tomato broth.

Unless you're dealing with the pink body meat or the dark tail meat from an alligator (both of which require extensive cooking to eliminate the powerful, gamey flavor), cooking with gator meat is just as easy as cooking with boneless, skinless chicken breasts. My fillets were more clear than pink, with an appearance that was more like fish than poultry, though the flavor tends toward the latter more than the former. In this case, all I had to do was cut the fillets into one-inch strips, brown them slightly in a buttered skillet, then leave them to simmer in the sauce, a mixture of tomatoes, bell peppers, onions, celery, bay leaves, garlic, chicken stock, fresh herbs, and, naturally, plenty of cayenne pepper. When it came time to serve it, the sauce piquant smelled every bit as delicious as I'd hoped, and I was just bursting with satisfaction at having whipped up this traditional Louisiana dish all by myself, and for the first time to boot.

But once more, the folly of my pride would soon be exposed. When I ladled the meat and sauce over the individual beds of long-grain rice, it didn't look quite right—the smell was there, and I knew I'd followed the recipe's proportions and cooking time to the letter, but the sauce was thin, more like a *minestra* than a proper stew. But my guests were getting hungry and a little restless, what with all the smells of simmering meat and vegetables and herbs wafting from the kitchen, so I decided to go ahead and just serve it anyway and hope for the best. It wasn't until after people had started eating their portions that I recognized, in horror, that I had committed one of the cardinal sins of Louisiana cuisine, a grievous oversight that should be viewed with every ounce of contempt and disgust a true South Louisianian can muster:

I forgot the butter.

Of all things, the *butter*! Not only had one of the most crucial elements fully escaped me and my sauce piquant, it dawned on me that I had just served my friends and colleagues a health-conscious version of an old Louisiana favorite. I groaned in regret and profound shame— no, no, no, this wouldn't do at all. I raced back into the kitchen to see if I could salvage what was left of the stew by adding a generous block of butter to the sauce, all the while muttering "Idiot!" repeatedly to myself, but the effort was mostly for naught. My repaired sauce was indeed worlds better, but everyone had already eaten most of the first course and passed judgment on it, and now had no desire to eat any more. "It's good," they tried to reassure me, but the damage, both to my ego and the dish itself, was done. I fumed for a few minutes while I put away what was left of the sauce and rice, though I didn't let myself become too distraught at the alligator oversight. The night wouldn't be a total wash, I knew, because I still had an ace up my sleeve—a thick, insanely rich and artery-clogging one at that—and dammit if I wasn't ready to throw it down. It was time to redeem myself with turtle soup.

On vacation back home several weeks earlier, my mother and I had spent a solid two days preparing a vat of turtle soup au sherry, a New Orleans classic, from scratch. And, like any good son of the Crescent

City, I'd smuggled several frozen blocks of the stuff with me on the plane trip back to New York.

Turtles, it turns out, are eaten almost everywhere in the world where they are available. In the United States, turtles have an interesting history on the dinner table, having been so popular in the nineteenth century that, like alligator and the American bison, their numbers plummeted and they were almost entirely wiped out. Fortunately for the turtles, people's tastes shifted, as they are wont to do, and turtle soup dropped out of fashion at some point during the early twentieth century, resulting in a more stable, protected turtle population. In some places, however, the taste for turtle never waned, the most famous being New Orleans. One of the city's most popular restaurants, Galatoire's, has been serving turtle soup from the same recipe since the establishment opened in 1905, which makes this particular dish something of a historical icon. The Galatoire's cookbook has this to say, in its introduction to the section on gumbos, soups, and stocks: "In October 1956, New Orleans writer Shirley Ann Grau recorded in *Holiday* magazine a comment she heard about one of Galatoire's most famous soups: 'Whenever I pass Mr. [Justin] Galatoire on the street, I really don't see him. I just see his turtle soup.' " Yes, it really is that good. So, in the interest of shameless carnivorism, not to mention my own homesickness, it was from this very same recipe that I decided to make my own turtle soup.

Doing so, however, would be neither quick nor easy, nor cheap, mostly because of the soup's main ingredient. No, not turtle—that part would be simple enough, believe it or not. In order to make a true turtle soup, the kind you get in New Orleans that makes you weak in the knees with your first decadent spoonful, you have to make veal stock. True, you could buy a premade stock or combine some hot water with those expensive little tins of veal demi-glace, but in my experience there's simply no way to coax the same flavor out of the dish without preparing the whole thing from scratch, from soup to nuts, as it were, and that requires bones. Ten pounds of veal marrow bones, to be precise, at a cost of over twenty dollars.

Making the stock isn't particularly difficult, but it is time consuming. It's a solid morning of work, followed by a minimum twelve hours of simmering, but in the end you'll find it well worth the wait. Plus, you have the added bonus of filling your entire kitchen, perhaps even your entire home, with the heady scent of simmering meat, bones, and vegetables. I suggest trying to stay away from the kitchen at this point, maybe go out into the garden or run an errand or two, because the smell alone is enough to drive you flapping bonkers. That thick, beefy aroma had me salivating continuously until the following day, when Mom and I would finish the soup to be served for dinner that night.

The rest of the turtle soup ministrations weren't difficult per se but required the utmost care and attention. First was the turtle, which, as I mentioned, wasn't a problem—we had no trouble procuring two pounds of boneless turtle meat from a local seafood store, one of the best things about being in Louisiana. Even in a place like Shreveport, sequestered in the northwest part of the state and a solid five- to six-hour drive from New Orleans, you can still find all of your classic N'awlins cooking provisions with little fuss or trouble.

While culinary history holds that the most prized turtle meat and eggs come from the diamondback terrapin (*Malaclemys terrapin*), a seafaring turtle common to the mid-Atlantic region of the United States, our meat was all *Chelhydra serpentina*, or snapping turtle. What does turtle meat look like? Strangely enough, it's nothing like its swampy cousins alligator, snake, and frog, which are all lighter in color (you know, like chicken). By contrast, the meat in our plastic tub was a dark, liverish red and possessed of a faintly fishy odor, not enough to cause concern that the meat was tainted, but just enough to remind you that this red meat actually came from an animal that spent much of its life in and around water. It's worth noting that these snappers are, like us, omnivores, known to eat all sorts of plant and animal matter—fish, frogs, even birds. True to their name, they also have a fast and terribly powerful way of snapping their jaws if provoked, often with enough force to quickly turn you into an amputee should you be silly enough to go poking at one of the larger members of the species with your fingers. Given that information, it's a safe bet that you can cross snapping turtles off the cute factor list.

Now that the veal stock was ready to go (we'd removed the bones, of course), the next step was to mince the meat and vegetables—onions, celery, bell peppers, and so forth—and sauté it all until nicely browned. At this stage, the turtle meat essentially looked and behaved like normal ground beef. I even tasted a bit before it went into the stock and found that while it did in fact have a beefy flavor and texture, there was something just a little bit "other" to it, a subtle aquatic note that differentiated it from every other red meat I'd eaten. The meat and vegetables went into the stock along with some spices and seasoning (bay leaves are a must, naturally), as well as parsley, lemon juice, chopped hard-boiled eggs, and, of course, a cup of dry sherry. Then there came the roux, a staple of the Louisiana kitchen used as a thickening agent for soups and stews, made by stirring flour and oil over very high heat. Very simple, and very dangerous—one spill on the toes and say au revoir to jogging for a while. Fortunately, I did as instructed, didn't flinch too much when I caught a spritz of oil on the hand, and managed to successfully add the entire roux without maiming myself. And that was it—the dish was done, and ready to be served.

After two days in the kitchen, it would have been a grand disappointment if our efforts didn't pay off in tastiness, but neither Mom nor I had any complaints: after all our roasting and deglazing and chopping and mincing and sautéing and roux adding, we agreed that our turtle soup was every bit as good as what we might find at Galatoire's. Then again, after all this effort, we were clearly biased. Still, there was no denying that the soup tasted fantastic, especially when, as tradition dictates, you spike your individual bowl with an added jolt of sherry, which for some reason intensifies all the flavors and gives the soup its unique character. I've always puzzled at this, since I can't stand drinking sherry—I love all kinds of liquor, but for some reason sipping dry sherry makes me want to gag—but I'd be utterly disconsolate if I didn't have any to add to my turtle soup. Go figure.

When it came time to share this sleeved ace with my New York friends, the reaction was just as I'd expected. As they tucked into the thick, mahogany-colored liquid, the room was filled with choruses of "ooh"s and "mmph"s and occasionally an "oh my God" or two. The secret, naturally, is that homemade veal stock, so rich and deeply beefy that it qualifies as decadent. Combine that with the spices, the lemon (I always add extra lemon, because I enjoy the way the acid cuts through the stock's richness), and the dry sherry, and you have something truly special. The strangest part is that the turtle seems to be the least important facet of the recipe, outside of the name. No one ever really complains that they "can't taste the turtle." I've never tried it, but I am fairly certain that one could replace the turtle meat with ground beef and it would make little difference. Skimp on that veal stock, though, and you're in serious trouble. This is one wonderful thing about being a carnivore: there isn't a single vegetarian soup I can think of or imagine that could compete with this recipe.

There were plenty of comments on the soup that evening, which luckily for me totally eclipsed my failure with the alligator sauce piquant. The most amusing note came from Brad, who, after finishing his second helping, told me, "Dude, your turtle soup gave me a boner." I took him to mean this metaphorically, or at least so I hoped—you never knew with Brad. The really fascinating part about that comment is that it came from a guy who keeps three turtles as pets in his apartment, and has for years. No congnitive dissonance there—if you can prepare a dish good enough to delight a person who keeps its main ingredient as a *pet*, I think there's little doubt that you've done a good job in the kitchen.

Like a number of animals on my meat list, frogs have never really caught on as food in the United States, not widely, anyway. Other than in certain areas of the Deep South—most notably Louisiana, where frogs' legs have a long-standing and continued popularity, mostly because of the French culinary influence on Cajun culture—people just don't enjoy eating frogs. On the rare occasion that I find this item on a restaurant menu, I'm always surprised and delighted, and can't help but order it, in spite of the queasiness and finger-down-the-throat-in-disgust pantomimes of my dining companions. It's like going out to dinner with a bunch of four-year-olds, sometimes. In fact, I once dated a woman who would only accompany me to a particular restaurant if I swore to her that I wouldn't order the frogs' legs, because they grossed her out so completely. I acquiesced, because I loved her, but I can't say I wasn't disappointed. Not that it mattered much; I made sure to hit that spot a number of times without her in tow. What can I say? When I have to get my frog on, I have to get my frog on.

I've always found American frog squeamishness to be one of those strange culinary mysteries, especially because frogs' legs really do taste great. It's not as if they're an acquired taste, like sea urchins or crickets or something. Quite the contrary: They're mild and tender and, yes, they do taste a bit like chicken; plus, they're often served breaded and deep fried, a major bonus when attracting the American appetite . . . You could deep-fry just about anything and make it compelling to Joe U.S.A.—chicken, beef, seafood, Twinkies, Oreos, bull testicles, what have you. Plus, you're not served the entire animal, à la guinea pig. So why the big fuss? I'm not the first or only one to ponder this little puzzle of the palate, either. Even his majesty Auguste Escoffier, one of the most renowned figures in the history of food, couldn't figure it out. He mused that Westerners balked at frogs either because of their appearance—granted, even I don't look at a frog in the woods and think "snack time"—or their name. Escoffier, who like many of his countrymen was a fond believer in the superior nature of the French language, found the word *frog* itself to be much less appetizing than its French counterpart, *grenouille*, and actually suggested that we replace it in English with the word *nymph*. I don't know about you, but I find the thought of eating "nymphs' legs" significantly more terrifying than eating "frogs' legs." But kudos to Auguste, bless his soul, for the effort.

Unfortunate nomenclature aside, I headed to a Thai joint in my neighborhood that offered frogs' legs prepared not one but two different ways, grilled or sautéed with basil and chile. I always went with the sautéed, since I always found the grilled ones to be severely lacking in butter content. I don't go out to eat frogs' legs to be healthy, that's for sure, even if they are naturally low in fat and cholesterol.

As I sat there at the Thai place with a cold Singha beer at my side and a big plate of juicy, golden brown frogs' legs in front of me—garnished delightfully with green and red peppers and basil leaves—it struck me just how deliciously barbaric this practice is. Oddly enough, I never feel this way when I'm eating chicken parts, but as I worked my way through one pair of legs after another, greedily devouring the meat and casting off the slender bones, I felt kind of monsterish, like some sort of great beast or ogre in a cave, as though I were the Cyclops Polyphemus, blithely chomping down on Odysseus's companions without a second thought. Ancient lore and popular culture alike are filled with images of the carnivorous cave creature, his den piled high with the skeletal remains of the unfortunate people and animals who've crossed his path—everything from *The Lord of the Ring*'s spider, Shelob, to the giant in "Jack and the Beanstalk" ("I'll grind your bones to make my bread!") to the wampa, the snow monster that nearly makes dinner out of Luke Skywalker in *The Empire Strikes Back*. And now, I noticed, the monster was me—when I was finished, I was confronted with a dish filled with the leg bones of five or six dearly departed frogs, giving me the distinctly powerful feeling of being the dominant creature. "Mess with me, frogs," my plate seemed to cry, "and this is what you'll get!" I was also given to thinking about that biblical plague of frogs in the book of Exodus, which, if viewed in a slightly different way, could have easily been seen as a great boon, had the Hebrews or the Egyptians had the good notion of using frogs as food. It would be like having a plague of buffalo wings. What's next, turning all the water into . . . beer? *Dayenu,* as the Hebrews say—it would have been enough!

Speaking of buffalo wings, I see no reason that frogs' legs couldn't be turned into a more popular dish here in the United States. The only thing keeping frogs from gaining ground on the American table is misguided prejudice and blind ignorance about the inherent joys of these amphibians' jumpy parts. Breaded and deep-fried, they bear a strong similarity in taste, texture, and size to chicken wings, so why not go with that angle? Slather them in a little Frank's Red Hot and serve them with some bleu cheese sauce and a couple of celery sticks, and voilà: buffalo frog wings! Genius! Frogs are also cheap and easy to raise, much more so than chickens, I'd imagine, so if you're on the fence about the idea, the cost-to-benefit ratio alone should be enough to make popularizing them worth earnest consideration. Seriously, someone should do this.

Dibs on the first KFF (Kentucky Fried Frog) franchise. We're gonna make a mint, dude.

Nice Rack!

By this point in what I was now referring to as simply The Month, I was on a roll. I had a number of animals down, plenty to go, and both my appetite and enthusiasm for all sorts of meaty deliciousness grew with each passing day. I was up to my gills in carnivorous history, trivia, science, recipes, and preparations, and meat was now constantly on my mind. Which, of course, is a good thing. I felt like a man possessed, and with each new animal I'd fork into my mouth, I couldn't wait to get to the next one.

Still, I was haunted by the memories of my various displays of culinary ineptitude (the missing butter, the dumpling wrappers, etc.), and in spite of several successes, I felt that I needed to start getting serious in the kitchen. I knew I wasn't a total imbecile when it came to cooking, but I was far from the confident, attentive cook I knew I had it in me to become. Now, I thought, was the time to really test myself in the kitchen. I wanted to buy an exquisite piece of meat, something expensive and fancy, the kind of purchase you'd only make if you were looking to either impress someone special or just have a fantastic, celebratory meal. And, God help me, I wanted to cook it myself. After due thought and careful consideration, I decided to go for a whole rack of lamb, which I'd prepare in my friend Tina's house and serve to her, her husband, and another friendly couple of carnivorous friends.

When I dug into the culinary history of lamb, I was shocked to learn that it's yet another one of those tasty animals that simply hasn't become all the rage here in the States. My surprise probably has something to do with the fact that my mother regularly cooked lamb for my family when I was growing up, usually as a nice change of pace from the perennial baked chicken. Sure, Americans eat plenty of lamb, much more than any of the more exotic animals on my list, but still nowhere close to the quantities of beef, chicken, pork, or turkey consumed. According to the USDA, the average American eats only 1.1 pounds of lamb each year, as opposed to 65 pounds of beef, 51 pounds of pork, and a whopping 84.5 pounds of chicken. The strangest thing, when looking at these numbers, is seeing that this amount has been steadily declining since the early twentieth century, when Americans were eating well over six pounds of retail-purchased lamb meat every year. This isn't just astonishing to me but also counterintuitive; as our country grows with a steady influx of foreign immigrants, many from countries in which lamb has been a dietary staple for years—particularly Northern Africa, the Middle East, and parts of both eastern and Western Europe—not to mention the rise of the Food Network and the increase in the average American's interest in and attention to new and different foods, one would imagine that the numbers would go up, not down. Perhaps this is because lamb is seen as vaguely un-American ("We love our beef, pork, and poultry here in the States, boy howdy, but lamb is something for foreigners") or as snooty high cuisine to be enjoyed by the fancy moneyed set instead of the average working family. That's only conjecture, of course—you could just as soon ascribe lamb's decrease in popularity to its strong flavor, particularly in older animals and in the fattier cuts (lamb meat is marbled through with fat, like beef), which, like goat, tend to give off an impression of musky foreignness. After all, what do you see when you walk into most Arab/Greek/Israeli restaurants if not a massive cylinder of lamb meat languorously revolving on one of those huge vertical spits, ready to be carved from at a moment's notice and filling the establishment with the pervasive heady aroma of faraway continents.

To tell you the truth, that distinct, powerful smell and flavor are the primary reason I and most other lamb lovers are so fond of it, but I suppose it's not for everyone. For me, I'm head over heels for it, everything from a classic rack or a leg roasted with rosemary and thyme, to those balls of savory goodness known as kibbeh, a simple gyro from a street-corner halal vender, classic Greek moussaka, or Moroccan tagine of lamb and a long link of grilled merguez sausage. And it's not just the taste I love—one of the wonderful things about lamb as a food is that it spans a number of cultures that are known to have centuries of dramatic political and religious friction between them. No matter how long the tension between Palestinians and Israelis goes on, their shared appreciation of a good shawarma isn't something that's likely to vanish in the near future, if ever. But who knows, perhaps that one beautiful commonality could be the basis for a road to peace? Maybe one day some gallant soul will declare, "Enough of this shooting and bombing and rock throwing, guys. Can't we all just have some nice lamb and get along?"

On the practical end of things, my big lamb dinner first required a trip to the butcher shop, which for me is always the start to a good day. All I had to do was say "rack of lamb," and Frank Ottomanelli was on the case, heading straight to the refrigerated back room of the shop and eventually emerging with the entire rib section of an animal. When Frank held up the huge rib cage and asked me what exactly I wanted, I stalled. Never having ordered a full rib rack from a butcher before (I'm very sad to say), I didn't know that there were options. "Well," I eventually asked, "I'm having about four people for dinner, not including myself, so can you make it enough for five and, you know, uh"—I struggled with trying to describe what I remembered a rack of lamb to look like—"make it look good?" I felt myself reddening a little then, embarrassed once again by my own ignorance.

"Cleaned and frenched," Frank replied, smiling. He was referring to the traditional French preparation, whereby a butcher or chef will take the rib rack, about eight ribs from the most tender section of the animal (between the loin and the neck), and trim away one to two inches of meat from the upper part of the rib bones, leaving them bare and exposed. Once cooked, the frenched rack is then divided into individual chops and served, which is what I'd planned on doing later that evening. My alternatives, I later discovered, were to have the rack either cut into individual chops before cooking (French-cut or not, great for pan-searing, like pork chops) or cooked whole as a rib roast or, if you're feeling ambitious, a crown roast, the impressive "special occasion" preparation of lamb, beef, or pork that involves tying the rib section in a circle, facing outward with the ribs up, so that the resulting roast does indeed resemble that unmistakable piece of regal headgear. You can even add paper frills to the rib tips after cooking to accentuate the crown effect. However, I seriously recommend *not* actually placing the roast on your head, prancing ceremoniously around the room, and declaring yourself Magisterial Monarch of Meat. People tend to get weirded out by that sort of behavior, for some reason.

So Frank got to work cleaning and frenching my rack of lamb, and it was a real pleasure watching him go about the process with practiced, near-effortless mastery, not to mention a variety of sharp, scary-looking tools ranging from a gigantic hacksaw to an oversized cleaver to a small paring knife. When he'd finished, I was rewarded with two gloriously trimmed, eight-rib racks of lamb, as well as a healthy portion of lamb trimmings—it would be a tragedy to waste any of that prime meat—which Frank noted could be used to prepare a fragrant stock that does particularly well as a base for barley soup. As for the finished racks: pink, well marbled (but not overly fatty), and with a good amount of meat, they looked unbelievably appetizing even in this raw state. I could only imagine how good they were going to taste once they were cooked. If you begin to get this kind of feeling before you've even left the butcher shop, you just know you'll be happy with what you've purchased. Not that it was cheap; indeed, this section of lamb is easily the most desirable, and hence costly, part of the animal. A leg of lamb, a sirloin roast, or spare ribs would of course be cheaper, but while still delectable these cuts lack the delicate subtlety and incomparable tenderness of the rib rack. As in all things, you get what you pay for, and I couldn't have been more pleased when I walked out of Ottomanelli's that afternoon, not just with the quality of the product but with the care and attention to detail of a consummate professional. Try getting that at MegaMart, I dare you.

I arrived at Tina's apartment that night armed with my beautiful racks of lamb and a bag filled with an assortment of fresh herbs and spices. Because of lamb's strong flavor, for centuries chefs have counterbalanced the natural taste of the fat and meat with a variety of seasonings. In this case, I planned on preparing my racks with herbs—fresh (always fresh!) parsley, oregano, thyme, and rosemary as well as minced garlic—blended together with breadcrumbs and olive oil to make a mixture that I'd use to encrust the meaty outer layer of the ribs, sticking it in place with a layer of Dijon mustard.

Every now and again I am reminded, in vivid detail, that I am not an expert chef. Or even a novice chef—or even a chef at all, for that matter, but rather an enormous, galumphing kitchen dunce. True, I'm not immune to the occasional culinary victory, but only when I do my best to remain humble. These moments of full-blown idiocy generally present themselves as I am attempting a particularly complicated or ambitious recipe, most often just when everything seems as though it's coming together perfectly, reminding me of my rightful place. To wit: after an hour of preparation in Tina's kitchen, when all the herbs were chopped and the garlic minced, and we'd mixed them together with

the olive oil and breadcrumbs to produce a fluffy, fragrant green concoction with which I'd carefully coated the two racks of lamb, it was finally time to place them in the oven. After that, all that stood between
the five of us and a succulent lamb dinner was time. Time and my own
foolishness, it turns out. So pleased was I with how everything had
progressed thus far, I stopped my careful attention to the recipe; after
the meat had been in the oven about five minutes, my friend Ben's fi-
ancée, Margot, noticed that something was amiss.

"Are you sure it's supposed to be cooking at that temperature?"
she asked.

"That's what the recipe says," I replied, a little huffy at her insinu-
ation that I was somehow screwing things up. Then I thought about it
for a second. "Um . . . at least I think that's what it says. Doesn't it?"
We took the sheet I'd printed out on my computer and inspected the
instructions.

"Nope," said Margot. "It's supposed to be cooking at 450 degrees—I'm pretty certain that 130 is supposed to be the final internal
temperature. Here, look."

She pointed to the bottom paragraph of the recipe and, sure
enough, the lamb was to cook at 450 degrees for ten to twelve minutes,
or until the *internal temperature* reached 130 degrees.

Oops.

My mother once told me that all it takes to know how to cook is
knowing how to read. Apparently, I couldn't even get that right—according to that dictum, I was functionally illiterate. Obviously, you
can't cook much of anything at 130 degrees—at more than 300 degrees
below the allotted oven temperature, I wasn't baking those two racks of
lamb so much as giving them a nice warm sauna to relax in, a crowning
achievement in my personal history of boneheadedness. Thank goodness for Margot.

Now rightly abashed, having been put in place by kitchen karma or
whatever cosmic force is responsible for smacking down my foolish
pride every time I start to get ahead of myself, I removed the two rib

racks, let the oven heat to 450 degrees (or close to it, I didn't want to leave the racks sitting out, partially cooked, for too long), then replaced them to cook to the appropriate temperature. Even in spite of my gaffe, everything worked out okay. Because we were hungry and didn't let the oven get to a full 450 degrees, the racks came out a little on the rare side, but that was fine with me. Not only is lamb one of those meats that benefits from a slightly rare preparation, at least I hadn't done the unthinkable and overcooked it, effectively ruining nearly seventy dollars' worth of prime lamb. No, rare was fine with me, as well as with my compatriots that evening. Along with a simple Greek salad and a side of couscous, a traditional accompaniment to lamb in North African cuisine, as well as a couple bottles of nice vino, it was a lovely meal. Sitting back, enjoying the company of my friends and a final glass of wine, staring dreamily at the twinkling lights of the Brooklyn Bridge and southern Manhattan (Tina and her husband's apartment has, I must note, a disgustingly gorgeous view), it was the kind of warm, congenial evening that makes me look back a little wistfully but with great fondness, counting myself truly blessed to have such opportunities. And such good meat, of course.

Herb-crusted Rack of Lamb

¼ CUP PLUS 2 TABLESPOONS EXTRA VIRGIN OLIVE OIL
½ CUP BREADCRUMBS
⅛ CUP EACH (ALL FRESH) CHOPPED PARSLEY, ROSEMARY, SAGE, THYME

4 GARLIC CLOVES, MINCED
1 RACK OF LAMB, APPROXIMATELY 2 POUNDS, TRIMMED AND FRENCHED
SALT AND PEPPER
1 TABLESPOON DIJON MUSTARD

Preheat oven to 450°F. Combine the 1/4 cup olive oil with the breadcrumbs and herbs and garlic in a food processor and process until combined yet crumbly. Set aside.

Season the lamb with salt and pepper, then brown quickly in a skillet with the remaining 2 tablespoons olive oil. Remove the lamb from the skillet and slather the outside (except for exposed bones) liberally with the Dijon mustard. Coat the exterior with the herb-crumb mixture, and place in an oiled roasting pan. Roast uncovered for 12 minutes, until the internal temperature is at least 130°F, or to your desired level of doneness. Carve the rack into chops and serve, preferably with couscous, salad, and a nice bottle of wine.

Serves 2 (double with an extra rib rack if you have guests)

Game Night

After narrowly averting disaster with the momos and the lamb, I felt it was time to get back on solid ground by doing what I loved best—grilling. I decided to have a Game Night, wherein I'd cook up several different game animals and let my panel of hungry carnivores weigh in on what they thought of each one. But what animals to include? Some of my meat pairings so far had been a little odd, to say the least (Asian dumplings and jambalaya? Hot dogs alongside kangaroo steak? Huh?), so I wanted to find three or four animals that were relatively similar to each other, but that would have their own distinct, inherent flavors. And then an aha moment: a survey of venison.

Now, most people know that the term *venison* means deer meat and assume it refers only to your basic whitetail variety, i.e., Bambi and his family. In truth, *venison* is a fairly broad term. It once referred to any "furred game" but now can be applied to almost any animal in the family Cervidae and a number in the order Atriodactyla, everything from moose to the pronghorn, which is apparently the fastest animal in North America. (Eat that, Road Runner!) For my meaty purposes, I chose four of the deer that were most available and that I thought most interesting: elk, antelope, caribou, and, yes, whitetail. One trip to the butcher shop and an order from ExoticMeats.com, and I was in business, ready to kick off the big game with four different animals in my fridge.

Once my esteemed panel—actually a motley group of friends and acquaintances—had gathered in my back courtyard and were suitably availed of beverages and hors d'oeuvres (potato chips and beer, naturally), the procession of game commenced. I worried initially that I should have varied my preparations with each of these animals as I'd done on previous occasions—say, a different marinade for each—but my friend Marigny disagreed vigorously with this notion, and with good reason. "You should season them exactly the same, then cook them to identical degrees of doneness," she suggested. "Let the integrity of the meat speak for itself." I fell immediately in love with that phrase: *the integrity of the meat*. Genius. Following Marigny's suggestion, I'd season each of the four animals (all tenderloin sections) simply with salt and pepper, and grill until just under medium rare. Since all deer meat is low in fat and marbling, it's both healthier than beef and notably more prone to drying out when you cook it. This is why many suggest you either stew the meat for a long time over low heat (venison stew is a wintertime staple in places like Scandinavia), marinate it, or, if broiling or grilling, make sure to serve it slightly underdone, the latter of which was my "game plan."

We started out simply, with the generic venison, which had come from a farm in New Zealand, believe it or not. Growing up, it seemed someone always had a bit of deer meat in the freezer somewhere, a donation from a friend or a relative who'd had a good bit of luck out in the deer stands during hunting season that year. It was Louisiana tradition. Things didn't work quite the same in New York City, it turned out; if you want venison and you don't have a generous hunter friend upstate somewhere, your best bet is to pick some up at the butcher shop, and it just so happens that the venison I picked up had been farmed in the Land Down Under. This does make sense, when you think about it—

hunted meat, or "bushmeat," is illegal to sell in the United States un-less your operation has USDA approval, which I'm sure most hunters don't go out of their way to get. And since deer farms appear to be do-ing swell business in New Zealand, voilà: Kiwi Venison. God bless those New Zealanders for their appreciation of fine game.

The farming of deer is both a good and bad thing, depending on how you look at it. It's a good thing, of course, because it means that if you don't hunt or have friends who do, you can still easily find yourself a nice piece of venison, both in and out of season. Call this the lazy man's approach to deer meat—don't want to bother with predawn wake-up calls, head-to-toe camouflage, and hours in the freezing cold brush? Don't have to! Isn't the modern world grand? On the downside (or upside, depending), farmed deer are mild, lacking the gamey flavor of their wild counterparts. Some people consider this preferable, but not me; I've long been fond of gamey venison. It's always felt to me as though you can really taste the animalness of the deer, rather than feel-ing like you're dining on something that could be, for all intents and purposes, a lean cut of beef. If I'm going to eat deer, then I want to taste deer, dammit! This was essentially the case with the whitetail tender-loin I served on Game Night. It was good, no doubt about it—we all found it to be tender and appealing to the palate, but not particularly flavorful, certainly not gamey or wild tasting. I was relatively pleased (especially since we had some left over, which I planned on placing atop a salad the following day for lunch), but not as much as I would have been were the deer wild.

Elk came next, which was a slight step up from the venison. Much larger than your average Bambi, the elk, also known as "wapiti," is a grand and rather noble animal found predominantly in the northern United States and Canada, as well as in Europe, although the European ver-sion is a different, smaller animal. Naturally, all things are bigger in America, especially when it comes to food. In going through a number of historical accounts of elk in the annals of cuisine, I found a few inter-esting notes: Firstly, it's commonly said to be one of the most nutritious of all deer meats, as well as the most "finely flavored," often said to land somewhere between beef and venison. More interestingly, it seems that Teddy Roosevelt had an affinity not just for elk meat, but the animal's tongue in particular, which he was fond of taking with him as his lunch on longer hunting expeditions. God bless Teddy, the most carnivorous president in the history of the United States—who else would take an animal's tongue for lunch while actively hunting for more of *that animal?*

Indeed, it turned out that our elk—this time in medallions rather than a whole tenderloin section—was just as described, a tender and only slightly gamey red meat analogous to beef. That would make us two for two on the "tastes like cow" scale. I couldn't help but be a little disappointed. The meat was good, yes, but none of it was really very special. Not that I was about to lose hope: we had two more deer varieties to go, and antelope was up next.

Like *venison*, the word *antelope* is something of a catch-all term, in this case referring to dozens of different ruminant mammals of Africa and Asia, and a word that, believe it or not, is originally derived from the Coptic term applied to the mythological unicorn. Now, though, the antelope category encompasses a number of leggy, graceful animals— as well as the gnu, or wildebeest, easily the least attractive of all the antelope—many of which have intriguingly exotic names: hartebeest, kudu, impala (the animal, not the Chevrolet often referred to in hiphop songs), springbok, addax, oribi, oryx, klipspringer, duiker, and the one that always makes me giggle: dik dik. The most famous type of antelope might be the gazelle, though as far as eating goes, in the United States you're most likely to get your hands on blackbuck (*Antilope cervicapra*). Otherwise known as Indian antelope, these creatures are among the smallest of the various antelope species and were imported from India and Pakistan to be raised on huge preserves, mostly in Texas, for hunting and other meat purposes. This, I assumed, was what I now had on my grill, slowly coming to perfect medium rareness.

I for one was very much looking forward to the antelope experience. Of all my favorite moments in nature television, I've always loved watching a lion take down a gazelle after an exciting, spirited chase. Watching similar animals attempt to cross a river filled with vicious crocs is a close second, but the lion–antelope scenario holds a special place in my carnivorous heart. It's like nature's own version of the action movie, just loaded up the wazoo with suspense. I root for the lion, of course, as I'm sure most folks do, if only secretly; I've always found the footage of haggard old lions dying of starvation because they can't hack the hunt any longer infinitely more sad than seeing a gazelle make a wrong move and quickly become breakfast for a lioness and her cubs. Either way, that's nature for you: hard and remorseless. So when it came to eating antelope myself, I was eager to tear into the meat as though I were the lion and this was my quarry, even though I hadn't hunted it, and, in fact, it came to me frozen in a plastic package, shipped the entire breadth of the country by airplane.

Sadly, despite the fact that I took my antelope loin off the grill at precisely the right moment, and rested it for just the appropriate amount of time so that it would be a beautiful, juicy medium rare, antelope turned out to be our one big disappointment of the night. I took my first bite, filled with playing the lion in my *National Geographic* daydream, sank my teeth into the meaty flesh, and chewed. And chewed. And kept chewing, for about five minutes, after which I had to let my jaws accept defeat and choked the rest of the masticated morsel down with a big swallow of beer. This result was most likely attributable to the meat being subpar in some way, either from an inferior cut or from an animal that had grown a little long in the tooth (or horn, for that matter). In retrospect, given the "integrity"* of this particular meat, I would have been very well served had I decided to give it a good long marinade instead of grilling it up quickly and simply. But in all

* Defined in the *Random House Unabridged Dictionary* (2006) as "honesty," "soundness," and "the state of being unimpaired," by, for instance, being overseasoned or overcooked, I surmised.

matters carnivorous, these things are to be expected from time to time. When you're eating specialty meats, you have to simply realize that not every cut is going to be perfect. Still, I couldn't help but be let down; we'd had three different varieties of venison so far and had yet to find one that really stood out from the herd, so to speak.

Then came caribou.

Ah, glorious caribou! Unless you've spent a fair bit of time in Alaska or Scandinavia, chances are you haven't availed yourself of the pleasures of caribou meat, known abroad as reindeer. That's right: Those magnificent beasts that pull Santa's sleigh provide what is, in my opinion, some of the tastiest meat in existence. On Donner and Blitzen, I say . . . right on into my mouth!

Before you get all huffy at me for wanting to ground Santa by eating his sled team and ruin Christmas for good, I'll have you know that I'm not alone in my appreciation for this animal. Reindeer and caribou have for centuries been a staple of life for the Alaskan Inuits as well as for Norwegians and other Scandinavian peoples, who have been hunting, trapping, and even herding them for their meat and skins (and sometimes for their antlers and milk, as beasts of burden, and as a means of transportation) since the Mesolithic era. Humans and reindeer go back a long, long way, and my small group of friends was about to be introduced to the unique joy of a meat that has sustained human life for over ten thousand years.

Raw, our caribou steak was much darker in color and finer in texture than any of the venison meats that preceded it that night, a deep red you'd more likely find in a cut of liver than in a venison tenderloin. Good reason for that—caribou and reindeer meat, like liver, is rich in nourishing iron, which I can imagine would be extremely beneficial to people living in the cold, inhospitable climates in which you'd find wild reindeer. Because of this, their meat, though lacking in tasty fats, had a much more distinct taste than either deer, antelope, or elk. And by *distinct*, I of course mean "awesome." Cooked to the same degree of doneness and with the same seasonings with which I'd prepared the other three venison meats, the caribou was much more flavorful than all of them combined, filled with a rich, dark unctuousness I'd never tasted before. It was a hit all around. "Oh my God," said Loren. "That's really, really, good." "It's fantastically rich," commented my friend Micaela. "Hard to say, but . . . it's kind of like eating chocolate meat." Chocolate meat, I thought. Now *there's* an idea.

All told, Game Night was a success, minus the antelope setback. At the very least, I knew I'd never be able to hear "Rudolph the Red-Nosed Reindeer" ever again without getting a little hungry.

GAME NIGHT SCORECARD				
Meat	*Tastes Like*	*Gaminess (out of 4)*	*"Integrity" Rating (out of 4)*	*Would Go Well . . .*
Whitetail venison	Mild, slightly wild beef tenderloin	*	**	Thinly sliced atop a salad of mixed summer greens.
Caribou	Chocolate meat	**	****	With nothing. Beautiful on its own.
Elk	Musty wild deer	***	***	As a stew, accompanied by wild rice.
Antelope	Meat-flavored bubblegum	****	*	With spring-loaded, titanium-reinforced jaws.

CHAPTER 7

Are Vegetarians the Enemy?

Like many carnivores, I occasionally refer to vegetarians by one of a wide variety of epithets, few of which are very kind: soy-heads, veggieburgers, communists, the enemy, and so forth. This, mind you, is almost always in jest, with the notable exception of vegetarians who are, in fact, members of the Communist Party. I don't actually believe that vegetable people are the enemy, of course. Some of my best friends are vegetarians, almost all of whom support my carnivorous endeavors (though they obviously don't partake in my meaty bounty), including several members of my band, my literary agent, even my own brother, Colin, because of his dedication to Buddhism (although many Tibetans eat meat, as noted earlier, most concede that avoiding it is spiritually preferable, though not essential). I may tease him for missing out on much of the food we grew up with—red beans and rice (with sausage and ham hock, naturally), crawfish étouffée, raw oysters, duck and andouille gumbo, Cajun boudin, and so on—but he's certainly not my enemy. He's my brother, after all, my blood and kin. I'd love him even if he decided to eat nothing but oats and hay.

I've spent years palling around with meat-shunning folk, and they've been good years, at that. I even worked for them: The summer after my freshman year in college, I took a job for a family friend's company, Wearable Vegetables, and spent a few months outside in the French Quarter flea market, selling vegetable-themed apparel and accessories to tourists. I'd spend nine hours a day sweating like crazy in the oppressive late-summer humidity, listening to the same four Fats Domino songs being played over and over by the guy selling CDs in the adjacent stall, and hawking T-shirts, aprons, baby bibs, and tote bags bearing slogans like "Shiitake Happens," "Desperately Seeking Spinach," and "Garlic Lover: Potent, Pure, and Proud." The wearable vegetables sold like organic, all-natural hotcakes, and I have to admit that I had a blast, although I'm still unable to hear "I Want to Walk You Home," without breaking into a thick sweat. For what it was worth, my vegetable job did right by me, and the vegetarians I encountered along the way were invariably kind, decent people.

When it comes down to it, people are free to feed themselves whatever they want, so long as they stay within state and federal law (no eating other people's pets, or other people for that matter). Or to not eat whatever they want. You on some new fad diet that has you consuming nothing but tree bark, dandelions, and kiwi juice? Fine by me—it's not my place to judge. And I would hope that most reasonable people feel the same way.

Problem is, they don't. There are more than a few vegetarians and vegans out there who feel that it's their job—a moral imperative!—to dissuade me from eating meat. This sort of veggie proselytizing, dear friends, I cannot abide. Pleading with a carnivore to quit eating meat is like telling him that he's praying to the wrong god. It's presumptuous and arrogant, and even though I'm not a violent man, it makes me want to go at these people with the claw end of a hammer.

For this reason, I think it's the duty of all true carnivores to respect the fact that vegetarians have chosen not to eat meat, and leave it at that. Granted, we don't have to understand that decision—to me, a life devoid of meat is more of a half life, a sad, deprived existence and hardly "living" at all—but we should at least respect it. I know for a fact that many carnivores can be just as presumptuous, hard-headed, and annoying to vegetarians as they can be to us. My friend Sarah often encounters such antagonism from some of her relatives, who are simply unable to let her do her veggie thing in peace, without mean-spirited heckling, especially during meat-centric occasions like Thanksgiving. "There are assholes on both sides of the fence," she's quick to remind me. "I've been a vegetarian for the last five Thanksgivings, and yet there are people in my own family who still give me the third degree about my tofurky. One person in particular reacted as though I was roasting an abortion in the Pyrex dish next to the turkey. Vegetarians also get attacked on a regular basis—it's not a one-way street."

So, as much as you and I might love meat, it's important to remember that it's not a carnivore's obligation to convert anyone to carnivorism, although I always find it immensely enjoyable on the rare occasions when my vegetarian friends break down and eat a little meat. Vegetarian Dan has a weakness for German sausages, and even Sarah, in a moment of stress, frustration, and sadness, allowed me, at her request, to console her with a plateful of buffalo chicken wings. These are outstanding moments, and although I take care never to foist my beliefs on my veggie amigos, every time they take a little bite of meat, it makes me feel all warm and fuzzy inside.

So how do well-heeled, conscientious carnivores deal with vegetarians, other than making sure not to get all up in their respective grills for not eating meat? There are dozens of different types of vegetarians who shun meat for dozens of different reasons, after all, so the first step is to delineate the decent, friendly types from the extremist crazies.

Of course, it's important to note that people veg out for many reasons. Foremost in my mind are those who don't eat meat because it is proscribed by their religion. I have the utmost respect for these people and their beliefs, especially since I imagine how difficult it must be to keep the faith in this manner, what with the delicious meat all around. Meat, meat everywhere, and not a bite to eat. Also, all of the religious vegetarians I've met are just as accepting of my carnivorism as I am of their vegetable ways, knowing that it doesn't affect their karma or faith or piety for me to eat meat. "Go ahead," my Hindu buddy Tanuj said when I first asked if eating a hamburger in his presence would offend him. "Makes no difference to me." Needless to say, he's a dear friend. Then there are those who decide to cut meat out of their diet for purely ethical reasons. Again, this is something I can fully get behind, so long as you're not aiming to cram said ethics down my carnivorous gullet. Clearly, I don't feel that eating meat is inherently wrong, but if that's what you think, more power to you for sticking to your beliefs and abstaining. More meat for me. I do hasten to add, however, that if this is your deal, you'd best not be wearing any leather or other animal parts—it's animals or no animals, if you're talking about ethics. You can't have it both ways.

Others become members of the tofu tribe for so-called health reasons. Unless you have a meat-specific allergy (and lo, what a tragedy that would be), this rationale is, in my humble opinion, a big steamy pile of elephant shit. There are dozens, maybe even hundreds of ways to have a totally healthy diet that contains all sorts of delicious meat, milk, eggs, and cheese. So long as you're focused on a balanced, portion-controlled diet, there should be no reason to convert to broccolihood. The people who claim they got healthier when they made the switch to vegetarianism did so for a different reason—they had been filling their bellies with large amounts of crap, and all of a sudden they were forced to pay attention to what they were shoveling into their heads. As a consequence, they realized that if they ate more whole grains and vegetables instead of, say, deep-fried chicken strips and French fries, they would lose weight and feel better. But simply keeping away from the meat does not in any way guarantee you'll soon be transformed into a svelte, sexy, athletic person. I know a number of vegetarians who are overweight, out-of-shape slobs, mostly because they consume a ton of cheese, soda pop, potato chips, and snacks loaded with sugar and high-fructose corn syrup, which has no meat in it, last I checked. Meat alone will not make you obese, or keep you there if you're that way already. You really want to lose weight and feel good about your body? Eat right, eat less, and exercise more. I can't say that's easy, not with the brontosaurus-sized portions we're used to here in the United States, but it's the truth.

Next, there are some people who, for reasons that confound me in a million ways—could they be masochists? extraterrestrials?—do not eat meat because they don't care for the taste. Again, I'll respect that decision, but I guarantee you I won't understand it, or say that it doesn't make me sad. Some people just don't like the taste of good food, I guess. Finally, there are those who go veg for other reasons entirely. George Bernard Shaw once noted, "Animals are my friends, and I don't eat my friends." Good point, George—I don't eat my friends, either. I eat steak, though, because, in my opinion, a cow will never be my friend. What kind of friend could a cow make, really? A cow won't pick you up at the airport, won't lend you money when you can't make the rent, won't talk you through a bad breakup, won't take a bullet for you (not willingly, anyway). A dog can be my friend, sure, because a dog will fend off an assailant, chase away the bad guy, and bite him in the ass. A good dog would go to war with you, as the Romans knew. Can you imagine a cow doing that? As far as I'm concerned, the best way a cow can be my friend is by being delicious.

Reasons aside, you also have to recognize that not all vegetarians are the same. Confused about who eats what, why, and how? Well, look no further—here's a quick primer on the various species and subspecies of vegetable folk:

1. *Ovo-lacto Vegetarians (Vegetarianus eggycheesygoodnus):* By and large, most people who claim to be vegetarians fall into this category, in which one eats no animal flesh but still consumes eggs and

dairy products. Most of my veggie friends are ovo-lactos, because let's face it, it's hard enough to abstain from meat these days, since it's less expensive and more widely available than at any point in human history. This way, at least they can eat pizza, chocolate cake, and bagels with cream cheese. According to my friend Vegetarian Nicole, "If I couldn't have my egg and cheese on a roll, I think I'd have to shoot myself." I couldn't agree more. All things considered, this breed of vegetarian tends to be the most amenable to having carnivorous friends, and is able to engage in spirited discussions about the meat-eating lifestyle with good sense and judgment.

2. *Pescetarians (Vegetarianus loxshmear):* Technically, pescetarians are not really vegetarians at all, since they habitually or occasionally consume fish and other tasty creatures of the sea. They have a good reason for referring to themselves as veg-heads, though: most people, when informed of one's pescetarianism, are apt to look like a dog staring at a ceiling fan—bewildered inquisitiveness. It's just much easier to designate oneself as a "vegetarian who eats fish every now and again," as my agent says. I like these faux vegetarians, because I also like eating fish, which, after all, is meat. Pescetarianism is often the first step of a vegetarian's eventual full-blown relapse back into the carnivorous fold. It's easy for them to eat fish, since fish are all but impossible to anthropomorphize, even despite the success of *Finding Nemo.* Real live fish are scaly and smelly and thoroughly uncute—unlike adorable little rabbits or big-eyed cows.

3. *Vegans (Vegetarianus soyburgerus):* Vegans do not eat or use any animal products or by-products whatsoever. No meat or fish, naturally, but also no eggs or dairy, not even honey, which they sometimes refer to as "bee vomit," or Jell-O, which is made from gelatin, which is derived from an animal's connective tissue (more on this later). These people, in my experience, are easily prone to irritability, especially when engaged in a discussion about their dietary habits. Ask with simple inquisitiveness why a vegan chose to be a

vegan, and you have a good chance of coming away with an angry philosophical screed against the evils of the meat and dairy industries. In my experience, this decision is largely a political one, rather than one spurred by health concerns or religion or taste, and people who believe passionately about political issues are generally prone to argue their case whenever given a chance. Not that I have anything against veganism per se—and, once more, I do have some lovely vegan friends—but vegans, as a vegetarian subphylum, have been the ones most prone to exploding at me in volcanic torrents of screaming rage when it comes to all things meat. All logic and reason goes galloping out the door. These people believe what they believe, and no counterargument or rational debate, no matter how sound, will ever convince them otherwise. In such cases, the carnivore is advised to be complacent, not provoke the vegan any further, and quickly disengage from this intractable position. Back away, and find yourself a reasonable human being to talk to.

4. *Batshit Crazy Lunatic Fundamentalist Wacko Nutjob Vegetarians (Vegetarianus fruitcakeus):* A number of subfamilies of this category exist, though I readily admit that, unlike the above vegetarians and vegans, I can't count any of them as personal friends, as their connection with reality is often tenuous at best. I'm speaking here about people who follow nutty, cultlike philosophies such as the raw food movement, adherents of which believe that we shouldn't cook any of our food because doing so robs the foodstuff of vital nutritional agents and fundamental enzymes, and that eating only raw food will make you live longer and avoid disease. One word for this: horseshit. Not total horseshit, though, just mostly horseshit—a lot of raw foods are fantastic, like sushi, which some raw foodies do in fact eat. But really, why live longer if you can't have a nice, hot bowl of soup, for crying out loud? Such beliefs are anathema to anyone who actually cares about food and the way it tastes, and you know that I do. Even if it turns out that a raw food diet is the fountain of longevity and youth, you can keep it. I'll eat

my grilled steaks with roasted potatoes and sautéed vegetables and have a much more fulfilling life, that's for damn sure.

But raw-foodism, while reeking of new-age hippie nonsense, isn't the most insane dietary practice to exist, not by a long shot. I present to you: *breatharianism*, a school of thought professing that human beings don't actually need to eat food or drink anything at all, and can get all of our nutrition from the air, the sun, and some sort of mystical cosmic force. Talk about horseshit! I'm quick to think that these are the members of the human species destined to be naturally selected out of the gene pool after they die of starvation and thirst. Some people, for profoundly idiotic reasons I can't even begin to comprehend, continue to believe this twaddle, even in spite of breatharianism having been discounted as a hoax when, in the 1980s, one of its foremost proponents, a man named Wiley Brooks, was caught secretly eating chicken potpies, an act he attributed to "air pollution." Of course pollution was the inciting factor there. Everyone who knows anything realizes that chlorofluorocarbons, smog, and methane in the atmosphere are inextricably linked to clandestine potpie binges. Isn't that, like, the first thing we learn in fifth-grade earth science?

5. *Cheeseburger Vegetarians (Vegetarianus quarterpounderus):* I was introduced to the concept of Cheeseburger Vegetarianism by a friend named Liz Adele, who is by all normal standards your average ovo-lacto vegetarian, except for when, occasionally, she gets an intense craving for a cheeseburger, which she's quick to satisfy. Such cravings happen infrequently, but she feels no misgivings about indulging in the odd burger now and again. "I don't eat meat because I don't particularly agree with the modern agricultural practices of the meat industry," she told me. Fair enough, I think— if you don't agree with something, don't support it. That's her right, and given her beliefs, I think it's the reasonable thing to do. "Only sometimes," she says, "I start to feel a little ill. I become tired and sluggish and it's hard to think, and I'm pretty sure it's because

I'm getting anemic. So I have a cheeseburger, and I feel right again." The Cheeseburger Vegetarian appellation actually applies to all vegetarians who sometimes, for whatever reason, eat meat, and don't feel that doing so every now and then means they've failed as vegetarians. Some people refer to such behavior as "flexitarianism," but I prefer Cheeseburger Vegetarian, which is much more descriptive and doesn't reek of corporate marketing-speak. Plus, it's hilarious.

6. *Lapsed Vegetarians (Carnivorus postvegetarianus):* These are my favorite kind of vegetarians, probably because they're not vegetarians at all but once were. The stories of lapsed vegetarians, all of which are vastly intriguing to a carnivore like me, could fill a book of their own. My favorite, though, is that of my own little brother, Eric. Like many Americans who become vegetarians, he did so in his adolescence as a kind of act of rebellion against authority, in this case represented by my meat-adoring parents, as well as a way to feel morally superior. He didn't just get up and quit cold tofurkey, however; he had to work up to it, starting first by eliminating beef and pork from his diet, then, eventually, chicken and other fowl (he's never liked fish). By the time our family took a big, long-anticipated vacation to Mexico, he had been a full-on veg-head for about six months and was having a pretty good run of it, lecturing and moralizing to the rest of us about the horrors of animal slaughter at seemingly every opportunity. Until we went to Xcaret, that is. A nature preserve of magnificent and varied beauties, Xcaret is a big tourist draw in the Cancun area, and we had a blast swimming in the coves, snorkeling the underwater caverns, and hiking through the trails, all of which built up a significant appetite when lunchtime rolled around. We were starving. As luck would have it, there were a number of concession stands around the park offering a variety of snacks and meals, including freshly grilled hamburgers. A single whiff of the grill was all it took for Eric to renounce vege-

tarianism for good—the poor kid was powerless in the presence of that intoxicating aroma, a siren's song of meat that produced in my younger brother a profound, uncontrollable lust for flame-broiled beef. He demanded a burger as soon as humanly possible, bouncing back and forth on his heels in desperation, barely able to contain himself as the cook prepared his sandwich. When finally he got his hands on the thing, Eric inhaled it with such speed and focused intensity, you'd think that he was terrified someone was just about to snatch the burger right out of his hands and leave him to starve in the Mexican jungle. It was gone in a matter of seconds. Now, I had one of those same burgers, and it was pretty good, but Eric was totally enraptured with the experience. To this day, he claims that the Xcaret hamburger is the single best hamburger he's ever had in his entire life, and that's saying a lot, since Eric's particularly fond of burgers, and he's certainly seen more than a few in his day. This one tops his list, though, hands down. It makes a carnivore wonder: Does going without meat for a certain period of time make it taste that much better when you return to it?

As the Magic 8 Ball says, "signs point to yes." Of the many lapsed vegetarians I spoke with in my research, all of them were quick to say how wonderful that first piece of meat, whatever it was, tasted when they finally gave veggiehood the old heave-ho. For some, it was chicken. Others opted for grilled fish, which most profess is the easiest thing for a newly former vegetarian to stomach. On the opposite end of the fence are people who'd done their best to hide their true nature as red-blooded carnivores, and just all of a sudden "needed a steak." Lord, can I understand this feeling. For these people, there's only so long you can fight against your natural instincts, and if those instincts tell you that the thing you need most in your life is a twelve-ounce, dry-aged, medium-rare porterhouse, go for it. Your body will be happy that you did, believe you me.

While I'm on the subject of vegetarianism, let's take a second to get to the bottom of this whole "Meat is murder" phenomenon. As a sort of joke, Vegetarian Sarah gave me a T-shirt for my birthday, bright pink with blood-red lettering that reads: "Meat is Murder. Tasty, Tasty Murder." It's a funny slogan, but I can't say I agree with it 100 percent—not that meat isn't tasty (I think we all know my position on this subject by now), but it's not murder. *Murder* by definition is a uniquely human activity, and most reputable dictionaries will define it as one human being ending the life of another (according to the *American Heritage Dictionary*: "The unlawful killing of one human by another, especially with premeditated malice"). Since fish and pigs and cows and chickens and so forth are not humans, they are de facto exempt from being the object of murder. Consider the following example: Some deranged maniac, lit up on a binge of PCP, malt liquor, and sleep deprivation, decides he's had enough of the neighbor's dog pooping on his lawn and blows the poor pooch to smithereens with an assault rifle. As horrible as this act is—and make no mistake, it's behavior that should result in some biblically harsh torture for eternity down in Lucifer Land—the dust-head will not be charged with murder. The most serious charge that can be leveled at him is animal cruelty, maybe destruction of property and criminal mischief, too. Why? Because killing an animal, in the eyes of the law, is not on par with killing a human being. Still, hard-core veg-heads will contest this, dredging up the argument that ending the life of any sentient being is an act of murder. My question for them is, how do you know what's sentient and what's not? Where do you draw the line? Given the current state of human knowledge about the workings of the universe, which is pretty wacky when you get into quantum physics (Schrödinger's cat being simultaneously alive and dead, for instance—that must be a *real* conundrum for animal rights activists), how are we to definitively and conclusively rule out the possibility that carrots or turnips, say, don't cry out in silent existential horror and terrible pain when you rip them from the ground? Maybe they do, and we simply haven't arrived at a way of recognizing it. Sure, it's unlikely, but impossible? I wonder. Ultimately, a more appropriate slogan would be "meat is death," which is undeniable. But by the same token, so is salad, since in most cases you have to end the lives of vegetables before you eat them. So, if you're going to ascribe the term *murder* to meat, I think in all fairness you have to ascribe it to vegetables as well.

Of course, the original purveyors of the "meat is murder" slogan is PETA; it's a phrase they've employed for years to entice impressionable young people to join their ranks. In the course of researching the philosophies of vegetarianism and carnivorism and how the two relate to one another, I learned a good deal about these People for the Ethical Treatment of Animals, some of which was downright disturbing. As a dedicated carnivore and someone who wants to keep the meat debate as fair and rational as possible, there are a few things I feel I need to get off my chest . . .

The Shameless Carnivore

3/18/08

People for the Ethical Treatment of Animals
501 Front St.
Norfolk, VA 23510

Dear PETA,

You might be inclined to think that as someone who calls himself a "shameless carnivore," I consider yours an enemy organization, and you couldn't be more wrong. To be frankly honest, PETA, you and I have many of the same thoughts and aims, since I, too, believe that all animals should be treated ethically and cared for with dignity and respect. It pains me as much as any decent human being when I see photographs or video evidence of tortured, abused creatures. It makes me feel sick to my stomach. And don't even get me started on the topic of testing cosmetics on animals—whether they're adorable bunnies or mean-eyed subway rats, I consider it reprehensible to gouge their eyeballs with mascara brushes so ingénues can look more appealing. It should be a crime, as far as I'm concerned. And yet, I obviously have no problems eating and enjoying meat. Which is where we part ways, ideologically speaking. The sticky wicket here is that I don't believe that these two concepts—ethical treatment of animals and carnivorism—are mutually exclusive. In your rulebook, based on what I've gleaned from PETA press releases, website copy, advertising campaigns, and other marketing materials, all meat eating is wrong, it's all barbaric, nothing but cruelty and malice. Then again,

Scott Gold
scott@shamelesscarnivore.com
www.shamelesscarnivore.com

you seem to have no qualms whatsoever about euthanizing thousands of animals that are left in your care, simply because there is no way to provide for them, even despite the millions of dollars in your coffers.

I'm sure most folks aren't aware that PETA kills animals. Lots of animals. *Tons* of animals, in fact. Not that it's a secret; I imagine you're aware of the 2005 article in the *San Francisco Chronicle* that said this:

> Don't be fooled by the slick propaganda of PETA, People for the Ethical Treatment of Animals. The organization may claim to champion the welfare of animals, as the many photos of cute puppies and kittens on its Web site suggest. But last week, two PETA employees were charged with 31 felony counts of animal cruelty each, after authorities found them dumping the dead bodies of 18 animals they had just picked up from a North Carolina animal shelter into a Dumpster. According to the Associated Press, 13 more dead animals were found in a van registered to PETA . . . This is not the first report that PETA killed animals it claimed to protect. In 1991, PETA killed 18 rabbits and 14 roosters it had previously "rescued" from a research facility. "We just don't have the money" to care for them, then–PETA Chairman Alex Pacheco told the *Washington Times*. The PETA animal shelter had run out of room.
>
> The Center for Consumer Freedom, which represents the food industry, a frequent target of PETA campaigns, released data filed by PETA with the state of Virginia that shows PETA has killed more than 10,000 animals from 1998 to 2003. "In 2003, PETA euthanized over 85 percent of the animals it took in," said a press release from the lobby, "finding adoptive homes for just 14 percent. By comparison, the Norfolk (Va.) SPCA found adoptive homes for 73 percent of its animals and Virginia Beach SPCA adopted out 66 percent."

So I'm inclined to ask, what's the difference between your organi-

Scott Gold

scott@shamelesscarnivore.com
www.shamelesscarnivore.com

zation putting down all of these poor cats and dogs and leaving them in the Dumpster to be collected by sanitation workers and discarded unceremoniously in a landfill and a farmer humanely dispatching a pig, cow, or chicken so that his family can eat? I'll tell you the difference: no one benefits from the poor PETA animals' deaths, that's for sure. Except for you, since you save a bunch of dough by not having to keep the critters alive and healthy. I wonder, how does one ride the moral high horse while simultaneously killing its brother and sister horses, so to speak? And why is your euthanasia rate so high when the SPCA's is so low? Surely you have resources similar to theirs, if not greater. It doesn't seem to add up.

I'd also like to bring up the fact that, like your buddies in the Animal Liberation Front, some of your members enjoy conducting a little guerrilla warfare against your opponents, notably by throwing fake blood, flour, and other unpleasant materials on law-abiding carnivores and wearers of fur (many know that *Vogue* editrix Anna Wintour has long been one of your favorite targets). Here's my question: Why don't you go after Native Americans and Inuits? If you're genuinely opposed to all use of animals for their meat and fur, it would make a really big statement if some of your most enthusiastic members made their way out to the reservations and busted up the rituals Native Americans conduct while wearing those gorgeous, intricately decorated animal skins, hosing everyone down with red paint, and denouncing these horrible people for their callous cruelty to our animal friends. Wouldn't that help prove your point, PETA? Or, if not a guerrilla attack, why not publicly denounce the practices of every Native American and Inuit tribe that uses fur and meat as inextricable components of their culture and tradition? Or how about the Massai in Africa, who are wholly dependent on cattle, animals so important to them that they're viewed as currency, and without which they

Scott Gold
scott@shamelesscarnivore.com
www.shamelesscarnivore.com

would all surely die? And while you're at it, why don't you lump in the Jews as well? The egg and the lamb shank are important symbols for us on Passover, after all, and our most sacred document, the Torah, is traditionally written on a parchment derived from lamb skin—aren't you just steaming mad at us for employing these things in our religious practices? Wouldn't coming out publicly against it send a big message that you're serious about what you profess to believe, and help you cast off this—admittedly hard to argue with—shadow of hypocrisy that's been following you around lately? Don't you want to walk the walk instead of just talking the talk?

No? Not going to do that? Hmph . . . I wonder why. Maybe it has something to do with people thinking your plea to Yasser Arafat to have Palestinian suicide bombers quit employing donkeys to convey their explosives—while not actively decrying the murder of innocent Israeli civilians—was a little distasteful, to put it mildly.

Oh, and by the way, PETA, while I have you here: have you ever even *tried* bacon? It tastes really, really, really good. Seriously.

Yours Sincerely,

Scott Gold,
The Shameless Carnivore

There. I feel much better now.

t Gold
@shamelesscarnivore.com
.shamelesscarnivore.com

CHAPTER 8

Behind Enemy Lines: The Bet

"You can't do it," Vegetarian Nicole said to me.

"Of course I can," I replied, offended at the implications of what she'd just said of me. I'd apparently crossed some sort of invisible event horizon of meat talk, and, despite usually being tolerant of my rants and raves about whatever meat I was eating that week, Nicole had simply had enough. I don't know exactly what I said that finally made her speak out, but suffice it to say she was fed up, and decided to show it. So she called me out, slapped me in the face with the proverbial gauntlet, and tossed it to the floor.

"There's no way," she said, "that you can go a whole day, twenty-four hours, without talking about meat." I couldn't believe she was saying this. Yes, of course I love meat, and I love talking about meat almost as much as I do eating it (*almost*). I delight in conversations about dry-aging methods, the strange meats of exotic cultures, the relative merits of various sausages, the underappreciated wonders of organ meats, or

which is the best hamburger in New York. But to have someone imply
that I couldn't control myself was too much to bear. It's not as though I
have a compulsive need to talk about meat all the time; it just so happens that, writing about meat being my job and everything, it's a subject
that frequently comes up in conversation. What kind of spineless, weak-
willed, jelly-constituted, no-self-control-having sap did she take me for?

"Come on," I scoffed. "You're so wrong, it's not even funny."

"Okay then," said Nicole, knowing that I was quickly falling into
her trap. "Let's make it an official bet."

"Fine," I replied, defiant. "What are the terms?"

"How about this: if you can keep yourself from talking about meat
for a whole twenty-four consecutive hours, I will eat . . . a cheeseburger."

Whoa, I thought. *This is serious.* For someone like Nicole, who'd
been a faithful vegetarian for years, eating a cheeseburger is kind of like
poisoning yourself. After a prolonged period of meat abstention—it
varies from individual to individual—a person's body sort of "forgets"
how to efficiently process animal flesh and fats. This is why most vegetarians, and especially vegans, often experience a bit of gastrointestinal distress when they fall off the vegetable wagon (or climb *on* the meat
wagon). For some, it's not much of a problem at all, but for others—and
Nicole knew she'd be one of the others—it means days of upset stomach, heartburn, and frequent trips to the toilet. If she lost, she'd eat a
burger and have to pay the consequences, which were bound to be
something less than pleasant.

"And if I lose?" I asked. "Not that I'm going to, of course."

Nicole thought about this. It wouldn't be enough for me to eat a
veggie burger or something. That would hardly be fair, considering the
potential gastric jeopardy she was facing. Soon enough, it came to her.
"You become a vegetarian. For a *week*."

I winced at the prospect. No meat for a week? For the Shameless
Carnivore? Not a pleasant idea. We agreed that this would be a compa-
rable penalty. All I needed to do was simply not discuss meat for a day.
How hard could that be, really?

Now that we'd decided our terms, we had to parse the verbal con-
tract to make sure that we both agreed on what would constitute a
breach, on my behalf. I was able to say the names of meat or meat
dishes, but only as a means of ordering said meat in a restaurant or grocery store, and only if necessary (pointing at menu items to indicate
that I desired them would be preferable). I could say the word *steak*,
but only in the context of self-reference, since *Steakbomb* and *Steak* are
nicknames of mine. I was strictly forbidden to discuss the taste of
meats; the agricultural process of raising animals for meat; the ethical,
environmental, religious, or sociological implications of meat consumption; and so forth. No meat discussion whatsoever. Again, I didn't
see any big problems with this. I had an interest in lots of other subjects, so I could just talk about them—philosophy, guitar playing, literature, television, movies, haircuts, coffee . . . There were plenty of
non-carnivore-related topics I could chat with my friends about without fear of having to suffer a week of veggiedom. Or I could simply
clam up and not say anything at all, just go mute for the day, which
would certainly result in my victory, but I didn't see it as the only way
I could win. We also had to pick a time when we'd actually be together
for an entire day, so that any slip-up on my part would be duly called
out. Since we're in a band together, we both agreed that one of the days
on our upcoming tour—when bandmates are practically glued to each
other 24/7—would be a perfect time. It would give me a few weeks to
bone up on my self-restraint, prime my willpower, and pick a restaurant
to take Nicole to for her "defeat-burger" after I inevitably won the bet.
By the time the day came, I was totally ready to go the distance—with
a mental picture of Nicole eating a cheeseburger lodged firmly in my
mind's eye, there was no way I'd let myself succumb to the temptation
of meat talk. First thing that fateful morning in Philadelphia, we shook
hands, started the clock, and let the game begin.

I lasted eight hours.

That's it, only eight out of twenty-four, a pathetic one-third of the
total distance I was supposed to travel. Even now, looking back on my

lame display that evening, I hardly know what it was that tripped me up. I was doing fine, moving along at a good clip, emboldened by each passing hour and every smart dodge when my friends, all in on the action, surreptitiously tried to make me fail. My biggest coup came when I somehow managed to order, consume, and enjoy a true Philly cheesesteak—in Philadelphia!—without giving in to the almost unbearable lure of talking about how good it was, its specific preparation and ingredients, all the things that made it so much better than the pitiable copycat versions cooked elsewhere. Like that amazing sandwich, I was on a roll. Then, unexpectedly, failure.

I said "bacon." Don't ask me why or how, because I don't really know. Looking back on that evening, as we sat around the upstairs greenroom of the rock club we'd be playing in a couple of hours, warming up on Jack Daniels and Yuengling lager, getting into our stage duds and generally horsing around in the way you'd expect an eleven-member band to do, it seemed like a daze. All of a sudden, out of nowhere and apropos of nothing, I said "bacon." It was like some sort of carnivore's Tourette's syndrome, the word leaping out of my mouth uncontrollably, a hard-wired tic impossible to contain. Of all the ways to fail, this one was pretty appalling, and I had only myself to blame. I tried to cover it up, of course, hoping desperately that no one had heard me, that nobody was paying enough attention to recognize that what I'd just said would toss me into a cell of full-on meat abstention for an entire week. No such luck.

"Bacon?" said Liz, tentatively at first. Then, realizing the implications: "Bacon! Ha!" She jumped to attention, rousing everyone in the room and waving them over to witness the shocking turn of events. "Hey, everyone, Scott said 'bacon'!" All eyes were on me, scanning my features for the telltale signs of embarrassment and disgrace, or possibly waiting for me to dispute Liz's findings, after which they would convene the bet-governing council to decide on a verdict. It didn't come to that.

"I did," I squeaked. It was only fair and honest of me to give myself up. Much as I yearned to feed Nikki a burger, I needed to remain a man of my word. "Oh God, I did, didn't I?" As everyone in the room laughed and shouted, taunting me ("In your face, meat man!") and offering up jubilant, celebratory high-fives to Nicole, I buried my head in my hands and contemplated my disgrace. They were right, apparently—I guess I can't control myself. I must really love meat so much that the subject has traveled beyond my own ability to contain it. But is that really so surprising? Though I was shocked, no one else seemed to be; they had zero confidence in me in this matter and had all expected me to fail. It now seemed as though they had every reason to do so.

Then, almost worse than wallowing in the shame of failure, I thought about its consequences. A vegetarian? Me? *An entire week?* I had no choice but to embrace my sentence, and to think about the possible upsides. At first I was stumped, and miserable at the prospect of having to avoid all my favorite meat treats for seven days, since I couldn't remember having gone sans animal flesh for more than about twenty-four hours at any given point in my life. There would be no pepperoni pizza, no baked chicken, no turkey sandwiches, for crying out loud. Then it came to me: I could use the week as a research opportunity, a chance to fully explore the weird, wacky world of meat analogues and simulacra. Yes, I thought, that's the ticket—I'd use my punishment to find out what in the world was going on with imitation meat, all that dreadful-looking stuff I'd seen my vegetarian friends bring out of their lunch bags when I was tucking into my ham and cheese. Also, surviving the week successfully would give me back a sense of self-control, much needed after losing a wager predicated on the belief that I didn't have any. I tried to perk up, thinking the week might not be as bad as I was making it out to be.

Truth be told, it wasn't. On the plus side, my vegetarian pals were delighted that I was keeping my word to Nicole and hopping over to their side of the fence, where the sprouts are greener. I'd imagined that they'd be full of self-righteous taunting and moralizing, maybe using my week of mandatory tofu imprisonment as a way to convert me to their ways permanently, but they were nothing of the sort. They all remained friendly, encouraging, and excited to take me out to all of their favorite veggie haunts, and they were delighted that I, the Shameless Carnivore, with all my incessant meat talk, was keeping an open mind.

Not that good company would make the week a total breeze. I have to admit, the first several days were pretty rough—not coming-off-of-heroin rough (from what I've been told), but certainly not a walk in the park. Fortunately, my Brooklyn neighborhood was friendly to vegetarians and offered up more than enough meat-free alternatives for me to get by without falling into a rut of eating the same things over and over. Problem was, most of these places also served all of my preferred meaty dishes as well. I *loved* the fact that I could still have pizza—I've always maintained that the New York–style plain cheese slice is a close-to-perfect foodstuff, one slice being the ideal snack and two making a satisfying but not disgustingly overfilling meal. But every time I walked into my local joint for a plain slice, I was inevitably forced to drool over the alternatives waiting there behind the glass: chicken rolls, sausage-and-tomato pies, pepperoni wheels, and so on. Meat was *everywhere*. Off to join my friends for a bite at a vegetarian restaurant in Alphabet City, I passed butcher shops with heaps of smoked sausage links hanging defiantly on display and Asian grocery stores with whole-cooked chickens and ducks in the window, tempting me. I could get a big and satisfying falafel sandwich at the Middle Eastern place around the corner, but while the guy behind the counter loaded up my pita with hummus, shredded cabbage, pickles, and onions, I had no recourse but to stand there and gaze longingly at the huge cylindrical hunk of spiced lamb rotating slowly on a spit, ready to be carved from at a moment's notice should someone call for shawarma. Or the kibbeh and meat pies beneath the glass, singing to me in Arabic.

Like Nicole herself, I'd thank the heavens for my morning egg and cheese on a roll, but the desire to add bacon, ham, or sausage was killing me. As was my neighborhood Chinese restaurant, where I'd snack on hot-and-sour soup and vegetable dumplings while some lucky bastard sat there nonchalantly forking large, glistening chunks of sesame chicken into his mouth, not knowing how much I wanted that to be *my* lunch instead. And at my favorite Tex-Mex takeout, I was happy to be ordering the tortillas filled with black beans, cheddar, and salsa, but the other menu items were still up there, goading me to order them instead, especially my favorite, an inexplicable quesadilla combining jack cheese with scallions, ham, turkey, *and* grilled chicken. It took every ounce of willpower I could conjure not to give in, but I managed, somehow, to keep up my end of the deal.

Physically, I fared okay. It's not a glamorous or attractive thing to say, but I certainly had no trouble going to the bathroom that week. So long as you're varying your diet and not eating only cheese fries, being a vegetarian is a great way to keep regular. I was having satiety issues, though. For some reason, filling up on vegetables and fake meats is not, well, very filling, not when you're used to loading up on meat calories. I'd pack away a huge plate of food, an act that would normally have me loosening my belt a notch or two, belching in satisfaction, and trying not to nod off at the table, and yet I'd still feel like I needed to eat one more helping. That sensation would fade after an hour or two, but still, it was a little disconcerting. I looked into this and found that what I suspected was true—meat *is* more satisfying. According to Mary Young at the National Cattlemen's Beef Association.

> There is a growing body of evidence indicating that lean protein foods, such as beef, make a meal more satiating, and research indicates that protein may be more satisfying than fat or carbohydrate. Protein-rich foods add satiety to a meal and help to stave off hunger longer, and research indicates that animal-based proteins foods are more satiating. In addition, studies show that people who consume diets moderately high in protein are less hungry between meals than those following a diet based on the Food Guide Pyramid. They also experienced more stable blood

glucose levels and reduced insulin response following meals, [which] could be related to more energy throughout the day.

Then there were the fake meats. Meat analogues, meat simulacra, whatever you want to call them, they are the substances created by food scientists to give noncarnivorous folks the comforting sensation of eating normal food, just like the rest of us. As an experiment, I tried out as much of this faux flesh as I could find. The results were mixed: some was good, some was bland and inoffensive, and some was just plain gross. My first experience came on my second night of vegetarianism, when I planned to meet up with three of my veggie friends at a downtown restaurant called Kate's Joint, known for its imitation versions of comfort food classics. To start were meatless buffalo wings, and I have to admit that when they arrived on our table they looked extremely appetizing and very much like the real deal—bright red, savory nuggets from which emanated that one-of-a-kind aroma of Frank's Red Hot wing sauce. I was hungry and excited . . . until I bit in. The sauce was tangy and authentic, but I was horrified to discover that underneath the succulent exterior was nothing more than a slimy rectangular block of tofu. It was like the people in the kitchen had pulled a fast one on me, a vegan bait and switch. I didn't know what I was expecting from a meat-free buffalo wing, but it certainly wasn't this. Tofu! Blech! As much as I've tried—and Lord, how I've tried over the years—I've never grown to enjoy the taste of bean curd. I'm told that aged tofu in the traditional Japanese style is a marvelous thing to behold, but judging by the tofu I've had in my day, I'm skeptical. To me, it's nothing but soft, slippery blocks of bland nonsense that meat-shunning individuals rely on for protein. It happened again with my fried "chicken," which turned out to be a beautifully golden, crispy exterior disguising, you guessed it, yet another block of tofu underneath.

As I sat there in Kate's, enjoying the company of my friends and trying to be a good sport, an old proverb I learned in my high school

Spanish class came rushing to mind: *Aunque la mona se vista de seda, mona se queda,* or "Even though a monkey's dressed in silk, it's still a monkey." An English equivalent might be "You can't make a silk purse out of a sow's ear," but that just wouldn't cut it in this case—given that tofu was masquerading as . . . well, everything in this restaurant. I'd have just about stabbed somebody for a nice, crispy sow's ear. But I did my best not to sulk, and to give good, honest consideration to every meat analogue that would come my way that week. This was research, after all.

I had better luck with tofurkey. I've long been skeptical of this stuff, not just for what it represents—a mad-scientist-like effort to produce turkeyless turkey—nor what it might taste like, but also because it sounds very much like a Scottish insult, which I discovered on a long car trip with my friend Dan Hewins. The two of us spent hours, much to the chagrin of our fellow passengers, trading barbs in our best Groundskeeper Willy accent. "ToFURKey!" I'd yell at him accusingly. "Tofurk—me?" he'd reply, scarcely believing that I'd say such things about him, to which I'd come back, filling my expression with as much spite and malice as I could conjure. "Tofurk-YE!!!" Strange things happen when old friends are in small spaces with each other for very long periods of time.

"Here, try this," said Liz Adele, handing me a tall triangular section of what appeared to be a standard three-decker turkey club on toasted wheat bread. On taking a healthy bite (sandwich protocol dictates that one must take a bite large enough to gather all the distinct elements of a three-layer sandwich), I had to admit that it tasted almost like the real deal. On examining the flavor layers and comparing them to the turkey clubs of my past—and there have been many—it wasn't a dead ringer, but close enough to actually be called an "un-turkey club" in good conscience. The unmistakable "turkeyness" of the meat protein was absent, of course (only turkey can truly taste like turkey), and replacing it with essentially flavorless tofurkey didn't disparage the sandwich's flavor integrity. Same thing with the faux bacon, a salted, smoky-flavored soy concoction also known as "Facon," which, if absolutely necessary, almost tastes like the real deal if you try not to think too hard about it, or if you've forgotten what actual bacon tastes like (and if you have, I'm dreadfully sorry for you). Imitation bacon is also occasionally known as "Smart Bacon," a title I'm surmising came about due to the staggering amount of scientific know-how that must be involved in the chemical process of making soybeans taste anything like pork bellies. Given these substitutions on my sandwich, I wondered, why did it still manage to somehow resemble a true turkey club? The answer is stupidly simple: mayonnaise. Liz had opted out of the vegan mayo and got the real stuff instead, which everyone knows contains good old-fashioned chicken eggs. Animal protein! Flavor! *That's* what was missing!

It was a good night—cold beer was a plus, for certain—but I couldn't help but be a little let down with my first fake meat outing, at least as far as the food was concerned. When I relayed this information to Nicole and her boyfriend, Dan (the one with the fondness for sneaking bites of German sausage when he thinks Nicole isn't looking), they were quick to explain. "I'm not surprised you felt that way," Dan said. "Kate's is, like, the first place newfound vegetarians or vegetarians new to New York are told to go, before they find out for themselves that there are better restaurants. It's supposed to be comfort food, but everything there is tofu."

"No kidding," I said, and regaled him with the story of my disappointing un-wings and fried un-chicken.

"We have to take you to Red Bamboo," Nicole added. She was pleased that I was keeping up my end of the deal, even a little proud of me, so the fact that I was dissatisfied with the food made her sad, and she felt as though she needed to make it up to me. "That's where the really good stuff is. You'll like it, I swear."

The next night we met at Red Bamboo, yet another restaurant offering up vegetarian versions of American comfort dishes. Here, however, the food was head and shoulders above what I'd had the night before. It was actually, dare I say it . . . good. For comparison's sake, I started again with the fake chicken wings. This time around, there were some very noticeable—and positive—differences from the "wings" at Kate's. First, the sauce. It was sweet, tangy, spicy, and thick, a world of flavor to savor and a massive improvement over the previous evening. Second, and the biggest difference, was the taste and texture of the "meat," which I was much relieved to learn wasn't just tofu in disguise. Red Bamboo did much of their meat substitution with textured vegetable protein (TVP). Mmmm, sounds yummy, doesn't it? I dislike using the abbreviation for this stuff, because it reminds me too much of PVC, and I hate the thought of eating the same material used to make tubing and lawn furniture.

In contrast to tofu, textured vegetable protein has a much fleshier feel to it, and even tends to have the sort of juiciness you'd expect from an actual cut of meat, though I'm quick to note that this juice is not tasty animal fat. The grain of it was a little strange, but astonishingly meatlike upon closer inspection. The interior of my fake wing resembled nothing if not a comparable cross-section of a chicken nugget, which is to say reconstituted meat slurry. But hey, anything's better than gussied-up tofu. Another big and somewhat shocking difference between these two nights of un-wings popped up on my first bite of the Red Bamboo TVP hunks: my teeth detected what appeared to be *a long bone* running through the middle, right where the bone in a chicken wing would be. This caught me off guard, seeing as how, the way I understand it, soybeans do not have bones. Taking the un-wing out of my mouth for a closer look, I discovered that the "bone" was actually a small bamboo dowel, strategically placed in the center of the food item to add further verisimilitude. Clever. The most notable advantage of that night's dish was this: I could eat a plate stacked full of the things and not feel ashamed and disgusting afterward. I love my buffalo wings, but overindulging in too many of them in one sitting leaves me fumbling for the Alka-Seltzer and feeling as though chicken grease might start oozing out of my pores. Not the case with fake wings, it turns out. Half a dozen of the things and I was still raring to go; and

I had to remind myself to stop with one helping, due to the delayed satiety effect I'd noticed during my vegetable week. It was nice to eat a plate of them and still feel like a champ, though, I have to say. Plus, I still had my main course on the way.

Next came a faux cheesesteak sandwich, the steak therein composed of wheat gluten (aka seitan, amusingly pronounced "Satan" . . . draw from that what you will), smothered in barbeque sauce, onions, mushrooms, and gobs of melted cheddar. Once again, not the real thing, but surprisingly similar. The "meat" had a firm, beefy texture to it, and given all the other ingredients in the sandwich it added up to a truly satisfying experience. That evening, as Dan and Nicole predicted, changed my mind about vegetarian cuisine and imitation meats. Sure, they didn't provide the exact same flavors and sensations afforded only by the flesh of dead animals, and they never would, but they weren't all bad. I wasn't rushing to become a vegetarian, but at least I now knew that if, through some strange set of circumstances, I was forced into veggiehood—if I were to be transported, Twilight Zone–like, to an alternate universe where eating animals was against the law and punishable by death, for instance—I would at least be availed of something close to my long-lost and beloved meat. Kind of like how I imagine vampires would go to the movies to experience scenes of daylight: not the same, but similar enough to get you by.

One last, alarming thing I learned during my vegetarian experiment was that some fake meats look disconcertingly like the real thing. I speak here specifically about something called vegetarian mock duck, often made from seitan and popular in Asia. I mean, this stuff really, really looks like duck, right down to the pocked "skin" where the nonexistent feathers once weren't. At one point, when I was hanging out over at Dan and Nicole's apartment, Dan whipped out a mock duck from a container he'd bought in Chinatown. True, I knew it was all wheat gluten on the inside, but *oh my God, it looked just like a dead bird!* Dan and Nikki were confused by my alarm, and I didn't know how to best explain it to them. There was something almost perverse about making a grain by-product appear to be a deceased, cooked animal. It's all fine and dandy if you don't want to eat meat for whatever reason, but if you're going to provide a protein alternative for vegetarians, why make it look exactly like a dead duck? And if you don't want to eat dead ducks, why eat something dressed up to look like what you're going out of your way not to eat? Does this not seem utterly bizarre to anyone else? I was flabbergasted.

Ultimately, I made it through my vegetarian week unscathed, decently fed, and feeling fine. I may not have won the bet, but at least I stayed true to my word and took my penalty like a man, with honor and dignity, or at least without a whole lot of whining. By the last two days, I wasn't even having those same satiety issues, and my cravings for animal flesh had become less than crippling. The longer I went without it, the easier it became, which frightened me a little when I started to think about it. I knew there was no way I was jumping to the green side of the fence anytime in the near future, though, a lesson I quickly learned on eating my first meat-inclusive meal after a week of successful animal abstinence. It was a turkey sandwich, and my stars if it wasn't one of the most glorious turkey sandwiches I'd had in my life.

Oh yeah, I reminded myself, *I remember now . . . This is why I'm a carnivore!*

A CARNIVORE'S FIELD GUIDE TO MEAT ANALOGUES

Analogue	Made From	Texture	Notes	"Meatiness" (out of 4)
Tofu	Soybeans	Soft, slimy	Very little flavor on its own, must be slathered in some sort of sauce	n/a
Seitan	Wheat gluten	Firm, hearty	Better texture than tofu, but still not quite "meaty"	***
Textured vegetable protein (TVP)	Soybeans, commonly	McNuggetty	Best of the bunch —I actually get occasional cravings for TVP "wings"	****
Facon/ Smart Bacon	Soybeans, possibly using black magic	Crispy when pan-fried, but notfatty (i.e., not "bacony")	It's not quite bacon-like, and it doesn't taste like soy . . . extremely disconcerting	*
Veggie burger	Mushrooms, grains, legumes, soy protein, wheat gluten, the kitchen sink	Like an extremely processed, mechanically separated meat patty	A sad thing to slap on the grill, but not wholly inedible, especially if you add real cheese on top	**

CHAPTER 9

Month of Meat, Round 4

Snakes on a Plate

The night of the rattlesnake chili was a night of many firsts. I'd never eaten a snake before, despite having grown up in a part of the country with a storied reputation for dining on swamp critters. Which of course means that I'd never cooked a snake before, another first. Nor had I ever made chili from scratch, much less served said chili to a party of about a dozen friends. Neither had I ever been persuaded by a chanting circle of drunken comrades to place a gun in my mouth, which would actually happen by the time my little chilifest concluded. That the gun was fashioned from hollowed glass and filled with Polish vodka is a detail worth noting, of course, but there *was* a gun, and I have photographic evidence to prove that it was, in fact, in my mouth (not to mention memories of an evil hangover).

This is what happens when you give tequila to otherwise normal people.

I'd known for some time that making chili with rattlesnake meat was standard practice in the American Southwest, and the dish had always intrigued me. People told me that the meat itself wasn't much to write home about, that it was relatively flavorless (another "tastes like chicken" scenario) and chewy to boot, but oddly enough it wasn't the flavor or texture of the animal that piqued my curiosity. It was the danger factor, the sheer manliness of eating a creature that could, and would, kill you if you had the misfortune of pissing it off. As Kurt Vonnegut remarked in *Breakfast of Champions*, "The Creator of the Universe had put a rattle on its tail. The Creator had also given it front teeth which were hypodermic syringes filled with deadly poison. Sometimes I wonder about the Creator of the Universe." No two ways about it: the rattlesnake is a terrifying instrument of death. I have seen photos of rattlesnake bites—and in one case of the many successive surgeries ultimately necessary to restore a poor guy's hand and arm to proper form and function—and they are horrible; the venom in those syringelike fangs is among the most powerful hemotoxins carried by any snake in the world, necrotizing flesh, halting blood coagulation, and shutting down organs as it courses through its victim's body. I wouldn't call the creature evil (though the writers of the Bible did famously choose the serpent to represent the forces of darkness)—it just behaves as nature intended it—but it's certainly a nasty piece of work. So eating one of these suckers is basically just a big show of carnivorous machismo, a display of man's power and dominance over one of Mother Nature's most vicious killers.* Which is to say that the operative question here was less "How will this taste?" than "*¿Quien es mas macho?*"

Granted, it would be way *muy macho* to go down to Nogales or Nacogdoches or somewhere in Nevada; snare one of these bad boys with my bare hands, deftly avoiding its feints and strikes, insinuating myself closer and closer, and waiting for just the right moment to snare its neck in my powerful grip; and then skin and clean it right there and bring the meat back to my cave dwelling, much to the awed admiration and respect of my clan—but that wasn't about to happen. I may love meat, and Lord knows I love feeling like a bona fide, chest-thumping descendent of great apes, but I am not fucking crazy. I'm a city boy, after all—I wasn't about to screw around with live pit vipers (the class of snake to which rattlers belong), no matter how cool I might look doing so, or how much fantastic copy it would inevitably provide. I did have to somehow procure myself a rattler for the chili, though. At the butcher shop, this request was the first I'd made that gave Frank Ottomanelli pause; it wasn't that he hadn't dealt in snake meat before, it's just simply not your everyday order for a Greenwich Village butcher.

"I'll ask my provider for you," he said skeptically, "but last I checked they were only selling them in ten-pound buckets." He pantomimed picking up a heavy pail from the floor to demonstrate its presumed size and weight. "There's a fair bit of meat in there, sure, but then, you know . . . you have a ten-pound bucket of snakes to deal with. That what you're going for?"

I thought about this for a moment, balancing the pros and cons. In the pro column was a definite abundance of meat, plus the joy of telling my friends that I had a ten-pound bucket of snakes in my kitchen, which would surely be great fun, particularly if done with abundant enthusiasm and hungry glee: *Check it out, guys, ten pounds of dead snakes in a bucket right here in my own home . . . how awesome is that!* It would also make for lively cocktail-party conversation at fancy gala-

---

* We humans have a bold claim on the number one spot in that category, with plenty of room to spare.

type affairs: *Good seeing you again, Chancellor/Senator/Reverend/Your Highness. What am I up to these days, you ask? Well, I got me this big ole bucket of dead snakes, you see* . . . On the con side, it would be expensive (a big lesson I'd learned from purchasing all of this exotic meat by the pound), and I would, as Frank noted, have to deal with ten pounds of the stuff, considerably more than I either wanted or needed. In the end, reason got the best of me, and I passed on the big-snake-bucket offer, opting instead to order a single rattler online from my new friends at ExoticMeats.com.

Option B turned out to be expensive after all. As a matter of fact, my three-and-a-half-pound rattlesnake was, pound for pound, the single most costly purchase of any meat I'd bought to date, well over a hundred dollars. The only thing that would come close was goose foie gras, but that—like truffles, Beluga caviar, and o-toro, the fatty tuna belly so highly prized by Japanese sushi enthusiasts and priced like gold—has long been perceived as a luxury item, a food widely assumed to be well worth the sticker shock for the amount of pure gastronomic pleasure it provides. But rattlesnake? I hadn't eaten it yet—maybe it'd end up being explosively delicious—but based on its reputation I'd hardly place it on the same list of delicacies. So why was it so damned pricey? Turns out, it takes a long time and a lot of live bait to lovingly raise a rattlesnake to this size and weight (the thing was nearly six feet long, uncoiled). And then, I'm guessing, there's the unspoken "hazard tax," added by the snake farmers because of the daily proximity to death.* It's one thing to go into the shed to milk a cow; it's something else entirely to go into a pen and fetch a fully mature rattlesnake.

After I received my rattler and dutifully thawed it, my first thorough inspection of the creature gave me pause, then concern, then downright worry. I don't know exactly what I expected; the photo of the package on the website showed only a coiled pink vacuum-sealed thing, hardly enough detail to make out what precisely was inside.

---

* And talk about a job title! Anyone who can list "rattlesnake wrangler" on his CV has, in my opinion, clearly earned the right to be referred to as a professional badass sonofabitch.

What I got was, quite simply, a snake. Not a snake fillet, not three and a half pounds of rattlesnake strips, not ground rattler meat. Nope—what you receive when you order a rattlesnake online is the whole animal, minus the skin, head, tail, and inner organs, its long, fat body coiled up tightly like a meaty pink spring. I was also crestfallen to discover that, at these exorbitant prices, they failed to include the rattle. Not that I had big plans for it—maybe put it in an old-fashioned mojo bag for good juju, as the Creoles might say, or fasten it to a length of leather to make a necklace—but come on, it's an important totem, a symbol of the vanquished beast, a talisman that, for a superstitious person, might represent the spiritual transference of the creature's power to whoever held or wore it. I didn't really believe that, but then again, I could use all the luck I could get. Plus, I paid for the thing, I might as well get to keep it, right?

Then there were the bones, which appeared to number close to 470 million. There is no real way to fillet a rattlesnake, I quickly learned—the meat is tenaciously attached to the animal's skeletal structure, and a snake is, if anything, just one long spinal column with a head at one end, a tail at the other, and a whole lot of ribs in between. If I wanted this meat, I would have to go in there and get it somehow, and cutting it easily from the bone in one deft motion was hardly an option. So what the hell was I supposed to do with this monster? My conclusion, later corroborated by online snake-cooking tips and recipes, was to hack the beast up into manageable hunks about five to six inches long and slow-cook the bejeezus out of it, after which the meat should be tender enough to remove from the bones and simmer in the chili. I'd have to do a hell of a lot of picking through those skinny ribs and vertebrae, but at least I would be spared having to stand in my kitchen with a sharp knife and an idiotic look on my face, flummoxed about how to successfully butcher a snake.

Strategy in place, I returned my snake to the refrigerator and started in on the chili. Like everything sold by ExoticMeats.com, my package arrived with a helpful sheet of colored paper filled with details about the animal I'd purchased, as well as several recipes contributed by fellow customers. I chose a recipe that looked good—three-bean chili with tequila—and went to work. The basic preparation of this chili was hardly daunting, even for me. Then about twenty minutes into the process, I learned the following Extremely Important Lesson About Dealing with Raw Chile Peppers:

I'm no Yoda, but I have, over the course of my life, learned a thing or two worth passing on. In this case, I learned that if you are going to be chopping up a bunch of hot peppers—jalapeños, poblanos, habañeros, whatever—you should wear gloves. And if you don't wear gloves, then it's essential to wash your hands *thoroughly*. Chile oil is a sticky, vindictive substance that was invented by Lucifer and is committed to staying on your hands with all the angry stubbornness of an irritated rodeo bull. If you do not spend at least a full minute scrubbing your fingers clean of the stuff, it *will* come back to cause you pain and grief the likes of which you have probably never experienced. Case in point: When I was done seeding, deribbing, and chopping my six ripe jalapeños into nice little bits, I gave my hands a cursory wash with warm water and soap. This, of course, did not do the trick, a fact I learned soon afterward when, feeling an itch up my nose, I wiped my nostrils with chile-oil-infused fingers and then—this is the worst part— *snorted sharply*, ensuring that the devil oil made it all the way up my nose, through my sinus cavities, and into the frontal lobe of my brain.

This is what it felt like: Imagine an ice cream headache. Now imagine that the ice cream flavor is "searing pain." It is not a pleasant experience. Your head is filled with what you assume to be boiling carbolic acid that is moments away from liquefying your gray matter, your nose begins to leak uncontrollably, your eyes redden and swell as though you'd been punched in the face by a gorilla, after which comes wave after wave of coughing and nausea . . . and there is simply nothing you can do but sit there and endure it. Spiciness has no complete remedy but time. So I sat down in a comfortable chair, took some long, measured breaths (through my mouth—my nose was still dribbling a clear, spicy liquid that, for all I knew, used to be part of my brain), and assured myself that the worst would be over in about thirty or forty-five minutes, which it was. At least I only touched my nose, I thought with great relief when the pain in my face had diminished to a moderate tingle; I couldn't bear to imagine what would have occurred had I instead tried to remove a stray lash from my eyeball or, God forbid, gone to have a pee.

Yikes.

Once I was back to sort-of-normal—that tingling would last for several hours—I continued with the chili by segmenting the snake as planned and adding it to the pot with the rest of the ingredients, then covering the dish and setting it to cook low and slow. Not that the cutting was easy. I had to whack at some of the thicker parts with heavy blows from my heaviest knife to get through the bones, but eventually they gave way. About eight hours later, I removed one of the sections to find that the meat was, as I'd hoped, tender and falling from the bones. For the following two hours, I proceeded to pick away at the snake meat and place it in a plastic bowl, doing my best to keep all of the bones on the cutting board and out of the stewing chili. For all my efforts I was provided with a healthy portion of meat, easily enough for the recipe, as well as a thumb and forefinger that would continue to prickle with spiciness for the next couple of days. In retrospect, there was really no need to cook the snake in the chili before removing the meat. Had I been a more thoughtful person (and I seem to begin many stories with this qualifier), I would have boiled the snake separately in salt water, so that not only would I have been spared spicy-finger syndrome, I could have been assured that no bones had sneaked into the final product.

Oh yes, there were bones. Despite my care and attention and a good half hour hunting through the Crock-Pot for anything more solid than a kidney bean, there was no way I would be able to catch each offending bit, as the chili was thick and texturally varied, making it hard to see the bones or differentiate them from small strings of rattlesnake meat. Oh well, I thought, my guests, who were to arrive within minutes, would just have to deal with it. I'd been through too much that day to care, and was desperately in need of beer. I grabbed a Dixie from the fridge, took one cold, beautiful swallow, and removed the cover of the pot to let the chili cook down a bit more before the feast began. I also made sure to take a preliminary taste of the meat, finding its texture indeed on the chewy side, even after stewing all day, but only enough to lend it a little "give." It was what I guess you might refer to as al dente meat, hardly the rubbery consistency people had warned me about. Tastewise it was mild, yes, but it did a wonderful job of picking up all the different flavors of the chili ingredients. I could tell by the first taste that this chili was going to be something special.

My friends arrived just as the sun was beginning its slow descent, hungry from a day of hearing live music at a summer concert series in a nearby park. My guests helped themselves from the pot, then added to their bowls any of the numerous toppings and extras I'd provided, including grated cheddar cheese, diced onions, sour cream, twelve different hot sauces, Fritos (always!), and, the most heralded addition of the evening, añejo tequila. Much like spiking turtle soup with sherry, tossing a shot of tequila into your chili gives it a fantastic extra kick, particularly if it's good, aged liquor. Try it—you won't be disappointed. On the other hand, it wasn't long before the bottle of tequila I'd placed on the table to be used as a condiment was drained, and I was well aware that most of it wasn't going into the chili.

Thus inebriated, no one seemed to care that they had to pick out snake ribs and small segments of spinal column from their dinner. They even turned it into a game, seeing who could find the most pieces of snake skeleton and drop them into the "bone bucket" I placed on the serving table (for the record, I think most of us were too sloshed by the end of the evening to decide on a proper victor, not that winning such a contest was going on anyone's résumé). Also, as a lucky coincidence or possibly serendipity, the Samuel L. Jackson film *Snakes on a Plane* would be opening in theaters the following weekend, a movie that famously proved once and for all that ubiquitous online buzz—you couldn't surf the Net for more than two minutes without stumbling on *Snakes on a Plane* fan art, fiction, homemade trailers, cartoons, ersatz posters, or visual gags—does not necessarily correlate to box office success. In the midst of all this hype, we couldn't help but make the connection between the forthcoming movie and our meal, referring to the evening as Snakes on a Plate, even though, to be fair, there was only a single snake and it was served in paper bowls. We took great pleasure sounding off about the chili using our best Sam Jackson voice: "I got to get this *mothafuckin* snake out of this *mothafuckin* chili!"

Then there was the gun.

My friends Christian and Alyssa, in appreciation for all the free meat they'd been enjoying at my carnivorous events, decided to thank me with a gift. Knowing my affinity for whiskey, they'd planned on bringing me a bottle of Jack Daniel's, but as soon as they took one look around the Polish liquor store on my street, they found something entirely more appropriate: Sniper, a two-foot-high glass bottle shaped like an assault rifle, including a handle, a magazine, even an orange faux-leather strap and butt cover, and the thing was filled to the brim with grain vodka. The logo even had a photo of a majestic buck's head, set against a backdrop of camouflage, smack between the crosshairs of a rifle scope. Awesome. Of course they bullied me into dramatically placing the "gun" to my lips to take a generous belt, gravity forcing the liquor from the tall bottle down my throat with unexpected velocity. When I'd finished I sputtered and coughed like an ancient tractor engine, but the display seemed to have appeased the mob, now cheering and clapping me on the back.

It was a triumphant moment. The night wasn't perfect—there were bones in the chili, my fingers were still numb from the snake-meat picking, and then there was that whole jalapeño-oil-up-the-nose business— but still, it was a grand time, a crazy time. It may have been that we were simply riding high from the long summer afternoon, from cold drinks, a hearty meal, and excellent companionship, but something special happened in my little apartment that night, a bonding, a communal experience that those in attendance would recall with fondness for months afterward. Perhaps we had actually gained a sort of power from eating that deadly viper, some transcendent property that moved swiftly through our systems and displayed itself in our bonhomie and youthful exuberance. We had conquered the venomous beast, consumed its flesh, and imbibed its spirit—could it be that we had inadvertently shared in some sort of mystical carnivorous rite?

Well . . . the chili was great, but my bet's on the tequila.

Three-Bean Snakebite Chili with Tequila

1 SIX-FOOT RATTLESNAKE, SKINNED, CLEANED, AND DE-RATTLED (APPROXIMATELY 1 POUND OF SNAKE MEAT)

4 CUPS FINELY CHOPPED ONION

3 GARLIC CLOVES, MINCED

2 TABLESPOONS CORNMEAL

ONE 15-OUNCE CAN TOMATOES, CHOPPED BUT NOT DRAINED

4 TEASPOONS CHILI POWDER

5 JALAPEÑOS, DE-RIBBED, SEEDED, AND DICED (WEAR GLOVES!)

1 TABLESPOON GROUND CUMIN

1 TABLESPOON CHOPPED FRESH OREGANO

ONE 15-OUNCE CAN KIDNEY BEANS

ONE 15-OUNCE CAN WHITE BEANS

ONE 15-OUNCE CAN BLACK BEANS

½ CUP AÑEJO (GOLD) TEQUILA

FOR GARNISH (OPTIONAL):

½ LARGE VIDALIA ONION, FINELY CHOPPED

2 CUPS SHREDDED CHEDDAR CHEESE

1 BAG FRITOS

1 CUP SOUR CREAM

EXTRA TEQUILA

HOT SAUCES OF YOUR CHOOSING

If the rattlesnake is whole, cut it into manageable segments roughly 5 to 6 inches long. Cook the snake pieces in lightly salted, simmering water for 1 to 2 hours, or until the meat is ten-

der and falls away from the bone. Pick the snake clean, making
sure no ribs or chunks of spinal column remain in the meat. Add
the remaining ingredients except the garnishes to a slow cooker
or Crock-Pot. Set on low and simmer for approximately 7 to 8
hours. Remove the cover and allow the chili to cook down to desired thickness. Garnish at will.

Serves 5 to 6

One for the Birds

With Game Night, I'd seen just how easy it might be to do multiple animals in one night, so I decided to be even more ambitious—noticing
that my list contained a large number of bird species, I thought what
the hell, might as well have a big bird taste-off: duck, pheasant, guinea
hen, quail, and squab, all in one night. And why not throw a nice free-
range, organic chicken into the mix as well? Maybe it was all this meat
I was consuming—leftovers from my previous tastings kept my fridge
well stocked with exotic meat treats—or maybe it was simply that I was
really coming into my own as a Shameless Carnivore, but I could feel
myself growing bolder. I was on familiar ground when it came to poultry, having cooked a fair share of chickens and ducks and turkeys in my
day, so I figured that while roasting up six unique animals in an evening
might be a challenge, it wasn't impossible. Plus, being able to sample
so many different creatures in one swoop had this tremendous feeling
of power connected to it, as though by doing so I was proving my human dominance over the winged beasts of the world. In contrast to the
venison night, however, I'd be ill advised to cook them all identically,
no matter how much I wanted to test out the "integrity" of each meat.
No, I'd have to devise a recipe for each, which would take a little time,
so I did what I always do when I'm hungry and ambitious and maybe
a little doubtful about my kitchen knowledge and skill set: I went to the

butcher shop. I consulted with Frank for some time about the relative merits of each of these animals, spoke about possible preparations and cooking times, and came away from the store that afternoon with not only a big bag of birds but also a bold and (should I succeed) delicious menu. I had no idea what I would serve as side dishes, and honestly, I can't say that I cared much. This was going to be my biggest, most ambitious cooking event yet, and I planned to let my guests bring whatever sides they felt like making, because I was going to be up to my ears with all of these poultry preparations, and I wouldn't have the time to think about vegetables and starches and so forth. Meat was my mission, and that was that. Let the poultry onslaught begin!

APPETIZER #1: QUAILSADILLAS

It may surprise many people—particularly Vice President Cheney—to learn that the quail (*Coturnix coturnix*), a small migratory bird of the partridge family, bears absolutely no resemblance whatsoever to a seventy-eight-year-old Republican lawyer's face, despite what the *Food Lover's Companion* refers to as its "white, tender, slightly gamey flesh." Can't really see how he got those two confused. Despite his questionable firearms safety skills, Dick was right for wanting to hunt quail, though, I have to say—they are seriously delicious little things. And they are little, the smallest European game birds, in fact, and though their appeal in the ancient kitchen was relatively scant (during classical times, many thought them to be unwholesome because of their diet, which included poisonous plants), they're now prized worldwide for hunting as well as fine dining. Which is not to say that quail don't have their rightful place in culinary lore. One of my favorite stories comes from, of all places, the Bible. Following their exodus from slavery in Egypt, as they wandered the desert for forty years, the Israelites understandably got a little hungry. Hearing their kvetching, God sent down some nourishment in the form of a miraculous foodstuff called manna, as well as, you guessed it . . . a "shower of quail." As a Jewish carnivore, this makes me particularly proud of my faith. When my people were exhausted and hungry in that terrible, lonely desert, it was meat that sustained them. And not just any meat—Divine Quail, straight from God! This "miracle of quail" has really got to be my favorite of all biblical miracles. At least it's the tastiest.

For my quailsadillas, I'd purchased a package of four semiboneless birds the day before Bird Night. If I hadn't been looking to take just the meat, I would have been more than happy to serve them whole, which is the traditional approach, and one that I adore. As with the guinea pig, the flavor and texture of which, you'll recall, is often compared to quail, there's really nothing quite like being served an entire animal to give you that splendid feeling of power, especially if you eschew cutlery and eat the thing with your bare hands, which, in quail etiquette, is considered standard practice. The grilling was simple enough. I washed each of birds, patted them dry, seasoned them with a little salt and pepper, then tossed them on a hot grill until they were just under medium doneness, since quail are often said best prepared a little underdone. After that, I let them rest for a few minutes to make sure they kept all their precious juices, then tossed them in the fridge to chill out until I'd need them the following day. When the time came and the other birds were roasting away in the oven, turning these birdies into quailsadillas was a snap. I picked all the meat from the bones—making sure to pop a scrap or two into my mouth in the process, as is the right of any carnivore in the kitchen—then assembled all of my ingredients. Okay, I'll admit, I cheated a little bit on the tortillas. After just barely surviving the flour debacle with the yak momos, there was no way I was going to make tortillas from scratch, so I did the next best thing and picked up six fresh flour tortillas from my favorite Chinese Tex-Mex place up the street (Chinese only in the ethnicity of its owners and operators, who decided to take up the restaurant game but take on a wholly different cuisine, and good that they did—they make unbelievable tortillas).

From there all I had to do was toss one tortilla on a heated skillet, liberally apply the quail meat and cheese (I used Monterey Jack with jalapeños, though had I given it a bit more thought, I would have added some *queso fresco*, maybe a little chopped cilantro, and a splash of lime juice), top with a second tortilla, and wait until the heat fused everything into one big, gooey, meaty sandwich. I repeated this process twice more to make three whole quailsadillas, which I sliced into quarters and arranged artfully on serving plates accompanied by sour cream and salsa for dipping. Not the fanciest preparation, true, but what it lacked in sophistication it made up for in taste. The quail meat, darker and more delicately flavored than your average chicken, gave the quesadilla a neat, new, and different spin. It may have not been a miracle from the heavens, but those plates were picked clean of everything but a smear of sour cream and salsa in just minutes. Score one for the chef; five more to go.

APPETIZER #2: SMOKED BREAST OF DUCK, SLICED
AND SERVED COLD

No, I did not smoke an entire duck, or even a duck breast, all by my lonesome. As much as I wanted to roast a whole duck or make a duck leg confit, duck à l'orange, or other variety of classical duck dish for my Poultrypalooza—even my favorite duck and andouille gumbo, in all its dark, savory splendor—there was simply not enough time, and I was roasting enough birds as it was. Not that having leftover duck would be a problem for me; as with many meats, duck is spectacular on that second day, after all of its fats and flavors and juices have sunk in and congealed. But I wanted to serve as many different birds as I could, so I took this as my opportunity to let someone else take care of the preparation and let me deal with the other birds I now had in the oven. I also loved smoked anything, especially poultry, so I picked up a whole smoked breast of duck at the butcher's as an impulse buy while I loaded up my bag with quail and squabs and guinea hens and so on.

Now, of all the birds that fill the skies and walk the grounds and swim the ponds of the earth, duck is one of my absolute favorites. First domesticated by the Chinese well over two thousand years ago, duck is one of the most popular meats of any bird in the world. There is a reason for this, and that reason is: *fat*. True, the meat of the breast and legs are deeper in hue and flavor than of most flightless birds and other poultry, but that heavy layer of subcutaneous fat is what makes the duck far more succulent than most of them. Duck fat kicks ass. Make sure to keep that fatty layer in place when you pop that bird in the oven, and you'll never have to worry about your duck drying out like chicken or turkey. And if you have any left over in your baking pan, for heaven's sake make sure you strain it off and save it in your refrigerator, because you'll want to make use of it later. Gourmets willingly pay top dollar for this stuff (eight or ten bucks for only a few ounces), so you'd be daft to waste it. If you're a doubter, try this: melt some duck fat in a pan and use it instead of cooking oil or butter in even the most simple of recipes, and what was once ordinary all of a sudden becomes extraordinary. Use a little duck fat in your sauté pan when you go to scramble some eggs, and all of a sudden you're riding high in Flavor Country, baby. Duck Fat Flavor Country. It's a country not recognized by the United Nations just yet, but I'm ready to start an intense lobbying campaign.

Speaking of eggs, I'd be remiss if I didn't mention that duck eggs are a tasty delicacy. Certain breeds of duck are raised specifically for their eggs, in fact. The Indian Runner, for instance, can lay up to two hundred each year, much more than your average domestic chicken. Sadly, duck eggs have never really taken hold in the American egg market, though you can still find them through specialty producers, and I highly recommend doing so. They certainly make for more interesting omelets and crepes, that's for sure. Throughout Asia, though, duck eggs are prized for a particularly horrifying dish called balut, otherwise known as "fertilized duck egg." You can find this dish in China, Vietnam, Cambodia, and the Philippines, among other places, should you be courageous enough to bother going out of your way to sample the virility-inducing properties of partially developed duck embryos. I'm not one to judge, of course, and given the opportunity I would probably give balut a go to find out what all the fuss is about, but I will say this: should I ever be in dire need of an aphrodisiac, I'll forgo balut and head straight for the oysters and alcohol instead. Nothing really says "I'm in the mood for nookie" like partially developed bird embryos, don't you think?

ROSEMARY-CRUSTED GUINEA HEN

When it came time to get into guinea hen, I was in a good spot. For years my mother had prepared a rosemary-crusted baked chicken for my family, and we'd all loved it. She loved it, too, since it was a cinch to make, and resulted in tender meat underneath a crispy, herbed skin. Lucky for me, I had a jar of the same rosemary rub and had been using it on chicken, but being availed of a three-pound Canadian guinea hen, which I was told should be cooked in the same manner as chicken, this one was a no-brainer for me. Which was good, because I needed my brain to deal with the other, trickier birds still to come. After washing and drying the guinea hen, all that was necessary was to coat it with a generous helping of the herbal rub, making sure to get some of it in between the breast meat and the skin, and let it sit in the fridge for a few hours to let the flavoring sink in. By the time I was ready to pop it into the oven, the only thing left to do was give it some salt, and I was good to go. Easy as pie. Well, easier than pie, really, considering how bad I am with dough. "Easy as chicken" is more like it.

You don't really see a lot of guinea hen these days, either in markets or in restaurants. Indigenous to Africa, these birds are said to be possessed of a delicate, slightly gamey meat, but to be perfectly honest, I have to admit that they do, in fact, taste like chicken. There was the slightest bit of gaminess there, but it was very subtle, and difficult to detect through the seasoning. It was also a bit on the dry side, everyone noticed, though they were polite enough not to complain. (And good they didn't, or no more birds for them!) In hindsight, I realized that I had erred less as a cook than as a culinary researcher—finding further information on cooking guinea fowl later on, I learned that while you are advised to cook them as you would chicken, they actually have less fat than your average chicken, which you have to compensate for in your cooking methods—baking covered with a little stock or water at the bottom of the pan, say, or better yet, larded with bacon—lest your guinea hen dry out. Big whoops on my part, but not too big. The duck and quail had been a hit so far, and there were still three more species of bird to sample before the night was through, so I soldiered on as best I could and tried not to pout at my dried-out hen.

A BRACE OF SQUAB

There are a number of animals whose names differ from those of the meat they provide. Instead of eating pig, we eat pork; cows become beef; and so on. People may not know what you're referring to when you tell them that you enjoyed a delicious braised squab, so you can tell them that the term refers to either a young, unfledged pigeon or dove. When you do, you'll see why I believe this alternate terminology is employed. Either they get disgusted that you're going to eat the same sordid animal found loitering on streetlamps and in parks—"rats with wings," as those who despise them often say—or appalled that you took so much pleasure devouring the one animal that represents peace. "You're going to eat that beautiful little peace bird?" someone actually asked me once. Yes, I'm going to eat it, and yes, I'm going to relish eating it. And oh, did I say that I was eating a *baby* peace bird? To some, this is distasteful ("Eating baby birds, for shame!"), but we carnivorous connoisseurs know them to be particularly tender.

As far as whether the term *squab* refers directly to dove or pigeon, it actually encompasses both, so long as they are young and have never flown (i.e., "unfledged"). Of the two, I prefer to think that I am eating pigeon (genus *Columba*), for a number of reasons. First, believe it or not, pigeons have a storied history in the annals of food, beginning with the ancient Egyptians, who are most responsible for bringing them to the table, prizing them for their "delicate, dark meat." They were, in fact, among the first birds to ever be domesticated. Later introduced to Western Europe, squab became beloved by both the French, who called them *pigeonneau*, and the English, who often baked them into a savory pie. You can keep your four and twenty blackbirds—I'll have four and twenty squab instead.

The other reason I delight in eating young pigeons, other than the marvelous flavor, naturally, is *revenge*. When I sink my teeth into the rich, dark flesh of these birds, it is a conscious act of retribution for every pigeon in every tree, on every lamppost, and in the air that has ever taken aim at me with that vile natural ammunition of theirs. Some people claim superstitiously that you're granted tremendous luck if you happen to bear the brunt of a direct hit, though I'm guessing these are not the people wiping pigeon shit out of their hair. It's a horrible thing to do to a person, and I want pigeons everywhere to know that. "So you want to have a little target practice on my new coat?" I ask the cooked bird, laughing maniacally as I tear off its leg and slowly work the meat away from the drumstick. "Not anymore, you little bastard! See my wrath, pigeons! Know my great and terrible vengeance, and despair!" I make sure not to do this in restaurants, though, at least not at full volume; vengeful declarations to one's entrée generally tend to make fellow restaurant patrons a little uncomfortable.

NEXT COURSE: DISASTER CHICKEN

Having so many people over for dinner, and already going gonzo with the number of birds I was cooking, I thought it would be a decent idea to throw a chicken into the mix as well. Doing so would ensure that everyone—and there must have been about twelve of us—had enough meat, but I also have a load of fun every time I cook a Beer-Butt Chicken. Yet another Cajun invention, this recipe involves taking a can of beer, drinking half of it (the best part!), filling the remaining liquid with whatever sauces or spices you want—I'm partial to Worcestershire sauce, a couple of fresh garlic cloves, sometimes a little liquid smoke—then shoving the can right up the raw chicken's ass, keeping the whole thing vertical to make sure you don't spill any precious beer. Cork up the neck cavity with a small potato or an onion and bake or barbeque it upright, and what happens is that all that flavorful liquid steams out of the can and into the meat itself, resulting in an uncommonly juicy chicken. It's sometimes a challenge to keep the bird from losing its balance and falling on its side (it's been drinking, after all); however, there is a company that sells a stainless steel ChickCan stand precisely for this purpose, and I happened to have one. I love cooking a chicken in this fashion for the flavor, naturally, and because it reminds me of home, but also because, with the chicken standing upright like this and a potato sticking out of the neck hole looking every bit like a replacement head—I sometimes like to carve a little smiley face on it to exaggerate this effect—the thing looks like a funny little guy.

"Check it out," I said to Katie, as she came into the kitchen for another glass of wine and to check on my progress. "It looks like a funny little guy! I kind of half expect him to wave to me, or get up and start dancing."

"Well, of course you think that," she said. "Our whole lives we've been bombarded with images of dancing chickens." I did think about it, and was amazed that I hadn't considered this before. She was right—I started remembering countless cartoons, commercials, and other media featuring dancing birds. The music video for Peter Gabriel's "Sledgehammer," with those two plump roasters spinning around to the beat in stop-motion animation, sprang to mind. Then I thought how twisted it was that this was such a ubiquitous image, since it is never live, happy chickens we see dancing (with the exception of those chicken puppets beloved by Gonzo in the Muppet movies), but dead chickens. Raw or cooked, they were always plucked clean of feathers, and absent of both head and feet. It's pretty warped stuff, when you think about it—all things considered, I'd prefer my dead chickens not getting up and doing a jig, thank you very much. I'll just have them stay dead and delicious.

By the time my Beer-Butt Potato-Head Chicken came out of the oven, it was looking pretty fine indeed, and was showing no indications that it might break into a tango anytime soon. It was a glorious sight, and even though I was rapidly filling up with all the squab and quail and guinea hen meat that preceded it, I am hopelessly and irrevocably programmed to become hungry every time I set my sights on a chicken right out of the oven. But it was a deceptive vision of chickeny goodness—all was not right here. The problem, I was soon alarmed to discover, was the smell. There was a distinctly funky odor emanating from my chicken's general direction, and further inspection confirmed that this splendid-looking bird was in fact the source. I hadn't noticed anything amiss when I removed the chicken from its packaging, though that was most likely due to what Katie referred to as a recent "garbage problem" in her kitchen that, while now completely taken care of, nonetheless left behind a faint but noticeable trace of its malodorous past. Now, however, there was no doubt about it: no matter how succulent it looked, this chicken's aroma was definitely *off*.

"Why don't you try it?" asked Katie. "See if it's okay. It might be okay, right?"

"Maybe," I replied, skeptical. Then I got another wince-inducing whiff of funky chicken. "But I doubt it. I don't think anyone should try it." I sighed dejectedly, knowing that there was only one solution to this problem—we had to throw it out. I wasn't totally surprised by this tragic turn of events, though, seeing that the chicken was the only bird I'd purchased at my local grocery store instead of from the butcher shop. Now, I hate, hate, *hate* to ever waste any meat, but in my opinion that maxim only refers to good meat. In this case, there's only one thing to do: chuck it. I know how difficult it is to dispose of an entire bird, but it must be done: before you have too much time to think about it, dump the thing in the trash can and order a pizza. Then make certain to give your purveyor a good, hard what-for the following day for burning you. Trust me, it's worth it.

LAST COURSE: DUCK-SAUSAGE-STUFFED PHEASANT

Pheasant (*Phasianus colchicus*) is yet another bird that owes its fame to the classical world. Though the animal's ancestry can be traced back to China, Greek lore has it that Jason and the Argonauts returned from their adventures in the Caucusus not only with the Golden Fleece but also with a bounty of pheasants as well. According to the *Oxford Companion to Food*, "The pheasant, with its close relations, is possibly the most important game bird of the world and great efforts have been made to maintain artificially large populations in those parts of Europe where natural conditions are favorable to the species. Without human help, the pheasant's presence in Europe would dwindle greatly." I know now that this particular outcome should be considered criminal, based solely on the natural flavor of pheasant flesh. It's largely agreed that the meat from the female of the species, being more plump and tender than that of cock pheasants (refrain from sniggering, please), is preferable, although one is warned that it is also relatively lean, meaning that you'd do best to introduce additional fat to the bird when cooking, a process known as "barding." One way of doing this is to wrap the pheasant in bacon and let that fantastic pork fat sink into the meat, which I would have been more than happy to do—hell, I wrap just about anything in bacon, given the opportunity—but Frank Ottomanelli offered me an alternative: stuffing the interior cavity of the bird with raw duck sausage. Two words for that notion: *damn* and *straight*. I bought a couple of links along with a nice plump female pheasant. This, it turns out, was a really good idea: once prepared, the combination of the intense, spicy duck sausage (I'd removed the meat from the natural casing and shoved the soft brown contents inside the bird prior to roasting) and the delicate, mild pheasant breast was a one-two punch of avian succulence.

It was the perfect finale to a big night, the last, triumphant note in a celebration of poultry that began with an overture of grilled quail and smoked duck and continued on to a first act of mild guinea hen, where it coasted until squab made its dramatic arrival and took things to an entirely new level, and now, finally, concluded with a duo of duck sausage and pheasant. In the end, Bird Night, with its ambition, scope, and narrowly averted food poisoning from a spoiled chicken, was a great carnivorous success. *Beware, birds,* I thought to myself as I stretched out on the couch, too filled with meat to even begin to consider moving, much less cleaning up the wreck I'd made of Katie's kitchen. *Now that I know how delicious you all are, you will have no rest—if you can find a way to escape, you'd best do it soon, because it won't belong before the Shameless Carnivore will once more be coming for you.*

The Finer Points of Decapitating a Baby Bird

I find myself in a small store in a suburban Seattle business park on a clear, hot late-August day. The walls here are lined almost exclusively with top-down freezer cases, and in those freezers, a carnivorous paradise: hundreds of pounds of various steaks, rib racks, hamburger patties, sausages, and jerkies from almost two dozen different animals, from kangaroo to caribou, pheasant to rattlesnake and seemingly everything in between. Displayed above each freezer is a laminated placard bearing an illustration of the animal contained therein, as well as a brief description of that creature, its meat, and its nutritional makeup. Sample: "ELK (111kcal; 22.95g protein; 1.45g fat; 12.45% calories from fat; 55mg cholesterol). Elk is the second largest member of the deer family. Elk is very dark and coarsely grained. It can be described as the sweetest of the deer meats. Elk can be cooked in the same way as venison. Considered by many zoologists to be the same species as moose." In the center of the room is a pair of wooden tables, draped in red felt and bearing a strange display of objects and wares both food and animal related: a vase filled with peacock feathers, a preserved alligator head, various barbeque sauces, books on grilling and smoking, and pamphlets with titles like "Why Bison?" There is a wooden quail, a stone leopard, and what appears to be a Scandinavian St. Nicholas doll, decked out in fur pajamas and hat. And behind the scenes, an employee dutifully boxes up pound after pound of frozen meats into packages filled with dry ice, to be shipped to adventurous carnivores across the nation.

I had made it. I was here. This was the headquarters of Exotic Meats.com.

I arrived at this place on a whim, actually. At the end of the Month of Meat, I paid a visit to my younger brother, Eric, who moved to Portland, Oregon, not long after Katrina put a rather sizable kink in his studies at the University of New Orleans. Never having been to Seattle, Eric and I took the opportunity to pay the city a visit, have lunch at one of the many fine local brewpubs, and of course check out the home base of the country's premier online retailer of uncommon meats (they've since moved the flagship store to San Antonio, as the central location provides more favorable shipping rates for customers). We browsed the store for a while, poring over the bewildering bounty of the stock, trying to decide what we might purchase to grill up for dinner back in Portland that evening. By this time, even though my thirty-one days of different animals had expired and I'd only made it to twenty-eight, I'd ceased caring about the deadline of my Month of Meat. Granted, I was a little deflated by missing out on the potential bragging rights—if you're into meat, being able to say you ate thirty-one animals in thirty-one days is pretty impressive-sounding—but you also have to consider my reasons. First, as I learned more about the creatures I'd listed, it turned out that some had to be crossed off due to lack of availability or for legal reasons, such as nutria, which try as I might I couldn't manage to find anywhere. Thus the final list numbered thirty instead of the intended thirty-one (though I'd get there eventually . . . I had to wait for a certain "season" for that last one). Also, of the remaining two still on the list, I promised to eat one with my younger brother, who, being all the way across the country, had entirely missed out on all of my carnivorous explorations so far. That would turn out to be partridge. The other, goose, I held off on cooking because my friend Julia claimed to have a fabulous, supersecret recipe handed down by her mother, who guarded the thing as cautiously as though it were a matter of national security. There's no chance I was going to miss out on that, deadline or no deadline.

As we hemmed and hawed over the wild boar strip steaks versus ostrich burger patties, we took in some kind words and funny stories from Dave, the store's operations manager, who told us the history of the business and the multiple vandalisms they'd suffered at the hands of the Animal Liberation Front and similar vegetable terrorist numbskulls. Eric and I stood there, mouths agape, as Dave regaled us with tales of these dirtbags trying to disrupt their business, an act that, when given even the slightest bit of thought, boggles the mind in its idiocy. What were these people trying to accomplish? I wonder if they would continue their efforts, no doubt inspired by evenings of monster bong blasts and pseudo-intellectual stoner rambling about "the Man," if they knew that most if not all of the meat these folks purvey is 1) not produced by them, as they are solely the middlemen in this process, retailers who acquire products wholesale and sell them at a markup to customers, and 2) high-quality, high-priced specialty food that is raised by conscientious farmers around the globe, people who care deeply about the welfare of their animals, not just because doing so increases the quality of the product they take so much pride in, but because they're good, honest people who heed the principles of responsible agriculture. These are the good guys, for crying out loud! Listen: I don't care how you feel about meat—you can say that it's the food of Satanists and that anyone who eats it is going to have their skin boiled off in the ninth circle of the Inferno, and I won't think twice about it. That's your opinion, and you're welcome to it. But when you start messing with a person's livelihood by committing acts of terrorism—against the wrong people, and for bad reasons, at that!—we're at war. You are an enemy combatant, and I hope the riot cops rain gas grenades, nightsticks, and Mace down on you. You should be ashamed of yourselves. Want to make a difference? Write a letter, make a movie, conduct a little civil disobedience, if that's your thing. Hey, it worked for Gandhi. Go to Washington and try to change some laws, for crying out loud. I draw the line at vandalizing an honest man's place of work, though.

After our thoughtful conversation with Dave, we returned to Eric's house in Oregon with a bounty of meat treats in tow: some goat and llama burgers, a few links of wild boar sausage, and, of course, two young partridges. It was early September, and, in contrast to the lingering heat and humidity of New York, the weather in Portland was stunning, all bright blue skies, temperatures in the low seventies, and very little moisture in the air. It would be a perfect day to have my brother invite over a few of his friends, fire up the grill in the backyard, and set about the beautiful business of carnivorism. We had a grand time of it—the goat burgers were a big hit (very beefy, with a touch of lamb-iness to them), while the llama meat proved to be exactly as divisive as my jamballama had some weeks ago, which was perfectly fine by me, because my taste for llama meat seemed to be growing exponentially with each bit I tasted, and I was more than happy to polish off the patties eschewed by those who found the meat a little too strong-flavored. Also as expected, the wild boar sausage went over like gangbusters, literally bursting with deep, smoky, rich piggy essence. Eric told me that his friends and roommates couldn't stop talking about it for weeks.

By the time we got to the two little partridges—and little they were, tiny young things no bigger than your average quail—I was in for a surprise. Like quail, the partridge (*Perdrix perdrix*) is a European game bird, popular everywhere from England to Russia, Turkey, and parts of Central Asia, and is said to be plump and stout-bodied, with highly flavorful meat. None of this information seemed particularly new to me, now that I had gone the distance with all sorts of avian characters on Bird Night, and I assumed these birds would be "more of the same." But when I opened up the packaging on these little fellas, there were two very large and noticeable differences between them and any of the birds I'd sampled before: First, there were still feathers on them. Feathers! Dark, stringy things at that, firmly planted in the animals' flesh. Was this some sort of error on the part of the producer? Were we intended to pluck them off ourselves, or should they stay on as the birds roasted? We were a bit flummoxed by this, but not as much as we were by the fact that, second, one of the birds still had its head and neck attached to its body. Nice surprise, I have to say. Nestled up as it was, and with the remaining feathers there, it looked like a sleeping little baby bird not long out of the shell. Only, you know, cold and dead. A quick glance at this sight was all it took for the young women among us (and, admittedly, a couple of the guys) to run screaming from the kitchen. As I'd discovered with the guinea pig, we Americans are simply not accustomed to our meat having faces. "Get rid of it!" one girl shouted from around the corner. "Just do away with it already!"

"No problem," I replied in my best capable-man voice, and asked my brother for a good, sharp knife suitable for decapitating a young bird.

"Here, use this," he said, an evil smile stretching across his face as he handed me a meat cleaver the size of a ceiling fan blade.

"I suppose this will do," I said. And with all appropriate solemnity, I held the tiny bird's body still and whacked off his noggin with one big, loud swoop, the cleaver smashing into the cutting board below it with a *crack* that echoed through the house like a thunderclap. Then silence.

"Did you do it?" one of the girls asked nervously, clutching her friend's arm for moral support.

"See for yourself," I told her, turning from the cutting board and presenting her with the freshly severed partridge head. The long, shrill screams that followed could have been recorded for stock use in any number of horror films, the kind featuring elaborate torture scenes of innocent college-age people that involve rusty power tools or dental implements. It might as well have been a human head I'd been holding; these girls were mortified out of their wits. I'm not usually this macabre when it comes to preparing animals for the table, but the inner third-grade boy in me refused all inclinations to resist. I'd like to say that I've matured, that I've grown past the desire to chase girls around the schoolyard with a fistful of worms as they shriek in terror, but, sadly, that didn't turn out to be the case. It's still just too much fun.

With the partridge thus de-nogginized, I pulled as many of the remaining feathers from the two birds as I could—they were tenaciously attached—sprinkled them both with salt and pepper, and set them in the oven to roast until the flesh was appropriately firm. When we later sampled the meat, no one was particularly blown away. True, the flesh was plump, albeit less flavorful than my research had led me to believe, which I attribute to the birds being both farm raised and young. Also, we had to pretend we didn't care about having to pick the odd feather or two out of our teeth, not an entirely appetizing procedure. In retrospect, it would have been nice to try an older bird prepared with, as suggested, juniper berries and other seasonings, or at least one that had been fully plucked. But at the end of the day, it was less the meat that will cling to my memory than that sustained, high-pitched scream those two girls let loose upon seeing a severed bird's head, which makes me chuckle softly to myself every time I think about it. I wasn't fully done with the birds on my list, though. There was still one to go, and it was a doozy.

My Goose Is Cooked

For the record: I am a fan of pie. I love peach pie, pear pie, blueberry pie, pecan pie (especially with freshly gathered Louisiana pecans, and topped with vanilla ice cream), you name it. But the pies I love best, of course, are meat pies. Regrettably, meat pies, or "savory pies," as they're referred to elsewhere, aren't particularly popular in the United States, which confounds me to no end. I mean, we adore pie—the apple pie is a quintessential symbol of American-ness, for goodness' sake—and I think there's no disputing our feelings for meat. So why is it, I often wonder, that the combination of the two has never really caught on here? With the notable exception of the chicken pot pie and shepherd's pie—which I don't consider to be a pie at all, since, for all of its hearty deliciousness, it lacks a proper pie crust—meat pies are conspicuously absent from the American table. The British, on the other hand, are smart enough to take advantage of a good thing. Savory pies, from mincemeat to poultry to the steak-and-kidney variety, are a staple of good old-fashioned English cookery. Also relatively sparse in the States is goose. It's a rare occasion indeed that you see goose on a menu, on a banquet table, or roasted in holiday celebration here, despite its being long known for the robust flavor of its meat, as well as the copious amounts of precious fat these birds offer. As an American carnivore, both of these facts make me sad. So, when my friend Julia (she of the dumpling-wrapper mastery) informed me that her mother, an Englishwoman, makes an out-of-this-world goose pie, I asked if she wouldn't mind sending me the recipe.

"I can't," she told me. "It's a secret."

"Secret goose pie? Really?" I was even more intrigued.

"Oh yes," confirmed Julia. "She's writing a cookbook on savory pies and is notoriously protective of all her recipes. She's been working on this one for years—it's pretty complex—and she would just die if someone managed to steal it." I promised her I'd never do such a thing. "All the same," she said, "I can't give you the recipe." This was killing me, knowing that there was this recipe that had more than enough keywords to reel me in—*secret, complicated, savory, goose,* and *pie*—and I wouldn't have a chance to try it. I begged Julia once more, pleading with her that I'd keep it safe, that it was all in the best interest of carnivorism—for the good of the people!—but she refused to budge. "I'll tell you what, though," she said. "We can make it together, but I won't let you see the whole recipe. Will that work?" A million times yes, that would work, I told her. I didn't need to see the recipe, so long as I got to savor the results. She could have blindfolded me and plugged my ears with wax during the preparation, for all I cared, though I was quick to remind her that doing so would probably impede my kitchen skills somewhat. Fortunately, the recipe wasn't *that* secret.

So it was that, a few weeks later, I showed up at Julia's apartment carrying an eleven-pound goose and a few other goodies. On the ten-minute walk over, I really started to feel the weight of what I was carrying, both literally and metaphorically. I had a giant bird in a bag, and damned if it wasn't getting heavy. I could scarcely wait to roast the thing and start eating. I'd have to wait, however—it takes time to bake a bird that large, not to mention making the other dishes involved in the elaborate, clandestine goose pie recipe. All told, we would spend about eight hours that first day (this would be a two-day process) preparing six separate dishes, not counting the goose, all of which would be combined to make the pie filling the following afternoon. Most of these involved fruits and vegetables, ranging from mushrooms to parsnips, onions, apples, pears, and so on. It would be a sneaky and unfair thing to relate all the details of the cooking process here, but to tell you the truth, either I wasn't made aware of them or I honestly don't remember. True to her word, Julia only gave me and our friend Marigny small, specific tasks—dicing garlic, chopping onions, cleaning pears, or, my favorite, flambéing mushrooms in Armagnac—but never once let us see the recipe itself. But, as I said, I didn't feel an overwhelming need to. So long as I got a big, fat slice of that goosie pie when our work was done and we were finally able to enjoy the fruits (and meat, and vegetables, and mushrooms) of our combined labor, I'd be a happy man.

Without the bird itself, though, all those other ministrations would be for naught. Our goose was a big sucker, and at the outset seemed somewhat larger than your average Thanksgiving turkey. This vision turned out to be deceiving—geese are less meaty than most turkeys, especially those Schwarzenegger-sized monsters modern science avails us of these days, the kind that make you wonder, "How do they even get around with breasts that big?" But although there was less meat, there was also more fat. Much, much more. Like ducks, geese (*Anser anser*) are migratory birds that store up fat to be used as warmth and protein on that big flight they take just prior to winter. More than any other part of the goose—the dark, deeply flavored meat, the quills (used for ink pens), or the feathers, which were put to great use in arrows during the Middle Ages—this fat is prized. Also known as "goose grease" (a term I love), it is often considered the creamiest, highest-quality fat of any bird, or indeed any animal, and has been sought after for use in the kitchen for centuries. One historical note even mentions beating it into a cream, then combining the stuff with vinegar, lemon juice, onions, and parsley and using it as a sandwich filling. This isn't the sort of recipe that would make a cardiologist very happy, but I'd be keen to try it, were goose grease not so expensive. It's a big part of the price you pay when you buy a goose, in fact. Once you set the thawed bird out on the table and start removing all the giblets and so forth from the interior cavity, the fat, thick and white as fresh snow, comes out in large, fist-sized clumps. It looked kind of like cake frosting. And indeed, knowing how savory all this was going to taste, I almost felt as if it were my birthday.

Once our goose was fully cooked (baked tented in liquid first, then uncovered for a short time to let the skin brown) and we'd dutifully plucked all the meat from its bones, Julia was kind enough to give us all a little taste of things to come, whipping up a simple pasta using the goose fat as a base, sautéing a few tomatoes and fresh spinach, and tossing in some linguini and scraps of goose meat when the sauce was just right. It was insanely good, a rich, potent pasta dish that, even thrown together on the fly, just exploded with umami. If goose fat and meat could make a trifle of a recipe so meltingly delicious, I could scarcely fathom the pleasure to be found in the elaborate goose pie to come. I was giddy with anticipation.

The next day, still a little jumpy with eagerness at the meal to come, Marigny and I met up at Julia's place with a small gaggle of friends (pardon the pun), all primed and ready for the big pièce de résistance. Julia took out the pie filling, a combination of the various independent dishes we'd made earlier, which had been resting in the refrigerator overnight in order to let all of the different flavors coalesce, and placed it in a large, heavy baking pan. Sealing the top with dough, she artfully decorated the uncooked pie crust with fanciful pinwheels and polygons of dough. Obviously, I left this all to her; I'd had enough experience with dough by now to recognize that any help I might provide would rapidly turn into a force of destruction and chaos. Once the enormous thing was stuffed into the oven and our party was left with a little time to hang out and contemplate the big dinner, I took the opportunity to whip out a little goodie from my goodie bag: one small, terrifically expensive can of goose pâté de foie gras. If you're going to do goose, I figured, *do goose.*

A BRIEF INTERLUDE ON THE NATURE OF FOIE GRAS,
AND WHY YOU CAN EAT IT WITHOUT SPIRIT-CRUSHING
GUILT AND WITHERING SHAME

Yes, I love foie gras. I can and will freely admit it, with no sense of embarrassment or disgrace, no matter how many people look at me with horror and revulsion when I do (they don't call me "shameless" for nothing). More than any other single kind of meat, foie gras—defined by the *Larousse gastronomique* as "goose or duck liver which is grossly enlarged by methodically fattening the bird"—is the constant subject of the most emphatic, violent invectives by the self-righteous green army, the enemy. Say to your run-of-the-mill vegans that you adore foie gras and you can count the seconds (it won't be many) before their boiling blood turns their faces steaming scarlet and they begin to berate you for supporting such an evil practice at the expense of all those poor, cute little ducks and geese. A pox on your house! This is a high point of moral superiority for them, an emblem of everything they stand against. Trouble is, most of them have absolutely no freaking clue what they're talking about. Most of their ideas and opinions about this subject are, quite simply, based on ignorance.

"But haven't you seen the pictures?" they ask. "All those animals in squalid cages, not being allowed to move, having a metal tube forced down their gullets against their will, feeding them until their livers are diseased and explode? The horror! The horror!"

Yes, I've seen the pictures. And yes, they are pretty grim, which is why they make fantastic propaganda. But these pictures do not convey all the facts. Or most of the facts, for that matter. So before you try to rip into me for advocating the senseless, sadistic torture of innocent waterfowl, let me give you a few facts to consider.

First, it's important to note that those anti–foie gras exposé photos are not indicative of the practices of the industry as a whole. They evoke deep, unsettling emotions in anyone who sees them, for certain . . . especially in proud and faithful farmers of high-quality foie gras ducks and geese. In fact, very few foie gras producers keep their animals in this fashion, for a number of reasons, the first being that animals farmed in this manner do not provide a quality product. As in all things agricultural, the better, more conscientious care you give your animals, the better their meat, eggs, and milk are going to be. Trust me, no one who truly cares about the taste of their foie gras is going to buy the stuff from people whose production methods themselves are so disgusting. You can taste the difference in the meat.

So what is the life of these ducks and geese really like? That was a question the American Veterinary Medical Association (AVMA) sought to answer in 2005, when a resolution came to its House of Delegates (HOD) aiming to officially oppose the practice of force-feeding ducks and geese to produce foie gras. If the horrifying picture we've been force-fed, so to speak, is true, then no one should doubt that these veterinarians—doctors whose professional lives are dedicated to the good health and care of animals—would approve the resolution. But instead of going with the knee-jerk reaction most people have when they learn about the practice of gavage—automatically denouncing it as cruel and inhumane on the spot, no more evidence needed—they decided to approach the matter scientifically. They read countless studies on the subject, and even sent a delegation to visit farms that produce foie gras in order to observe the process firsthand. Could it be as terrifying as everyone says it is?

Their professional opinion was: no. According to the AVMA, as stated on its website, "Limited peer-reviewed, scientific information is available dealing with the animal welfare concerns associated with foie gras production, but the observations and practical experience shared by HOD members indicate a minimum of adverse effects on the birds involved. Therefore, delegates decided it is not necessary for the AVMA to take a position on foie gras production at this time." That's right: neither scientific evidence nor empirical observation of the process was enough to prove to an objective panel of *animal doctors* that foie gras is, in fact, worth officially denouncing. Their findings while visiting two farms in New York—two of the three major operations in the country that produce this specialty food—were particularly remarkable. One vet, Dr. Robert Gordon, even reversed his stance on the issue completely. He was keen to be scientific, especially in the face of those infamous pictures, about which he stated, "We've all seen the pictures. Seeing with your own eyes and penetrating the issue is worth a thousand pictures." So penetrate the issue he did. "On July 5, he visited a farm in New York. 'After being on the premises, my position changed dramatically,' Dr. Gordon said. 'I did not see animals I would consider distressed, and I didn't see pain and suffering.' *He said it is more distressing to take a rectal temperature in a cat*" (emphasis mine).

Score one for shameless carnivorism.

According to one observing member of the HOD, "In contrast with what some critics claim, [Dr. McCarthy] said that the esophagus of the birds used for foie gras is lined with a cornified epithelium, 'a very tough esophagus that can accept a great deal of abuse.' He said it is very elastic and pliable, so the birds can swallow a huge amount of fish or grain." The veterinarians even objected to the term *force-feeding*, since the animals willingly accepted their large rations, preferring the phrase *tube-feeding* instead. Plus, the AVMA concluded that the resulting fatty liver from the gavage was not the result of an induced disease process, referring to it as "physiologic, not pathologic," and were quick to note that modern cattle farmers feed enriched diets to their animals that often result in a number of diseases, and that practice has yet to be denounced.

So, to recap: judging by the investigations conducted by the AVMA, on the farms from which we get the majority of our foie gras, the ducks and geese are overwhelmingly 1) not harmed by the tube-feeding process, 2) not put in distress by this process, 3) not averse to either their feeders or the feeding, 4) well cared for, 5) not diseased, and 6) delicious.

Oh yes, did I forget to mention that foie gras tastes spine-meltingly good? You can argue the agricultural ethics of foie gras production until the cows come home (or the ducks, or the geese for that matter), but you simply cannot deny that the stuff is gratifying to the palate. That is a stone-cold fact, and one that even the most vitriolic PETA-head couldn't argue with. Make a short list of the finest, most expensive culinary delicacies in the world, from Beluga caviar to white truffles and o-toro, and you simply have to throw in foie gras, not just because of the flavor, which any gourmet will tell you has an incomparable richness that borders on lethal (the caloric, cholesterol, and fat content is enough to make your heart all but explode), but also because of its fascinating history. People have been eating the fattened livers of geese and ducks for not hundreds, but *thousands* of years. Most historians agree that the practice dates back as far as 2500 BCE in ancient Egypt, where a number of archaeological sites show illustrations depicting the hand-feeding of birds in this manner. The Hebrews were also instrumental in carrying on the tradition, picking it up from their Egyptian captors and eventually bringing it to Jerusalem, where the conquering Romans found out about the delights of fatty livers, and were later known to gorge their birds on honeyed figs. From Rome it spread to the rest of Western Europe and was fondly adopted by the French, who have become keepers of the tradition, proudly considered a national dish to this very day. Foie gras is in fact illegal in a number of countries, including Israel, though I've always imagined that the continued popularity of chopped liver (mostly from chickens) in contemporary Jewish cuisine descends directly from hundreds of years of making foie gras. But you have to hand it to the French for carrying the torch all these years, and for not backing down an inch when, today, it seems like everyone and his cousin is clamoring to get rid of the stuff once and for all. To that end, I think this passage in the *Larousse gastronomique* puts it best: "The goose is nothing, but man has made of it an instrument for the output of a marvelous product, a kind of living hothouse in which there grows the supreme fruit of gastronomy." Snap!

MEET THE ORTOLAN

When it comes to cruel gourmet delicacies, fatty liver pales in comparison to one of the most heralded—and abhorred—dishes ever devised: ortolan. Illegal to produce, serve, or eat in France, the ortolan is an adorable little songbird that has the dubious distinction of being an icon of both sublime gastronomy and humankind's brutality against its animal friends. Why is ortolan so beloved and so reviled? In both cases, it's all in the preparation: First, the bird—a precious, tiny little thing (also known as a bunting) with a lovely song, no less—is either blinded by having its eyes gouged out or simply set inside a dark box, in order to create disorientation and confusion. With its natural rhythms thus disrupted, the ortolan has no idea when to feed, so it feeds constantly and, like those delicious goose and duck livers, plumps up to many times the size nature intended it to be. This is when things get really mean. Once it's nice and fat and ready to go, the bird is then drowned in Armagnac, then roasted and served whole—head, bones, you name it—to the lucky diner, who eats the animal with a napkin draped over his head to fully experience its intoxicating aromas and, some say, to hide his shame from God. One is supposed to place the entire bird in one's mouth, feet first, then bite the head off and let it fall to the plate (*plonk!*), and eat the whole animal in one go, slowly masticating skin, fat, meat, and bones for up to half an hour until finished. To the gastronomically inclined, it is said to be one of the most exquisite dining experiences that exist, though obviously not for the faint of heart (or jaw). Eating a simple foie gras seems pretty tame, by comparison. It's no wonder the practice is outlawed, although ortolan is still served today in secret, speakeasy fashion, and the law often turns a blind eye. Maybe it has something to do with the fact that the late former French president François Mitterrand, in the end stage of his struggle against cancer, ate not just one but two ortolan during his infamous final feast. Shameless carnivorism? Whoa, Nelly! It bears noting that the late president's meal also included Marenne oysters, roasted capon, and, you guessed it, foie gras. I think it's a fair bet that if the cancer hadn't sent him six feet under, that menu alone probably would have done the job. Hey, if you gotta go . . .

Back at Julia's, we laid into the pâté, which I'd spread on toast points and topped with caramelized apple slices. A fruit pairing is generally a good idea when it comes to foie gras, as the clean, sweet flavors help cut into the decadent richness of the liver. Needless to say, we were more than a little biased on the subject: our conversation was continually interrupted by intermittent moans of pleasure. We also cracked up at the labeling on the can the pâté came in, which admonished overeager gourmands that this product was "For Internal Use Only: Do Not Rub All Over Body." Apparently, the producers knew just how good their product was and weren't above having a little fun with that fact, which is great—something as serious as foie gras deserves some levity, I think.

Soon enough we'd have even more reason to swoon—the goose pie was finally ready. After two full days of prep, one eleven-pound goose, dozens of ingredients, and at least six different individual recipes that spanned the culinary gamut from sautéing and flambéing to braising, roasting, and caramelizing, the baking dish emerged from the oven, topped with a glorious golden piecrust. After letting it cool, Julia cut the pie into large square segments and carefully laid them on our plates, the steaming, fragrant filling oozing out the sides of the crust in a gooey mess of meat, vegetables, fruits, fungi, and God knows what else. My first bite was a marvel, a three-ring circus of different flavors dancing around my palate: sweet pears and apples; dark, fatty goose meat; heady Armagnac; earthy mushrooms; crisp, buttery crust; and a variety of others that I couldn't quite place, given the staggering variety of tastes that were now playing around with each other like children in a schoolyard. After two heaping slices, I was done, finished, rendered kaput by this unbelievable pie. Contemplating the feast afterward, I was a little overwhelmed, not at how good everything turned out to be, but with bewilderment and sadness for my fellow Americans. How could it be that we haven't realized the magnificence of an excellently prepared savory pie? How could we let ourselves miss out like this?

Ultimately, Julia's mother had every right to hold this clandestine recipe close to her breast; now that I know how good it is, it's all I can do to keep myself from engaging in high-level espionage in order to get it for myself. Forget the diamonds, the microfilm, the bank vault combination, the nuclear key codes. I'd spy for goose pie.

CHAPTER 10

Killing with Mister Knuckles

I sit still on the floor of the thicket, letting the cool, predawn air steady my nerves. The weather is verging on cold, unseasonable for this time of year (mid-October) in this part of the country (northwest Louisiana), and I rub my hands against each other to warm my fingers, ensuring that they won't be stiff and clumsy with numbness when the time comes. The creature is out there, somewhere—soon enough the sun will begin to rise, and the animal will emerge to feed. That's when I'll have my chance. Until then, I remain motionless, calm, ready for action. It's been made explicit to me by my guide that any loud movement—the snapping of a twig or the potato-chip-like *scrunch* of dried leaves beneath a boot heel, for instance—will give away my presence, and in this situation, that's the last thing we want to happen. This beast is a clever one, possessed of nimbleness, speed, and phenomenal hearing, not to mention a healthy sense of paranoia; should it detect even the faintest sign that I am there in the woods with it, it will disappear, seeking sanctuary from me, the predator. I must be silent, stealthy. I must look keenly for any movement in the trees and bushes, and be prepared to raise and fire my weapon accurately and without hesitation when I spy him. I have only two loaded barrels, which means only two chances in a sitting, after which the shotgun's report will frighten the animals into hiding, and I will have to begin again from scratch. It is a difficult mission, if not a perilous one, where patience, timing, and accuracy are paramount, and any mistake spells failure. But I must prevail.

Because I'll be goddamned if I have to go back to New York without a bellyful of Louisiana squirrel.

I am not, by nature, a killer. Or at least I thought I wasn't. This bit of presumed self-knowledge changed not long after I went back home to Louisiana for the opening of squirrel hunting season. More accurately, it changed because of a man whose name, I kid you not, is Leroy Knuckles.

Leroy Knuckles. How's that for a handle?

To be fair to Leroy and his family, the name is actually spelled Nuckolls, but it's pronounced the same way, so it still invokes a skeptical reaction when I tell people about him; given that mantle, he might as well be called Frankie Fingers, Flattop Tony, or Eddie the Fist, and I have to admit that I love sounding like I'm associating with shady mob types. Based on name alone, you'd pretty much expect him to talk like something out of *Goodfellas*, just loaded with mafioso swagger and that distinctive wiseguy brogue: "How you doin', Leroy Knuckles, good to meetcha . . . Hey, fuggedduboudit . . . How's ya motha? Tell her Leroy Knuckles said hello. And ay, while you're attit, leave the gun, take the cannoli . . ." Truth be told, Leroy's more good ole boy than goombah, a successful, self-made entrepreneur who has lived most of his life in the Shreveport/Bossier City area, happily married to one of my mother's close friends from high school. When my parents moved to Shreveport—where Mom grew up, as well as the current home of her mother and a number of cousins—following the drowning of our family's New Orleans home in Hurricane Katrina, they quickly became reacquainted with the Nuckollses, who live in their new neighborhood. It wasn't long before my mother told them all about my Carnivore project, after which she gave me a call in New York.

"Leroy Nuckolls wants to take you squirrel hunting," she said.

"Who?"

"Leroy Nuckolls, a friend of ours. He's married to my friend Peggy, from high school."

"Peggy Knuckles?" I said. "You're yanking my chain."

"No, I'm serious. He wants to take you out for the beginning of squirrel hunting season. He's such a nice man, you'll really like him. Don't you think that'd be good for your book?"

I considered this for a moment. "You want me to drive off into the woods, God knows how many miles from civilization, in a car filled with firearms and a man named Leroy Knuckles?"

"He says it'll be a lot of fun."

"You sure you're not trying to have me whacked?"

"Oh, Scott . . ."

"Because I'm a big fan of *The Sopranos*, you know—I realize how these things work."

"Come on," said Mom. "I told you he was a friend, didn't I?"

"It's always a friend, isn't it? Didn't you see *Casino*?"

"Please. You're supposed to be this big carnivore and you're not going to eat squirrels?" Like it or not, she had me on this one.

"Well, in that case, for the sake of carnivorism, I don't see any way I can say no. But I'll keep an eye open in the back of my head, just in case . . ."

I told my mother to RSVP to Leroy, and to find out just when squirrel hunting season began. Until the details were all sorted through, I was pretty anxious. It wasn't that I was afraid of or inexperienced with firearms. As a child I was so obsessed with guns and gunplay, as most young boys are, that my grandmother became convinced that there was no way on earth I wouldn't grow up to be a bona fide terrorist. Not to mention that, to this very day, my mother claims our late family dog's skittishness and anxious bladder (poor thing would let loose all over the floor if you just said hello to her) were a direct result of my tearing around the house with plastic M16s, MAC-10s, Uzis, and various other armaments, yelling bloody murder and leaping behind the furniture for cover against 600,000 guerrilla warriors represented by my little brother. Guns came so naturally to me that during an eighth-grade retreat to the Y.O. Ranch in Texas, when I first got to squeeze off a few shots with a real revolver, the firing range instructor wouldn't believe me when I told her that I'd never shot a handgun before. "But you're such a natural," she exclaimed as I flushed with pride. We also got to fire a 20-gauge shotgun into a gallon milk jug filled with water, a gun-safety exercise intended to show us the approximate effect such a weapon might have on a human body. Needless to say, it was way, way cool.

So it wasn't the guns that worried me as much as the dozens of questions about hunting etiquette and protocol that cropped up soon after I'd volunteered to accompany Mr. Nuckolls. Believe it or not, as much as I enjoyed messing around with firearms, I'd never been hunting before, which is remarkable, considering that Louisiana's state motto is "Sportsman's Paradise," less for its famous athletes than for the stellar hunting and fishing to be enjoyed throughout the state. Growing up, it seemed like just about everyone's dad or uncle was either a hunter or a fisherman except mine, who preferred the more elegant manly arts of tae kwon do, fencing, and golf. Being a novice in the field of stalking and killing things outside of the odd palmetto bug (those gigantic, prehistoric flying cockroaches approximately the size of a dachshund that we have in the swampier parts of the country), I had to wonder: Did I need to buy camouflage? Face paint? My own gun? Would I require a hunting license? And what in the world do you hunt a squirrel with, anyway? Wouldn't anything bigger than a sling-shot just tear the bejeezus out of the poor critter? Where do you put the carcass, once you've done the deed: Carry it with you? Make your-self a small pile of dead squirrels and return to collect them when you're done for the day? Now that I thought about it, would I really be able to go through with it, to violently take the life of an innocent crea-ture, and an adorable one at that? And, most troubling of all—was I ac-tually going to have to wake up before dawn?

All of these questions, and quite a few more, would be posed and answered during this episode, beginning with the logistics of guns and gear. Upon arriving at my parents' house (after spending half an hour in fruitless argument with airline personnel who for some reason failed to appreciate my desire to have my luggage arrive when and where I did), I opened the guest bedroom closet to discover that Mr. Nuckolls had generously supplied me with the following items:

- One pair of heavy-duty, fully water-resistant Red Head hunting boots, sized men's 10 (my size), "mossy oak" camouflage pattern
- One camouflage jumpsuit, also in my size
- One matching camouflage baseball cap
- One matching camouflage hunter's vest, fully stocked with both insect repellent and 20-gauge shotgun shells
- One Browning twin barrel, "over-and-under"-style 20-gauge shotgun, cleaned and oiled, with carrying case

Apparently, this is pretty much everything I would need to transform myself from a pale, bookish foodie into a ruthless, squirrel-massacring

Terminator. The shotgun was of especially good quality, and I had no doubt that it would fire true should I be able to muster up enough guts to point it at a charming little animal and pull the trigger.

"Wow," I thought aloud to my mother, "he really did think of everything."

"Oh, let me tell you," she replied, "Leroy Nuckolls doesn't do *any-thing* halfway."

To make sure everything was really in order, I tried on the entire getup, including the gun, which I "broke" (weaponry terminology for popping the barrels of a shotgun open away from the handle and stock in order to load fresh shells or eject spent ones) and propped over my forearm in true gun-safety fashion, finding to my disappointment that once it was all in place, I bore less resemblance to John Rambo than to Elmer Fudd, minus the horn-rimmed glasses, of course, which made me look even more ridiculous. I stepped out of my room to give Mom a gander. She promptly erupted into peals of laughter. "Oh my God," she said, "look at you!"

"You realize that I'm armed," I reminded her.

"I know," she replied, doing her best to stifle the mounting giggles as her face went from pink to crimson.

"Okay," I conceded, "so I'm probably not the most intimidating-looking guy in the world, but guess what? The squirrels don't know that . . ."

My father had a similar reaction to the Elmer outfit, albeit a bit more restrained, though he was just as interested in examining the shotgun as I was; he'd been keen on firearms since his days as a battalion surgeon stationed with the marines at Camp Lejeune, North Carolina, some three decades before (we used to have a great photo of him in full-on GI Joe garb, dolled up in OD green fatigues and sporting an enormous M60 machine gun, a belt of live ammunition draped across his chest and everything, even a *mustache*). We stood in my room and took turns breaking the gun open and snapping it back into place to produce that satisfying mechanical *clunk*, examining the barrels, dry-firing it a few times each, and grunting in approval. You know, man stuff.

"Just make sure never to point it at a person, even if you know it's not loaded," he said sternly.

"I know, Dad, I know."

"And for God's sake, don't blow your foot off, son."

"Gee," I said dryly, "thanks for the vote of confidence."

"I'm serious," he replied, and judging by his expression, he was.

Before I'd have a chance to blast any of my appendages off, there were still a few logistics to take care of, the first being the acquisition of a Louisiana hunting license. This worried me: How long would it take? If it was anywhere on par with having to deal with state offices such as the Department of Motor Vehicles,* I was in serious trouble—I didn't have proof of permanent residency, nor had I completed any sort of gun-safety training courses (minus the Y.O. Ranch, but that was sixteen years ago and I had no physical proof of that experience), not to mention that I'd need it then and there, because the first day of hunting season was *tomorrow* and there would be no time for detailed background checks into my criminal history or any other serious investigation to ensure that I wasn't a serial murderer.

As luck would have it, getting oneself sanctioned by the government of Louisiana to assassinate its myriad precious woodland creatures is not a particularly difficult task. I made my way to the sporting goods store, which might as well be renamed Sporting Goods and Arsenal, as they purvey not only the usual assortment of gym socks, basketballs, and athletic groin protectors, but also an astonishingly diverse array of shotguns, rifles, handguns, knives, compound bows, arrows, quivers, BB and pellet guns, slingshots, and paintball supplies, and enough ammunition in every caliber, gauge, and shot size to fend off even the most fervent enemy encroachment on one's fortified compound or to stage a successful military coup against the government of

---

* I've always maintained that had Dante Alighieri lived to witness the rise of the automobile, he would have certainly reserved an especially gruesome circle of his *Inferno* for the DMV.

a modest-sized banana republic. One can also find camouflage *any-thing*, in all conceivable stripes and patterns, from "urban-combat gray" to my own "mossy oak," products running the gamut from bandannas, boots, and hats to beer cozies and baby rompers,* as well as an assortment of T-shirts with hunting-themed slogans such as "Backstraps rule!"† and "There's room on earth for all of God's creatures . . . right next to the mashed potatoes!" Suffice it to say, I was both delighted and transfixed.

After ogling the armory for a while, I stood in line at the cash register to order up my hunting license. The cashier took my valid Louisiana driver's license (I've never had the heart to change over to a New York ID, despite the fact that I've lived there for over six years) and asked me a few basic questions—Social Security number, phone, birthday confirmation, and so on—the answers to which she entered into a computer. I was a little worried when she inquired about having completed a "hunting safety course," and I told her, truthfully, that I hadn't. Not that it made much of a difference, because only a few minutes and fifteen dollars later, I was holding in my hands a basic hunting license, good until the following June. "Basic," of course, meant that I could hunt only fowl and small game—no deer for me, at least not until I ponied up for the "big game" license—but even so, there it was, and no matter how small it seemed (I'd thought it'd be a handsome, laminated affair, and it turned out to be little more than a gussied up, dot-matrix-printed cashier's receipt), my name and number were on there clearly for anyone to see.

It was now official: I was licensed to kill. For the first time in my life as a carnivore, I could hunt for my own dinner.

I called Leroy that evening to thank him for supplying me so am-

---

* Brand name, I swear, Li'l Hunter. I assume this is for parent–child bonding or hunting lifestyle indoctrination purposes rather than the need to outfit one's infant for an actual hunt. Then again, this was Louisiana, so you never know . . . At some point in the state's history, it's entirely possible that an overzealous daddy actually needed to utter the words "Quit with the cooing, Junior—there's a twelve-pointer out there!"

† *Backstrap* is the hunter's term for an animal's tenderloins (usually deer), the two long strips of soft flesh running along either side of the spine, oft considered the most desirable cut.

ply for our hunting expedition, and to clarify a few final details before we headed out the following morning. No need to wear anything under the jumpsuit except underwear and maybe a T-shirt, he told me; it can get pretty warm out there once the sun's up. And as for when to wake up, he'd be dropping by to collect me at 5:30 a.m. Now, I don't know whether or not he heard my aggrieved moan at that moment (five f'ing thirty!), but if so, he didn't acknowledge it. In fact, he was downright chipper about the prospect of having me as a hunting partner. "We're gonna have such a good time, man!" he told me before hanging up, his deep Shreveport drawl transmogrifying that last word into the two-syllable "may-yun." The guy wasn't anything if not enthusiastic.

True to his word, Leroy Nuckolls picked me up precisely at 5:30 a.m. the next day, all smiles and gusto. The sun would be coming up at half past six, and it'd take us about an hour to get where we were going, so we had just enough time. I grabbed my gun and breakfast (Mom was kind enough to supply me with a bagel loaded with honey-baked ham and cream cheese—a delicious combination that could only have been invented by my fellow southern Jews—as well as a fresh cup of coffee, a necessity at this unholy hour), piled my half-asleep bones into Leroy's SUV, and we headed out into the darkness.

Our destination was a nearly uninhabited stretch of about 480 acres in Plain Dealing, Louisiana (population 1,057), which Leroy and his family referred to as "the Hill Place." As we sped through Shreveport, Bossier City, and beyond, I got to know a little more about this mysterious man who was about to teach me the finer points of killing one's supper. He grew up in Benton, not far from Shreveport, and had been hunting at the Hill Place with his cousins nearly all his life: squirrel, rabbit, deer, various birds. "Back when I about fifteen years old," he told me (he's in his midsixties now, though his irrepressibly genial nature gives the impression of a younger man), "we used to go out to the Hill Place and camp, hunt, chase girls." He smiled and sighed at the fond memory. "It was so much fun."

We arrived at the Hill Place not long before the scheduled sunrise, turning off the main road onto a narrow dirt path that led us past a small cemetery (Leroy's great-grandfather was buried there, a man who fought for the Confederacy during the Civil War and who returned to the area to rebuild after the Union victory; his decendants had lived there ever since), through a series of grassy fields connected by ditches crossable only with four-wheel drive, and finally into a large clearing bordering the woods. We parked, and I got out to stretch my legs, finish my coffee, zip up my vest, and gather my munitions. When I walked around the other side of the car to see what my guide was up to, I found him standing with his back to me, taking a leisurely piss right there in the open. "When you're in nature," he said with delight, "everywhere's a bathroom!" How true, I thought, and I reminded myself to do the same at some point.

Now it was hunting time. The two of us loaded our guns (Leroy would be using a scoped .22 rifle—killing a squirrel with one of these requires significantly more predatory acumen than killing one with a shotgun) and walked carefully into the trees. It wasn't going to be an easy hunt for a couple of reasons, the man told me: First, the full harvest moon had been out that night—the point at which the moon is closest to the earth, and therefore brightest; farmers used the extra light to continue their work after sunset, hence the term *harvest moon*—which meant that many of the animals would be out feeding at night instead of their customary dawn breakfast time, drastically reducing the number of squirrels we were likely to see. Second, there'd been no rain for weeks, leaving the ground dry and crunchy and making it rather difficult, once you'd spotted your quarry, to sneak up on it unawares. That's why I had a shotgun, Leroy explained—using small number-four shot, I'd get better range and a good spread, perfect for the novice killer. Range was still an issue, though. I'd have to be within about ten to twenty feet of the thing, any more being too far away for an effective shot, and any closer resulting in some rather unappetizing squirrel confetti.

"Sit here," Leroy whispered once we were deep in the woods.

"Keep your eyes on the trees up there as the sun comes up. Look and listen for movement." I did as he directed, being as still as possible, gradually letting my eyes and ears become accustomed to the sights and sounds of nature—wind through leaves, a bird call here, a woodpecker there—readying myself for the moment of truth. It was a wonderful opportunity to think, being in the cool, quiet woods like that, and as I dutifully kept my eyes peeled for any signs of movement above, I had a chance to ponder why I was there at all. It definitely wasn't bloodlust, or the desire to experience the rush of killing something. In fact, I could barely convince myself that I'd be able to do it at all, silently hoping that at the end of the day Leroy would have bagged a couple of beasts and I, despite all my best efforts, would return from the field empty-handed. Then I would be able to enjoy eating the animal without having its death on my conscience. But, I then thought, that's precisely the reason that I *should* be there: like it or not, death is an inextricable part of eating meat.

Barring the successful advances of in vitro meat, there is simply no way to eat an animal's flesh without being complicit, no matter how far removed, in the death of that creature. Fail to recognize that, and you become at best a shameful carnivore, and at worst a cowardly hypocrite hiding from nature's cold, hard truths. Killing an animal yourself is the most direct way of appreciating the deeper meaning of carnivorism— you actually *become* the food chain. No farmer, no slaughterhouse, no butcher, no packager, no grocery store clerk, and absolutely no way to deny just where your food came from. It's just you and the animal, from start to finish, life to death, from the forest to your plate. Going through this process provides the hunter with an amazing connection to both humankind's primitive nature as well as its history; aside from the weaponry, this was the same behavior our ancestors were engaged in tens of thousands of years ago when they hunted buffalo or antelope or chickens or mountain goats, and the same behavior that most people around the globe display when they want to eat meat. We've been so dislocated from the food chain, so many links away from the source, that many if not most of us fail to appreciate it. There's something powerfully primal about participating in this ritual, almost as though you're going back in time. And if I really wanted to be the ultimate carnivore, it wasn't just important that I experience this, it was completely necessary.

"Scott," Leroy whispered, drawing me out of my philosophical reverie. "Up there." He raised his right index finger and indicated a spot just above and behind him, in the trees. I fixed my gaze there for several moments until, sure enough, I saw the distinct rustling of a tree branch. "See if you can get up close to it," he said. Slowly and with great care I stood and took three steps, heel to toe, as softly as I could, keeping my eyes trained on the spot Leroy had indicated. And then, right as I was closing in just within firing distance—*krack!*—a stick fractured under my boot. Leroy winced; I might as well have shouted at the thing that I was standing there. The squirrel was gone, hiding out for the next few hours until he was good and sure no more clumsy humans with shotguns were out there waiting for him.

This was pretty much the way things turned out the rest of that first day. Leroy went off in one direction and I in another, and neither of us had any luck. "Just too damned dry, and too damned bright out," Leroy claimed. "If only it'd rained a couple of days ago, we'd have armloads of squirrels right now." I did get off a couple of shots, but whether they were at actual squirrels, tree branches in the distance that I mistook for squirrels, or figment-of-my-imagination squirrels, I didn't appear to have shot anything but innocent and unsuspecting oak leaves. Even if I didn't hit anything, I have to admit that the booming report of the shotgun and its kick against my shoulder were tremendously enjoyable.

We'd have much better luck the following day. Leroy decided that I'd have more success with a 12-gauge, Russian-made Baikal shotgun, which would afford me much deeper range than the 20, though I'd have to be careful not to get too close and blow my prey into a bloody, formless ragout. I was just as ambivalent about whether or not I'd be able to go through with it, but I kept reminding myself of the one big, inescapable fact: no kill = no eat. Not squirrel, anyway, since I couldn't just go to any chain grocery store and buy myself a couple of squirrels all nice and quartered. To the best of my knowledge and research, there's nowhere in the United States—or possibly even the world—that one can find commercially available squirrel meat. I've heard rumors of squirrel farms, but have uncovered no evidence to prove their existence. So if you want this particular kind of meat for supper, either you or someone you know has to go out and shoot it.

Which is precisely what I did.

About two hours into our second day traipsing around the trees at the Hill Place, I was all but convinced that I'd be heading back into civilization with nothing to show for it but dirty boots and a few spent shotgun shells. The sun was climbing higher, the temperature rising with it, and soon enough there wouldn't be any squirrels feeding out in the open for the rest of the day. Then, just as I was ready to resign myself to having been outwitted by a cuddly forest critter, I saw it: the bouncing of a tree branch about fifteen feet in the distance. I raised my Baikal, aimed, and pulled the trigger. Half a second later, something— I couldn't tell what, exactly, but it appeared to be fauna, not flora, something with mass—fell from the branch onto the soft earth below, landing with an audible *thud*. I rushed up to take a look, and it was confirmed: I'd bagged my first squirrel.

Out of respect for the dead and a desire to avoid seeming morbid, I will not discuss the finer details of the kill, other than to say that it was about what you'd expect: violent, bloody, and sad. I looked down at that poor little creature, and I suddenly felt a great sense of melancholy. "What have I done?" I asked myself. It's one thing to enjoy handling firearms, but a wholly other thing to use one of them to steal the life of a relatively defenseless creature, and I was beginning to feel the weight of my actions. To paraphrase the poignant words of Clint Eastwood in *The Unforgiven*, "It's a hell of a thing, killing a [squirrel]. Take away all he's got . . . all he'll ever have."

Moments later, the initial shock of the deed started to wear off, and I realized again the inevitable correlation between death and meat. I said a quick prayer apologizing to the soul of the squirrel and promising that his death would not be in vain, put the animal in the lower back pouch of my hunting vest ("So *that's* what you do with them," I remember saying to Leroy when he instructed me on how to deal with deceased quarry), and made my way into the clearing, out by the car, where I would be able to rest assured that the hard part was over. I had completed the deed, my very first kill, a task that in many cultures over many hundreds, even thousands of years, has signified the ascent of a boy into the realm of official manhood.*

According to Leroy, I'd "done real good." The animal I'd dispatched was a large fox squirrel, so named because of its reddish fur, and the bigger of the only two breeds indigenous to North America. "They're very clean animals," my guide told me. "Out in the wild like this, they eat mostly nuts from these trees, so the meat has a real nice taste to it." He'd gotten out of the woods with one squirrel as well, what he referred to as a "cat squirrel," also known as an Eastern gray squirrel, the other type indigenous to this continent; you might recognize it as the sort of animal you'd likely find in your backyard tree or in a local park. It was quite a bit smaller than mine, and Leroy was somewhat disappointed with our modest success. "I shot at least two more, but whether they lived and were able to run away or if they got caught up in a tree branch, they weren't there on the ground. I'll tell you this— those squirrels have *a lot* of fight in 'em." He also attributed his lack of additional kills to the fact that he'd nearly stomped on a water moccasin as he was walking through the dry creek bed, just managing to shoot the venomous predator before it had a chance to strike him. "After that," he claimed, "I wasn't hunting squirrels anymore; I was hunting snakes!"

Fortunately, we would have just enough meat for our intended

---

* Technically, my bar mitzvah had accomplished this transition some sixteen years earlier, although I have to say that it was considerably less gory.

recipe. Leroy had at least one more squirrel saved in his freezer (the man vehemently opposed both hunting for sport and wasting any usable meat from any animals he or his relatives kill), as did his mother, the eighty-four-year-old "Mama" Nuckolls. The plan was to take the animals back to Leroy's place, clean them, then take them over to Mama's to be boiled with the others in preparation of making her famous "Squirrel 'n Dumplings." So we rode back into Shreveport in the bright, beautifully warm fall morning listening to Leroy's favorite music, the outlaw country tunes of Waylon Jennings and Johnny Cash, discussing everything from the previous days' hunt to his gun collection—which included not only a tiny, Derringer-sized pistol that he kept legally in the center console of his Corvette in order to thwart any would-be carjackers but also a Thompson submachine gun (an honest-to-God Tommy Gun, complete with thirty-round drum)—as well as his hobby restoring vintage motorcycles, particularly his prized 1964 Triumph. Also, he's a member of Mensa. If I wrote fiction, there's simply no way I could make these things up—Leroy Nuckolls had to be one of the single most interesting people I'd met in my life. And now, apparently, he'd turned me into a killer, a fact that I mentioned to him and that he brushed off, saying, "Oh, I don't think it's *sinful*. Now we get to eat!"

Upon returning to the house of Nuckolls, Leroy pulled a small metal table with a wooden cutting surface on its top out of his garage and set to cleaning the two dead animals with a penknife right there in the grass aside his home. He made short work of it, despite admitting that this was his least favorite part of the whole process, no matter how many hundreds of times he'd done it. Like the kill itself, it was literally a visceral experience (head and tail get chopped off, entrails and shotgun pellets removed and placed into a plastic bucket, etc.), but about halfway through the cleaning, something remarkable happened: once the fur and the inner organs had been removed and Leroy was cutting the squirrel into quarters, I began to think about what he had in his hands less as a dead animal, and more like, well . . . lunch. In the end, it was meat, and I was hungry.

We would not eat the squirrels that day, however. Our two critters, as well as Leroy and Mama's additional frozen squirrels, still needed to be boiled in salt water to make the meat tender enough to pick from the bone, and that would take time. Leroy picked me up again the following morning and brought me over to Mama's house, in nearby Benton, where all of the squirrels were done boiling and ready for the dumpling pot. As for Mama herself, she turned out to be just about the Platonic ideal of the gracious, mature southern lady. I don't think I can recall a single instance in which she wasn't either smiling, laughing, or verging on one or the other. She was eager to have me in her home to help her cook, though modestly afraid that she'd "mess up the recipe for the important food writer." I assured her that I might be a food writer, yes, but a very far cry from important; I was just happy to have the chance to cook with her, and to learn the ancient Jedi ways of cooking squirrel meat. She laughed at that.

Now, chicken and dumplings is about the most basic, inexpensive southern recipe in existence, and the addition of squirrel, aside from the fact that one can't buy the meat in a butcher shop or grocery store, does little to make it any more complex. There are essentially only five ingredients (plus the meat): stock (in which the squirrels were previously boiled), water, flour (though Mama preferred Bisquick or Pillsbury pie crust mix), salt, and pepper. And that's it—amazingly, beautifully simple. The key, as in any simple recipe, is in the preparation. After dutifully picking all of the meat from the squirrel's bones— the sectioned, cleaned animal looked surprisingly similar to a rabbit—I watched as Mama expertly mixed the dough, kneaded it, flattened it out on the kitchen counter, and cut it with a butter knife into strips about six inches long and three-fourths of an inch wide. These become southern "dumplings," which have very little in common with the momos I'd made before, since they're not actually filled with anything at all, but are simply small lumps of dough, making the dish easy even for dough-impaired people such as myself. "You don't want them too, too thick, though," she warned, "or they'll be doughy on the inside." Leroy, it turns out, likes his dumplings to cook longer than most people prefer, so that they almost fall apart, making the dish thicker, more like a chowder than a soup, which is how we prepared it. In addition to our squirrel meal, Leroy also decided to pan-fry some wild rabbit he'd shot a while back, just to have a little something extra to go with the dumplings. The preparation of that dish was similarly straightforward: quartered rabbit coated in flour and fried in vegetable oil until golden brown. "Not hare," he made sure to note, "but cottontail, the only true rabbit left." So it turned out that we'd be having Bugs Bunny as well as Rocky the Squirrel for dinner. Elmer would be so proud.

"But how did it taste?" everyone was dying to know when I returned to New York. It was fantastic, of course, and there was little chance that it wouldn't be—the meat was clean and unadulterated by processing, and the recipe was made with attention and care using the simplest of ingredients. The dish was hot and thick, meaty and thoroughly comforting. And squirrel meat happens to tastes almost identical to tender, dark-meat chicken, as did the wild rabbit; they are both mild meats with little inherent gamey flavor. If you were to dig into Mama Nuckolls's Squirrel 'n Dumplings under the assumption that it was chicken, you'd never know the difference, though this wasn't enough to keep my father from avoiding the dish as though it were plutonium stewed in hot tar—he simply couldn't get past his preconceived notion of squirrels essentially being oversized rodents, dirty animals that nobody should ever eat unless their very existence depended on it. It was a childish assumption, and I told him so, not that it made any difference. As hard as I tried to get him to take a taste, he would have just as soon eaten his own hand.

I love my dad, but I couldn't help be a little sad for him then, and for anyone who might feel similarly about squirrel or any other animal with a long-standing—albeit unorthodox—tradition of appearing on the dinner table. It was just so damned *good.* Okay, so maybe you won't see squirrel on the menu at Jean Georges or Daniel or Lutèce anytime soon (actually, I'd *love* to see that), but it simply doesn't matter— Americans have hunted and eaten squirrels as long as this country has been a country and well before that, and I have no doubt that they'll continue to do so as long as there are squirrels out there to hunt and eat. I was now part of that ritual, and proudly so. As for everyone else, the squeamish eaters who refuse to try something a little different and the elitists who feel that such an interesting and intelligent animal is somehow a poverty food, something beneath their golden palates, I'll say only this:

Fooey. You have no idea what you're missing.

Mama Nuckolls's Squirrel 'N Dumplings

4 LARGE SQUIRRELS (OR 6 SMALL ONES), SKINNED, CLEANED, SECTIONED, AND ANY STRAY SHOTGUN PELLETS REMOVED

2 PILLSBURY FLAKY PIE CRUSTS (THESE CAN BE FOUND IN THE UNFROZEN DAIRY SECTION OF A SUPERMARKET)

1 CUP FLOUR

SALT AND GROUND BLACK PEPPER

Put 4 to 5 cups water into a 6-quart pot and bring to a boil. Add the squirrels to the boiling water and cover. Boil until the meat is tender and can be picked from the bone. Save the stock and discard the bones. Return the boneless squirrel to the stock and bring to a slow boil. Roll out the pie crusts until very thin. Dust with flour to prevent sticking. Using a sharp knife, slice the pie crusts into strips about one inch wide and place them into the boiling pot one strip at a time until they reach the preferred consistency. (The longer you boil, the more tender the dumplings become, but do not allow them to stick to the bottom of your pot.) Season with salt and pepper to taste. Allow to boil slowly, stirring gently for 7 to 8 minutes. These are delicious served with hot buttered corn bread.

Serves "6 to 8 hungry guys," according to Mama Nuckolls

CHAPTER 11

Brave New World

The Future of Meat

We now venture from the primitive human tradition of hunting your own meal to the opposite end of the spectrum: the ultra-modern approach, namely laboratory meat.

Once upon a time, long ago, there was only one way for a human being to put meat in his diet: track an animal in the wild and kill it. The animal ate whatever it was supposed to eat, and it lived a life mostly devoid of human interference or interaction right up until the very end, when Caveman Sam caught it dead in the chest with spear or arrow and brought the beast back to his jubilant family. As the centuries passed, humans eventually learned how to domesticate animals, and soon thereafter discovered that their cows or pigs, sheep or birds would react differently to being fed different types of foods, in different quantities, and at different times of the year. Elsie gets big and fat if we stuff her full of corn instead of letting her graze? Corn it is! More milk, more meat! Cut to the present: we've gotten meat pretty much down to a science. Literally. Ranchers at the source of the food chain know precisely what and how to feed an animal in order to ensure the maximum possible yield and continue to selectively breed animals that offer the most product, with the highest quality, for the least amount of money. It's all about business ratios, price points, and profit margins; meat is a product just like toothpaste or gasoline or Barbie dolls. The question is: Have we come to the end? Have human beings finally reached the pinnacle of what we can do with the animals we eat?

Not by a long shot.

As our species advances and our understanding about science and nature grows, so does progress in the meat world. True, many people are now realizing the potential downsides to having inexpensive, plentiful meat—including risk of disease from overconsumption and less healthy meat—and there's an increasing trend of people opting instead for "natural" beef, chicken, or lamb, for which they're willing to pay a premium. On the other hand, there are plenty of agricultural scientists, even geneticists, who continue to make tremendous innovations in the wonderful world of meat. Truth be told, there's some pretty interesting stuff going on in food laboratories around the world, and these innovations are starting to raise concerned discussion, even alarm. So what, then, could stir up so much trouble? What's the meat of the future?

1. The Cloned T-Bone

Ever since a Scottish sheep named Dolly took the world by storm in 1996, the field of cloning has taken some serious steps forward. At some point in the last ten years, a very enterprising—and, dare I say, hungry?—geneticist realized that if you got all the kinks out of the cloning procedure, you'd be able to take a cow with the best meat on the entire farm and make an identical copy of it, rather than having to gamble on selective breeding. And just like that, the cloned meat controversy began. Unlike some other breakthroughs in food science, this

one came to fruition with stunning speed. It wasn't but a few years until geneticists were proclaiming that the cloned animals were just as
healthy and viable as their "parent" animals, and began to take the issue up with the U.S. Food and Drug Administration to try to get
cloned rib eyes into the supermarket as soon as possible. Unfortunately
for them, the FDA wasn't about to give in quickly; it commissioned
years' worth of intensive studies to validate the scientists' claims. After
all, the government didn't want to give the go-ahead, then find out a
couple of years down the road that Frankensteaks were causing unsuspecting Americans to sprout unwanted additional appendages on their
foreheads or start growing gills or something (actually, that would be
pretty cool). Our nation already has what many are referring to as an
obesity epidemic—who wants to add genetic freakdom to the mix, too?
Today, after years of comprehensive studies, cloned beef is still illegal;
however, the FDA is closer than ever to putting an end to that morato-
rium. In December 2006, it announced that, yes, milk and meat from
cloned cows are perfectly safe to consume, even presenting to the public an almost seven-hundred-page "draft risk assessment." This came
three years after the FDA's first approval, which was later withdrawn after consumer advocacy groups, bless their hearts, claimed that the science behind all this cloning was suspect. Not so, claimed the FDA after
reviewing said science. So here we are today, with an estimated five to
six hundred cloned cows in the United States (out of a whopping forty-
four million beef and dairy cattle, according the *New York Times*) waiting for final approval. The government and the scientists tell us it's
safe, but the question remains: Will people eat it?

Yes and no—the majority of consumers, faced with the option of
buying cloned beef, will stay with the old-fashioned stuff, and many
of them have grave concerns with the concept in the first place. Much of
this apprehension exists, according to a scientist from ViaGen, one of
the leading proponents of cloned meat, because people don't fully understand the science involved. It seems just about every innovation
breeds unease and skepticism, if not outrage—people spoke out against

pasteurization, organ transplants, and in vitro fertilization, all considered commonplace these days.

So it's understandable that some might be wary about the thought of turning Dolly into lamb chops. It's really not all that alarming, once you find out what's actually involved. Essentially, a producer discovers that a certain cow yielded a beautiful steak. "That's a beautiful steak," he might say, and, wanting more like it, he decides to spend the dough to send it over to ViaGen in Austin, Texas, to have it cloned. Here's where the big misunderstanding begins. It's easy to think that cloning beef happens like something out of a bad science-fiction B movie from the fifties, à la Ed Wood: a dank basement laboratory buzzing with the thrum of large, nondescript machinery, beakers all over the place bubbling over with smoke, and a brilliant but dodgy professor standing over two tables, one empty, the other holding a succulent porterhouse with a bunch of electrodes attached to it. Maybe there's a pretty assistant in a miniskirt version of surgical scrubs hovering nearby, standing at the ready. With a lot of anxious hand wringing and raising of his bushy eyebrows, Dr. Steakenstein throws the switch, showering the lab with a hail of sparks and lightning bolts, after which there appears, somewhat miraculously, an identical steak on the once-empty table.

Admittedly, that image is a lot of fun, but a little far-fetched.

Back in the nonfictional world, things are less dramatic. Scientists do take a tissue sample from the original steak, but they don't actually clone the steak itself. They extract the DNA and inject it into an unused egg from a slaughtered cow, "coax" the egg into producing an embryo, then implant that embryo into a cow to gestate, after which a steer identical to the original is born. This is called "somatic cell nuclear transfer." The same basic biological process happens with identical twins, which are clones of each other, only without a Texas biotechnology lab involved in the middle stages. The cloned steer produces offspring, and those perfectly ordinary-looking and ordinary-behaving calves grow up to be the cloned meat causing all the controversy. Other than how it came to be, cloned beef is all but indistinguishable from noncloned beef, and the few people lucky enough to have tried it (at their own discretion, seeing as how it's still technically out of bounds) claim that it is precisely as juicy and delicious as the alternative. But still, people balk, and that's fine—we'll let the market say whether or not cloned beef will be viable, though there might have to be some sort of government labeling system in place to let people know, so that they don't unsuspectingly order clone meat if they're opposed to it, an issue that still hangs in the balance. Plus, right now cloned cattle, at $15,000 a pop, are more than seven times as expensive as their farm-bred counterparts, which sell for about two grand. Eventually, if there's enough call for it, the cost might go down, which is entirely possible, given the huge demand for and limited supply of prime-grade beef. But only time will tell. I for one have no qualms whatsover about eating cloned beef, knowing what I do about it.

The future is now, my friends. I can almost taste it.

2. Healthy Bacon?

This is where things get still more interesting: given their control over an animal's genetic makeup in the cloning process, scientists are actually able to manipulate its nutritional content. Enter transgenic pigs that contain, that's right, meat loaded with beneficial omega-3 fatty acids, the good stuff everyone's telling you to get more of by eating loads of salmon or taking yet another dietary supplement (one day, we'll be taking supplements of just about everything). Problem is, all the wonderful things we're doing to our oceans have produced fish that also contain high levels of mercury, and unless you happen to be a thermometer, you do not want a high level of toxic mercury inside of you. So what to do? Amazingly, according to the abstract of a 2006 study published in *Nature Biotechnology* by scientists from Harvard Medical School, the University of Missouri, and the University of Pittsburgh Medical Center,

Meat products are generally low in omega-3 (n-3) fatty acids, which are beneficial to human health. We describe the generation of cloned pigs that express a humanized Caenorhabditis elegans gene, fat-1, encoding an n-3 fatty acid desaturase. The hfat-1 transgenic pigs produce high levels of n-3 fatty acids from n-6 analogs, and their tissues have a significantly reduced ratio of n-6/n-3 fatty acids ($P < 0.001$).

Of course, you know exactly what this means, just like I do, and you do not feel in any way that such an abstract might as well be written in a lesser-known dialect of ancient Sumerian (aside from that first sentence, of course). In layman's terms, this development heralds an era when a pork chop might actually help your heart instead of destroying it. Can you dig *that*? And given this big first step, milk, eggs, and beef with added omega-3s aren't far off, either.

But as far as controversy is concerned, these transgenic piggies— known also as genetically modified organisms (GMOs)—are more than a handful. Take the alarmist reaction over cloned beef, double it, and maybe you'll start to get close to the massive problems people have with the idea of genetically altered food. There are advocacy groups out there petitioning and protesting their hearts out to ban or limit transgenic corn, tomatoes, and other produce, and once you get into genetically modified animals being used for food, they cry foul as though we're only steps away from changing the entire earth into a planet of Dr. Moreau–like mutants, filled with catpeople and dogpeople and catdogs and duckpeople and whatnot. This, to me, is somewhat alarmist—in 2005, a Pew research poll showed that while most Americans still had little knowledge of the science or application of GMOs as food, the majority of them, surprisingly, were not out and out against them, opting instead to let the research continue, but making sure that there is strict government oversight to ensure that they won't, say, give birth to a litter of lizard babies after eating it. I think that's a pretty fair assessment, though that of course means that we'd have to just trust the government will do its job and not let things slide, which might seem naive considering that the multibillion-dollar company Monsanto has one of the biggest stakes in GMOs, and those deep pockets might be awfully tempting to crooked politicos. So it still might be risky.

Ultimately, I'm of two minds on the subject. I am of course a big proponent of meat au naturel—organic free-range hippie-style meat—because there's something pure and wonderful about eating wholly unadulterated food. Plus, it makes for a much more romantic and palatable mental image to know that the porc mignon you're tearing into was born in the wild, and not in the cold, harsh fluorescent light of a biology laboratory.

On the other hand, healthy bacon!

Okay, I think the other hand has it. As with similar developments in the science of food, more than a few carnivores are going to be soured by the idea of eating genetically altered pigs, whether or not their meat is swimming in omega-3s. No real reason for this, when you think about it. I mean, I see little difference between genetic modification and selective breeding in the grand scheme of things, as both are calculated human attempts to produce an animal with favorable meat. And if that meat is healthy as well as delicious? Double score. Then again, I'm biased. For me, the greatest thing about this whole deal, what I'm most dying to see, is the possibility of people actually being able to say with great sincerity things like "I'll just have the ham steak . . . I'm on a strict diet" or "Now, honey, you know what the doctor said . . . You have to eat your bacon if you want to lower that cholesterol." Never mind the jetpacks and flying cars that fold into briefcases; when I start to hear people saying things to the effect of "A pork chop a day keeps the doctor away," I'll know we've finally entered *Jetsons* territory.

3. Meat Without the Moo
(The Test Tube Tenderloin)

If we're talking about playing God and screwing around with nature to our benefit (and hey, really, what could possibly go wrong?), cloned beef and healthy bacon are only the beginning. No matter how those cows are bred or what's been done to the pigs' genes to modify them, if you want to eat these animals, you still have to kill them, which naturally sucks for the animals. I've said it before, and I'll continue to say it: you can't have meat without death. Or *can* you? Welcome, carnivores, to the wild, wonderful world of in vitro meat.

Pardon my English, but this is some serious upper-level shit. What I'm talking about here is meat grown in a lab, from a culture, instead of being taken from a living animal that has to be violently dispatched. That's right: no farms, no high-density feedlots, no processing plant, no butcher, not even a cow, for crying out loud. Just a few cloned cells, multiplied using a lot of slick science that I can only barely understand on my best day. According to the official website of New Harvest, a multinational scientific research collective looking to advance the cause of meat alternatives:

> One novel line of research is to produce meat in vitro, in a cell culture, rather than from an animal. The production of such "cultured meat" begins by taking a number of cells from a farm animal and proliferating them in a nutrient-rich medium. Cells are capable of multiplying so many times in culture that, in theory, a single cell could be used to produce enough meat to feed the global population for a year. After the cells are multiplied, they are attached to a sponge-like "scaffold" and soaked with nutrients. They may also be mechanically stretched to increase their size and protein content. The resulting cells can then be harvested,

seasoned, cooked, and consumed as a boneless processed meat, such as sausage, hamburger, or chicken nuggets.

The science is far from complete, but the foundation is there, enough to have some of these Petri Dish McNuggets available for human consumption in only a few years, not counting approval by the Food and Drug Administration. Sure, the idea is more than a little scary to a lot of people, who for some strange reason would prefer that their meat come from a once-living animal instead of a lab. Go figure. But assuming that the stuff won't give you cancer, turn you deaf, or make your intestines spontaneously combust or anything, the potential benefits are staggering. First, you'd be able to once and for all bid sweet sayonara to the ethical issues pertaining to carnivorism. Or, as you might be able to claim on the packaging: "No animals were harmed or killed in the making of these sausages." I'm crossing my fingers pretty tightly here, but the advent of in vitro meat might just toll the death knell for the vegetarian high horse, which would be a nice relief for outspoken carnivores, not to mention the fact that fewer animals would have to lose their lives for us to enjoy some meat. As I've said, I take no pride in the death of animals to satisfy my carnivorous habits, though I will take responsibility. Come the day that lab meat graces the supermarket refrigerator, that will cease to be an issue.

Another upside is environmental. It's been noted in numerous studies that the steadily increasing number of animals being raised for milk and meat does have a deleterious effect on the environment. Before you go thinking that farting cows are a significant contributor to global warming, I'll have to stop you right there—it's actually burping cows, which produce much more greenhouse-causing methane than bovine flatulence (hey, you learn something new every day). It stands to reason that lab-grown meat will reduce the quantity of livestock needed to feed the masses, and hence the damage that those animals are wreaking on our precious Mother Earth. And speaking of feeding the masses, as noted above, should the in vitro meat process evolve to a point where its end product is both tasty and inexpensive, we could have a viable way to combat starvation in developing or famine-ridden nations.

But wouldn't feeding the world's poor lots of laboratory beef be terrible for their health? Quite the contrary—just like our crafty scientists and their omega-3 pork, the good folks working on in vitro meat have a great degree of control over the nutritional content of their product, and could load it up with all sorts of beneficial extra vitamins and other nutritious goodies, and even alter its levels of harmful cholesterol and fat. Not only that, producers would be able to create a piece of meat with absolute consistency in marbling and flavor—no more being disappointed by getting a bad cut of steak, since every cut would be identically delicious.

So, theoretically speaking, in vitro meat could eventually be tasty, nutritious, inexpensive, plentiful, and beneficial to the environment. So what's the big fuss? Why are people so queasy about the prospect of something that seems like it could be the next great step for human beings, even the planet? For one thing, there are those who feel that it would be simply way too easy to clone human meat instead of cows, pigs, or chickens, a huge ethical issue. That's right: these people are terrified that in vitro labs might actually produce something akin to Soylent Green. I'll give them that one. I don't really care to be eating "long pork" anytime soon, either. Also, others fear the effect this technology might have on American agribusiness, because large-scale production of cheap, lab-cultured meat would inevitably result in a sharp decline in the old-fashioned stuff, which would almost definitely become hugely more expensive. No matter how you feel about it, it's difficult to deny that lab meat, if made on a large scale, would be worlds more efficient than raising a bunch of animals to provide a similar product. I don't think anyone worries that this will put American cattle farmers completely out of business—there will always be those who want an au naturel steak, myself included—but it would more than likely scale them down a fair bit.

As for me, I'm eagerly awaiting the day in vitro meat hits the shelves, if only out of sheer curiosity. True, it's much less romantic than eating steak from a grass-fed, free-range steer, but it's also considerably less sad. I'd also love to see if any of my vegetarian friends would dig into a platter of laboratory lamb chops, knowing that they'd effectively be "deathless." The science is still a long ways off—we're not anywhere near the days where dry-aged Wagyu strip loin is only a test tube away—but it might only be a few short years before laboratories offer us up nutritious, cruelty-free, cow-free burgers. And on that day, dear reader, I will be there, fork in hand, ready and waiting.

PART II

The
Tour de
Boeuf

The Geography of a Beef Steer: An Atlas of Primal Cuts

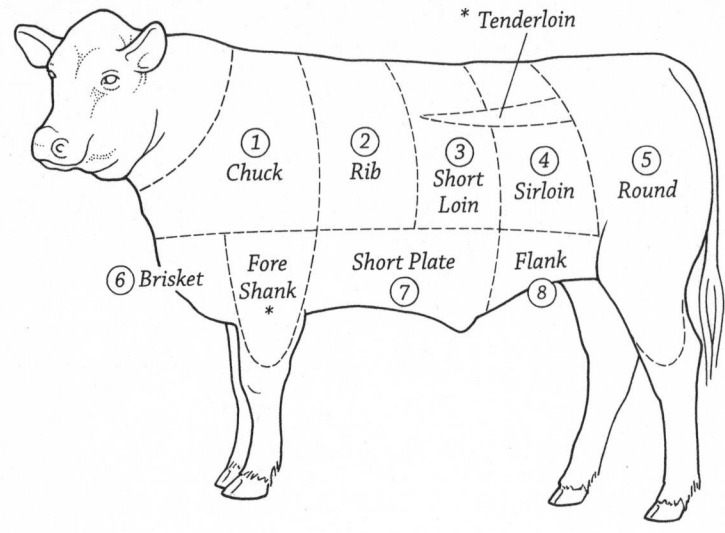

1. **Chuck:** Pot Roast (shoulder, arm, under blade, cross-rib), shoulder center, shoulder tender, flatiron steak.
2. **Rib:** Rack of ribs, rib steak, rib-eye steak, rib roast, rib-eye roast
3. **Short Loin:** Porterhouse, T-bone steak, NY/Kansas City Strip (shell steak), top loin steak, tenderloin steak (filet mignon, Chateaubriand)
4. **Sirloin:** Sirloin steak, top sirloin steak, tri-tip (i.e. "triangle roast"), tenderloin steaks/roasts
5. **Round:** Round steak, rump roast, top/bottom round roast, eye round roast, tip steak, ground beef
6. **Brisket:** Whole brisket, point half brisket, flat half brisket
7. **Short Plate:** Short ribs; Interior: skirt steak (fajita steak), hanging tender (hanger steak)
8. **Flank:** Flank steak ("London Broil," when marinated whole), flank steak rolls

*The diagram shows the eight traditional "primal cuts," as well as the tenderloin and the fore shank, which though both are important and delicious are not generally recognized as primal.

CHAPTER 12

The Ballad of Ernie the Cow

For a dedicated carnivore, remembering your first visit to a top-tier steakhouse is like fondly recalling your first kiss. In my case, it was Ruth's Chris. Located on Broad Street, the New Orleans Ruth's was the flagship store, the very first in a now dizzyingly franchised operation, and to many people (especially New Orleanians), the best. Now a local legend in the Big Easy's restaurant world, Ruth Fertel bought Chris's Steakhouse in 1969 against the advice of her lawyer and her banker, who obviously underestimated Ruth's gumption and, naturally, her dedication to the cause of carnivorism. She was contractually obligated to keep Chris's name on the establishment for a certain period of time, and later—even after a flood destroyed the initial location and forced her to move to the long-heralded North Broad Street locale—decided to retain the "Chris" to ensure that she kept her customers as well. Over the years, the restaurant emerged as a classic American steakhouse, with one very important difference: the oven.

All the steaks at Ruth's are flash-broiled in a hot-as-Hades 1,800-degree-Fahrenheit oven (that's *1,000* degrees centigrade) that sears the meat quickly on the outside to lock in all the savory juices, then transferred to a 500-degree heated plate along with an ounce of butter, which quickly melts. What comes out of the kitchen and to your table is a platter with a perfectly seared steak literally sizzling in melted butter. You can hear your meat coming before you can see it—it only takes a couple of trips to Ruth's before you're ingrained with a conditioned, Pavlovian response to that sound, causing you to immediately start drooling like a bull mastiff as soon as you hear the unmistakable crackle of superheated butter on meat. This experience is so distinctive, so important to the business and everything it represents, that gift cards to the restaurant actually include an audio recording of it. That's some serious sizzle.

This was the place I first learned to truly appreciate a fine steak. Ruth's was a perfect embodiment of my Platonic ideal of a steakhouse: a dimly lit, overtly masculine place with dark woods and white tablecloths; older men in expensive suits with their younger, décolletage-baring trophy wives or mistresses in tow; oversized martinis, tumblers of scotch, and enormous goblets of wine; tuxedoed waiters serving you with butleresque deference and attention; and, naturally, huge hunks of steaming meat, crispy shoestring potatoes, and a couple of vegetables (usually smothered in cream sauce or cheese), all served à la carte. This is the kind of restaurant, I remember once thinking, that Hindus might come to in order to renounce their religion. A T-bone Temple. A Sirloin Synagogue. I was about thirteen or fourteen years old my first time there, and, to me, the place was pure magic. One bite of that stately filet, salted and swimming in butter, and I was hooked like a junkie.

Of all the animals we've bred, raised, and slaughtered for meat over the course of history, the humble cow (*Bos taurus*) may very well be the most important, especially to Americans, and thus its prominence in this book, not to mention my life. In the British Isles, domestic cattle have been an important part of daily life since prehistoric times, and hence the British desire to bring beef and work cattle to North America when they settled here, though it took them some years before they had the means to eat beef on anything close to a regular basis (which didn't matter too much, considering the other natural bounty of America at the time—plenty of squirrels, deer, rabbit, and other meats to go around). The cows we have today are descended from a huge, extinct bovine known as the aurochs (*Bos primigenius*), a cowlike beast that historians believe to be originally from India—which makes perfect sense, given the Hindu reverence for cows and bulls. This animal and its ruminant descendants—ruminants being cud-chewing animals who have multichambered stomachs that evolved to help them properly digest grass—are said to go back up to 40 million years, making them way older than modern humans (*Homo sapiens* is assumed to be only about 200,000 years old, so we're evolutionary babies by comparison). Over time the aurochs made its way to northern Africa and Asia, and then on to Europe about a quarter of a millennium ago. If you happen to have a chance to check out those famous cave paintings at Lascaux, in southern France, you'll see a few aurochs on the wall. People began domesticating the aurochs about eight thousand years ago, a process that over time radically changed the animal's physiology, to the point where many believed we'd created a wholly separate subspecies, though that notion has since been refuted by taxonomists. New species, subspecies, or just a smaller version of their behemoth forebears, we now have cows, and thank heavens for that.

Because Lord knows, we do love our cows. But for most people outside of the upper class, beef was mostly an expensive and rare proposition for almost a hundred years of American history, especially in rural areas where pork was more prominent, until the rise of the Chicago meatpacking industry in the mid-1870s. Using ice from the Great Lakes to cool their warehouses during the warmer months, Armour and other large meatpacking companies were able to process meat year round and deliver it to an increasing number of other cities.

According to the *Oxford Encyclopedia of Food and Drink in America*, "Firms, such as Swift, set up branch houses that provided meat to urban butcher shops and established refrigerated railroad car routes that reached deep into the American countryside. By World War I, the distribution networks of the five dominant Chicago-based meatpacking firms touched 25,000 American communities."

Today, Americans consume over sixty pounds of beef every year per capita, a massive amount when you factor in all the vegetarians, pescetarians, and others who choose not to partake in our bovine bounty. Sixty pounds. The size of a middle-schooler. That, my friends, is *a lot* of beef. Sadly, it seems to me as though, like chicken, beef has become so commonplace that aside from the most expensive cuts—mostly from the short loin, including steaks and chops such as T-bones, porterhouses, and tenderloin filets—beef really doesn't get the attention or respect it deserves. A cow is a very large animal, which means there's a lot there to love, more than most people who enjoy meat might know. Not just underappreciated cuts (the chuck and flank come to mind here) but organ meats, too, which most Americans shy away from as though they're inherently diseased, and not loaded with delicious flavors and textures. One consequence of living in an affluent society is that most of us don't ever think about eating the parts and cuts of an animal that we consider undesirable. Don't want to eat the heart or kidney? Don't have to. Of course, this is a major luxury when you consider what people in either olden or hard times did with an animal, which was *waste nothing*. I was in a cooking class not long ago and met an older gentleman who brought up life during World War II. Rationing was on and money was tight, but his family did have a cow, which they proceeded to kill and butcher. "And that's what we ate that year," he said, laughing softly and shaking his head, "every last part of that damn cow."

I intended to do the same—I wanted to give each bit of the cow the attention and respect that it deserves, from filet mignon to blood, brains, and bone. But how? Would I actually have to eat an entire cow myself? A 1,200-pound steer yields 500 pounds of retail cuts from a 750 pound carcass, and while I have a healthy appetite, eating just under three times my total body weight is less a culinary adventure than a suicide mission. Plus, it seemed unnecessarily gluttonous, even wasteful. I really didn't need all that beef, so I decided to settle for a survey of each of the big primal cuts, eating as many of their components as I could, followed by a similar tour of each of the variety meats, otherwise known as organ meats or offal. This was a solid plan, affording me not only the chance to savor all the various, wonderful parts of a varied, wonderful animal but also giving me the opportunity to explore all things beef related, historically, socially, and culturally as well as culinarily. I'd had my Month of Meat; call this my Tour de Boeuf.

With my plan devised and settled upon, I was ready for beef. Bring it on, I thought, or, better yet, as the bullfighters say: "Toro! Toro!" But first, before I could embark on this bovine odyssey, I had one simple, extremely important lesson to learn. It was time to witness, firsthand, where beef comes from.

Sometimes, for whatever reason, opportunities come out of nowhere with such stratospheric serendipity, it's difficult not to wonder whether someone or something is out there in the ether playing around with your life as though it were a fun little parlor game. This is what occurred to me when, in the late fall of my meaty year, I received an e-mail from my friend Amy that had been forwarded to her by a friend who'd found an intriguing opportunity on Craigslist, the online bulletin board. This is what it said:

Subject: OMG! butchering!

Help with butchering in exchange for fresh veal

It's that time of year again when we will be butchering our cow. He
weighs nearly 700 lbs by now, so we're expecting about 300 lbs of meat.
The work required to wash, cut, trim, package and label that much meat
is more than we wish to handle by ourselves this year.

So, we are offering to anyone with basic butchering skills the opportunity
to drive two hours north and help us with the butchering, in exchange for
a nice quantity of the "grass fed, free range veal." (The cow is 10 months
old, so technically his meat is still veal.)

Please write for more information, this is going to happen as soon as the
weather stays a bit colder, which could be any day now.

Amy had sent the e-mail my way as kind of a joke. She didn't honestly believe that I was so into meat that I'd want to take this person—
who for all we knew was barking insane and didn't even *have* a
cow—up on his offer. She was wrong. True, I had absolutely no clue
who had posted the request for butchery aid, but the writing and information in the post seemed honest and sincere enough to warrant a reply, and maybe a chat on the telephone to see if this might be something
worth pursuing. I was enticed for a number of reasons. First was the
fact that I would be helping out the American family farm, a concept
that gets very little consideration these days when it comes to the subject of beef, as it seems people are focused on discussing the ethical, biological, and environmental implications of huge industrial feedlot
operations. It's easy to forget there are still people out there who, honest to God, live off the land. How could I *not* help out? Second was a
desire to observe and participate in the entire beef process, from living
cow to meat in my fridge and every step in between no matter how difficult, physically or emotionally. So many of us are prone to shying
away from where meat comes from and how it gets to the store,
wrapped snugly in those perfect little parcels, because of its inherent,
unavoidable violence. You can't blame folks for not wanting the image

of a cow's slaughter in their minds when they pick up their rib roast at the Safeway. My interest was far from being motivated by bloodlust or a fascination with gore, that's for certain—after my squirrel hunt, I was less than enthusiastic about watching another animal die. But for a concerned carnivore, I felt that witnessing this process was terribly important.

To really embrace meat, I felt, it was critical to know and experience exactly where meat comes from, whatever that entails. I was also intrigued by the techniques of the butchering process itself. After all, who besides farmers, butchers, or employees of meatpacking plants gets to see how a whole steer, cleaned and skinned, goes from being a giant hanging carcass to being all those trimmed and lovely-looking beef cuts we find in the butcher's case? And, finally, how could I pass up an offer of what the poster claimed to be grass-fed, free-range veal? To some, only a perverted psychopath eager for grimness and gore would respond positively to this post. For me, the more I turned the idea over in my head, the fewer reasons I could think of not to.

I wrote the person back and promptly got a reply. The anonymous farmer turned out to be a young man named Paul who owned and ran a small farm just north of New York City with his wife, Marilyn. They'd started up the operation, which they'd dubbed Beaverwood Farm, in the picturesque town of Ferndale, a charmingly bucolic area near Monticello and, I was surprised to learn, a body of water known as Swan Lake. Beaverwood wasn't a commercial beef, dairy, or poultry farm, even on the smallest of scales. Instead, according to Paul, he and Marilyn got along providing the more rustic services a wholesome family farm might offer. According to their business cards, this included farm tours, a petting zoo, pony rides, farm-fresh eggs, organic produce, dog boarding, and website design. That last specialty is all it should take to realize how difficult it is to make ends meet on a farm these days. They rely on twenty-first-century technological progress to help them get by in the lean months, when groups of field-tripping schoolchildren are difficult to come by.

But despite the modern conveniences afforded by the Internet, Paul and Marilyn lived off their small parcel of land as much as possible, which in this case meant not buying meat at a store. Instead, they had purchased, raised, slaughtered, butchered, and packaged at least one cow a year, as well as the occasional pig, for the past six years. As Paul told me over the phone, "It's a tremendous amount of work, and we're down one person this year, which is why we're really looking for someone to help out." It turns out that one of their close friends, a neighbor and a talented butcher, usually aided the two with the bigger, trickier tasks of turning an animal into steak, including the slaughter itself. Tragically, he'd become extremely ill with brain cancer in recent months, and the disease had progressed with terrifying swiftness, leaving their dear friend hospitalized and, of course, unable to do his traditional duties.

The longer I spoke with Paul, the more my intuition told me that he was an honest, conscientious person, and that his offer was genuine. They didn't want to spend the several hundred dollars (minimum) it would cost to transport the young steer to an independent plant and have it processed there, which would be difficult to do in the first place, since the rise of huge industrial agricultural facilities has resulted in a steady decline of smaller companies that can help out individual farmers. There's a tragic shortage of independent slaughterhouses now, much to the lament of "natural" farmers who want to provide an alternative to concentrated animal feeding operation (CAFO) beef, since more than 80 percent of the nation's beef is processed by four companies and they don't work with small producers (according to a 2006 report by National Public Radio). Nor did Paul and Marilyn desire to pay someone to come up and help, which left them in the position of having to seek aid on Craigslist, offering only some fine-quality meat and a valuable work experience for any interested volunteers. And oh, was I interested.

After a brief discussion of related matters—who I was (they, too,

were understandably wary of potential psychopaths), traveling directions, and what I should bring (warm clothes that I wouldn't mind getting sullied with dirt, blood, and other animal matter, something clean
to change into at the end of the day, a cooler, and, preferably, a sharp
knife)—we made plans for me to travel up to the farm the following
week. Fortunately for me, Amy's friend Brendan, the one who'd initially forwarded her the "OMG! butchering!" e-mail, was also keen on
helping Paul and Marilyn out and offered to drive me and his golden
retriever, Bode, up to Beaverwood Farm. We both agreed that, whatever happened, it was sure to be an interesting experience.

We would not be disappointed.

The two of us made the drive up there early in the morning the
next week, with Bode the golden happily panting away in the backseat
and two empty coolers in the trunk, soon to be filled with veal so fresh
it was still alive and wandering around the barnyard as we drove. After
a couple of wrong turns and calls for directions—the roads seemed to
get increasingly twisty and unmarked the closer we got—we found our
way to Swan Lake and then to Beaverwood, where Paul greeted us as
we pulled into the driveway. I can't say that, physically, he looked anything like I'd imagined; when I thought "family farm," my mind con-
jured an image of an older man, maybe well into his fifties and going
gray around the edges, clad in the requisite overalls and John Deere
trucker cap, hands as rough and strong as slabs of uncut granite, and a
fat wad of Red Man pinched in his lower lip. This, I quickly learned,
was pretty far off base. Paul was much younger than I'd thought, in his
early thirties if I had to hazard a guess, with closely cropped dark-
brown hair and wire-rimmed glasses, brimming over with positive energy and a sort of "esprit de farm." Despite the jeans and coat stained
with years of work outdoors as well as in (the house itself was in the
middle of a large-scale renovation, which Paul was undertaking himself, that included the installation of a fire pole in the middle of the living room, among other things), the overall impression he made was of

an enthusiastic graduate student rather than the co-proprietor of a working farm.

And speaking of work, we needed to attend to the day's task fairly soon, but Paul and Marilyn were happy to let us settle in and give us a tour of the grounds. Setting our belongings inside, we ventured out back to get a look at their operation. It was pretty impressive, exactly the kind of cozily rustic *Green Acres*-style farm you like to think about when you imagine a young married couple trying to live off the land, complete with horses, chickens, goats, pigs, and what seemed to be about four thousand dogs, most of which were being boarded at the farm while their owners were out of town, tearing about the grounds and going absolutely nuts when they got a load of Bode, who was more than keen to play with a bunch of new canine friends (after Brendan and Paul made sure to get him accustomed to the chickens, of course— we didn't want any unforeseen poultry slaughters today). We took a look inside the chicken coop, and Paul was happy to discover that one of his hens had just laid an egg, which he plucked from the nest and gently set in my hands. It was still warm.

"Talk about fresh eggs," said Paul. "Straight out of the chicken's butt!" Then he turned my attention past the pond and down the hill. "Meet Ernie," he said.

Here is Ernie's story: Paul and Marilyn had purchased the little guy at only a couple of months old, along with his brother, Bert (yes, Bert and Ernie—isn't that just cuter'n hell?), from a local dairy farm. Most male calves—"steers" if castrated—on dairy farms are sold for meat, should they not be grown to become stud bulls, which is more often the exception than the rule. In this case, both Ernie and Bert were slated to become dog food, of all things, before Paul and Marilyn swooped in and bought them to be raised at Beaverwood until they were large enough to provide a significant amount of meat, roughly seven hundred pounds. Essentially, it was a stay of execution; instead of having to be slaughtered unceremoniously at two or three months by the dog-food people, they'd get to spend the next six to eight months getting the care and attention of two conscientious farmers and have the opportunity to wander freely around Beaverwood's acres, eating grass and palling around with chickens and goats and hogs. Bert, sadly, didn't even make it those ten months. At some point during the summer, he contracted a cattle disease called "bloat," otherwise known as "gastric torsion," wherein the afflicted animal's gastrointestinal system is plagued by excess gas. Despite all efforts to save him, poor Bert became progressively sicker until, eventually, they had to put him down. On the upside, bloat doesn't necessarily affect the quality of an animal's meat (or at least that's what I was told), so they were still able to butcher him. We would actually be having some Bert ribs and filets mignon, wrapped in bacon, for lunch. This day wasn't anything if not all about meat.

Ernie, on the other hand, was still alive and thriving. At this point he was ten months old, which technically made him a veal calf, though veal terminology is largely elastic (the USDA has no specific definition for the term, making it the subject of much debate). By the broadest of definitions, veal comes from cows that are less than a year old, which would certainly make Ernie a candidate for the title, although most veal we eat today comes from animals somewhere between four and six months old. He did not, however, fit the image of veal most veal-shunning people have, which is to say that he wasn't an adorable baby cow isolated from its mother, shackled inside a tiny crate and kept motionless, then loaded up with steroids and antibiotics and fed an all-liquid, milk replacement formula. This, of course, is a process that conscientious farmers disagree with, even though it indisputably results in the softest, mildest meat, as well as a white color that's the result of an iron deficiency (anemia). "Veal," however, doesn't have to be the result of such practices. There is now a growing group of independent farmers dedicated to providing humanely raised veal, letting the young animals live their brief lives out in the pasture with their mothers. Even better, they claim that pastured calves that feed on mother's milk, grass, and/or grain provide more flavorful meat. (See page 281.)

So if you want to avoid supporting inhumane farming but can't avoid your cravings for *vitello parmigiana*, you're in luck. You can even go to Wolfgang Puck's famous Spago restaurant in Los Angeles for some humanely raised wienerschnitzel. And if you're going to cook for yourself or your family, be on the lookout for the "Certified Humane Raised and Handled" sticker when you're shopping (you can search for providers at www.certifiedhumane.com). This way, you can have your veal and eat it, too.

Ernie might not have been as big as a full-grown bull, but at his current seven hundred pounds, he was still quite a beast, a slightly lean but broad-bodied black-and-white picture of bovine beauty. What can I say, he was cute. Not very bright, though. Of all the things we can say about modern domestic cattle, I think it's safe to admit that they are not, on the whole, particularly smart. An aurochs might have been an astute creature, keenly attuned to its surroundings and the animals around it, but I imagine that, over the centuries, we've pretty much bred the smart right out of our domestic cows, which is probably for the best—we don't want our beef cattle staging a military coup, now do we? I walked down the hill to get further acquainted with Ernie, and Paul even gave me his food bucket (he was being fattened up on grains as well as grass during his last few weeks) and let me feed the steer, who took less of a liking to the contents of the bucket than to my coat, which he decided might make for a better meal, tonguing and gnawing at my sleeve as I tried to give him the bucket instead. He had the attention span of a mentally challenged three-year-old. He certainly was sweet, though, and I can't tell you that I wanted to watch him die. Neither did Paul, for whom it was hard not to delay the inevitable, or Marilyn, who hadn't decided whether or she'd witness the slaughter or not. Ultimately, though, there was much work to be done and little time in which to do it, and as sad and difficult as it was, we all knew that Ernie's life was soon to be only a memory.

The weather that day was cold, gray, and lugubrious, the type of atmosphere you'd expect from something out of Poe, when the feeling of

impending doom hangs in the air. Literary scholars refer to this phenomenon, when the weather perfectly matches the mood of the material, as "cosmic complicity." As eager as I had been to head up to
Beaverwood, meet Paul and Marilyn, and score myself some primo
veal, I was anxious, even a little scared, when it came time for "the
deed." None of us wanted to do it, least of all Paul, who'd not only left
the job up to his neighbor in years past but had naturally grown kind
of attached to Ernie during his stay on the farm and considered him
"my buddy," which is perfectly understandable—when you care for a
living thing for so long, it must be hard for any reasonable conscience-
equipped human not to feel a genuine connection. Nor did Brendan or
I want to do it, less out of a desire to avoid killing an animal than the
fear of screwing it up. The slaughter of any animal should be set about
with utmost care, conviction, and precision, in order to ensure the animal as quick and painless a death as possible, and there was nothing I
wanted less than to torture poor Ernie by failing to do so. No one in
their right mind actually enjoys seeing animals suffer, least of all the
farmers who raise them, not only because of the inhumanity involved
but also because it actually has a negative effect on the quality of the
meat—when an animal freaks out just before slaughter, its body reac-
tively dumps a large amount of adrenaline and other hormones into the
muscles and bloodstream, which causes a recognizable change in the
flavor of the meat that many people find undesirable. At farms and
ranches genuinely concerned with both meat and animal welfare (as
much as it seems that those two concepts are mutually exclusive, they
are not), panicked or anxious animals will be pulled from the slaughter
line until they are calm and relaxed.

In our case, Paul—who'd taken on the burden of the kill himself—
made absolutely sure that Ernie was feeling fine when he told me to
lead him over to the "killing tree," a large bare oak beside which were
the tools of the task—a garden hose, a stack of buckets, a table, and a
number of knives—and from which hung, via rope and pulley, a
wooden plank bearing two menacing metal hooks at each end, also

known as a "singletree." These are all standard farm implements, but to the uninitiated they look like the kind of gear you'd find in one of the CIA's "black site" interrogation chambers. Scary stuff, and a big reminder to all of us of what was about to happen.

As instructed, I enticed Ernie over to the killing tree using the feed bucket as Paul exited the farmhouse, prepared and equipped to accomplish the job that is, emotionally, the most difficult part of the entire process. Queasy as I felt knowing that I was the one literally leading the young steer to his death, at least I knew that, judging by all appearances, he was well fed, relaxed, and content, and that in all likelihood he'd never see it coming. Kind of like a mob hit on a cow. If all things went according to plan, the slaughter would be fast and painless, and Ernie would be wandering around a cow's version of the Elysian Fields eating heavenly bluegrass before he had any clue what had happened.

I've relayed this story a number of times in the weeks and months since it occurred, and when I get to this point, I'm usually interrupted and asked, "How did they do it? How did they kill the cow?" Answer: with a gun and a knife. As primitive as this sounds, this is all it takes to put down such a large animal quickly, and with a bare minimum of pain, if any. What happens is this: One is to shoot the animal with a large-caliber round (or shotgun slug) in a place just between the eyes and the horns and slightly off to one side, which is exactly where the creature's brain should be. This should effectively "stun" the creature, sending it instantaneously into unconsciousness and onto the ground, after which one should lay it on its side and draw a sharp knife across the animal's throat, slashing the carotid artery and jugular veins and allowing the animal to exsanguinate, or "bleed out." Done properly, this process is remarkably fast. In larger-scale operations, like CAFOs and abattoirs, employees use what is known as a "captive bolt stunner," a mechanism that shoots a large metal rod into the cow's brain. For all of its violence, this "stunning" process—also referred to throughout history as poleaxing, after the poleaxe, a large, spiked weapon once used for this purpose—is largely viewed as the most humane way of slaughtering an animal, since it almost instantly knocks the animal out, thus sparing it the pain of the bloodletting, or "sticking." Other ways of stunning include using electric shock or carbon dioxide to produce the same state of unconsciousness; both are methods approved by the USDA, though used less frequently. But on the farm, all the equipment you really need is a reliable gun and a sharp knife. Again, this stuff is not for the faint of heart or constitution, but it's unavoidably necessary in order for you to have that sizzling New York strip you've been dreaming about all week.

The slaughtering of animals, specifically with a focus on the most humane way of accomplishing it, is about as old as humanity itself. All one has to do is look at the most renowned historical and religious texts to see how seriously people have considered this issue through-out the ages. In the Jewish tradition, for instance, there is *shechita*, the series of livestock slaughter principles set forth in the laws of kashrut, or kosher diet. The process must be presided over by an ordained ex-pert in kosher butchery (a *shochet*), who inspects the animal for its fit-ness and health and ensures that it is not distressed at the time of slaughter, as well as reciting a series of prayers and performing the kill himself, according to a strict set of rules. While *shechita* prohibits stun-ning an animal, there are also prohibitions against anything other than a fast, clean bloodletting, including pressing (pushing down on the blade instead of slicing across), pausing during the process, stabbing or piercing the animal's throat, covering (i.e., slicing too deeply), or using a dull blade that causes tearing. Also, slaughtering an animal in front of other animals, especially its relatives, is strictly verboten. Muslims have similar laws, called *dhabiha halal*, with the similar aim of killing an an-imal as efficiently and hygienically and with as little pain as possible. As I've said, I can't claim to stick with a kosher diet (I'm way too in love with my porcine delicacies for that), but I commend anyone who fol-lows these principles, because honestly, this is very serious business, and it should be taken seriously. As far as I'm concerned, any animal that dies so that I might live deserves my respect, at the very least, and these practices convey a deep respect for the lives (as well as deaths) of these animals.

Now it was time to offer that respect to Ernie the cow. As with my squirrel, I don't want to linger on the grim details of his death. I will only say that it was, in fact, very fast, and over before I could fully wrap my head around what I was witnessing. It was all I could do to keep from turning my head or covering my eyes as Paul prepared to place the barrel of his rifle against Ernie's temple, but I held on, knowing that shying away from the hardest part of the day would be counter to the entire reason I was there in the first place. There was a crack of the rifle, which rang out across the trees and hills and scattered the birds, after which followed a loud *whump*, as all seven hundred pounds of the animal fell to the ground, and then Paul turned him on his side and quickly set about finishing the job with his knife.

There was a lot of blood. It stained the ground, and my shoes. I said a prayer for Ernie, vowing that his short life would not be in vain. And then, he was gone.

It's difficult to describe exactly how I felt at that moment. There was this sudden, profound intensity, an increase in the sharpness of colors and smells and sensations, as though everything around me had become hyperreal. I knew this experience wasn't anything like being at war, but for some reason that frenetic, harrowing opening sequence in *Saving Private Ryan* sprang to mind. It must have been the sudden proximity to death, the site of hot blood steaming on the ground, the pungent animal smells, the fatalism of it all. I tried to be stoic, to be the manly sort who isn't shaken in the presence of such a scene, not flinching when seeing with my own eyes the speed with which a life can be violently taken, and I don't know whether or not it showed on the outside, but I have to admit: I was rattled. Not ashamed or regretful, per se—like it or not, this had been Ernie's fate since his birth—but definitely stirred up. Once more, I was reminded that *this* is what happens to cows that become beef, and it's been happening for thousands of years.

For most of the people I know, which is to say middle-class people living in the most prosperous nation in the world during the most prosperous era in human history, this plain, unavoidable truth is something to be avoided at all costs. Why linger on such ghastly details when you don't have to? We have become children of the supermarket, of restaurants and delicatessens, where all of our meat is presented to us in beautiful packaging that has been cleverly and calculatedly designed by experts in marketing and food packaging to be as appealing as possible. Of course, this severs all connection with its animal history. The veal chops are a beautiful, rosy pink, steaks are red and savory, chicken breasts are boned, sliced, and glistening, just so. If you want to purchase a whole bird, you have to go out of your way to a specialty butcher or grocery store, usually one of the Asian variety, to even find the heads or feet of these animals at all. I've tried, during the course of my meat explorations, to engage in thoughtful conversation with a number of friends and acquaintances about this phenomenon, and most of them (the ones who aren't as shamelessly carnivorous as I am, I suppose) balk at the prospect of even talking about the unpleasant "meat = death" equation.

An excellent example of this attitude was relayed by my friend Dawn, whose family is of West Indian descent. She recalled visiting family in Jamaica who, come suppertime, asked her what she'd like to eat. "Chicken," she replied nonchalantly, knowing it to be a safe option, after which a relative took off into the yard. "Where are you going?" Dawn asked. "To go get a chicken," he replied, maybe thinking that she was a little slow on the uptake. Dawn was appalled, quickly realizing to her horror that he wasn't going to the store to pick up a preplucked, processed bird, but rounding up a live one just outside, one of the same chickens she'd been playing with earlier, and that he was going to *kill it* for their dinner. "I just wanted chicken," she remembers saying, "not, you know . . . *a* chicken!"

It would of course be preferable if that animal was perfectly happy to become braised brisket or chicken Kiev or buffaloaf, and was able to say so. There are a number of cultural references expressing this wish, my favorite being in Douglas Adams's *The Restaurant at the End of the Universe*, the second in the Hitchhiker's Guide series. At Milliways, the bistro in the title, our famished intergalactic-traveling protagonists are given the option of "meeting the meat." A large, bovine-ish animal arrives at their table and offers up the various parts of his own body that the dinner party might find most pleasing, having been specifically bred to *want* to become a meal. Arthur Dent, the book's resident human—and thus the only one with any ethical qualms regarding the situation—is visibly terrified by the prospect, hemming and hawing and attempting to order only a salad, much to the animal's profound disappointment (" 'Something off the shoulder, perhaps?' suggested the animal. 'Braised in a white wine sauce?' 'Er, *your* shoulder?' said Arthur. 'But naturally my shoulder, sir,' mooed the animal contentedly, 'nobody else's is mine to offer.' ") Eventually the "meat's" dignity is preserved intact by another member of the party insisting on "four rare steaks please, and hurry!" a notion that greatly pleases the animal, which happily saunters back to the kitchen to shoot itself. In the world we live in, however, things are quite a bit more complicated, as I was experiencing firsthand.

Once we were sure that no life lingered in the late Ernie (postmortem kicking, a common reaction, having injured more than a few ranchers over the course of history), the real work began, starting with cleaning. Paul sliced the cow evenly up its belly and removed the inner organs, saving the heart and liver, which Marilyn placed in one of the plastic buckets and carried inside the house, to be vacuum-sealed and frozen for later consumption. Next he removed the head, and with it we discussed whether or not any of us felt like cutting out the tongue or the cheeks, both delicacies. Properly skinned, in fact, the entire head could be boiled to make "head cheese," which would make use of every last scrap of meat on the skull. We decided to do that later, if at all, opting instead to get as much of the big work done while we still had enough light. This meant first carefully hanging Ernie from the single-tree. Looping the steel hooks solidly through the gambrel space—the small area near the hind knees between the gambrel tendon and the bone—we cautiously winched the carcass up using a rope pulley, until it was just above our heads.

It was now time to remove the hide, a delicate, time-consuming process that had to be undertaken with great care, since Paul wanted to preserve the skin to fashion a throw blanket, a memento mori of the dearly departed Ernie, which meant that we had to cut it from the carcass cleanly, without any punctures. The farmer showed Brendan and me the process, which was both simple and exhausting. "All you need to do is pull down on the loose flap of hide, like this," he said, grabbing a fistful of skin and firmly stretching it down, exposing the white, web-like fascia between the hide and the meat, "and run your blade gently across the connective tissue. Just keep pulling and cutting, and before you know it we'll be done. And once the skin's off, it gets much less emotional—you'll stop seeing a cow and start seeing steak. Trust me, it's not so bad."

He was right; it wasn't so bad, though it was a fair bit of work. I was literally up to my elbows in Ernie for the next hour, as Brendan and I pulled and cut, pulled and cut, working the hide down the carcass until, finally, the skin was hanging down around the forelegs. Paul took a look at our work, pronounced it good, and let us know that we could clean up in the basement sink before lunch. Seeing that my arms were now covered in tufts of cow fur, and my sweatshirt's sleeves were soaked through with blood, I could certainly stand some soap and water, that was for sure.

Once relatively clean and dry, we headed in for a big steak lunch and a nice discussion of all things meat related. We began talking about the Swan Lake area and how it's such a boon during hunting season, when gun-happy, cavalier marketing executives and bankers come up to bag a big kill. According to Paul, a local woman makes a fortune—both in money and meat—processing deer carcasses for these yahoos, who don't want anything but the backstraps and the head, the former for eating, the latter for mounting in their wood-paneled rec rooms as a confirmation of their masculinity. The woman gets to keep the rest of the venison, a true bounty. As much as those poseurs represent everything I find reprehensible about hunting—killing for trophies and sport rather than for true sustenance or concerned conservationism—at least the deer lady makes up for their wastefulness, and the carcass isn't simply left in the woods to rot. "But even though you can shoot a deer," Paul continued, "if you happen to accidentally hit one with your car, you can't legally keep it. Isn't that crazy?" I agreed—if the animal is going to die, it might as well feed your family. "In fact," he continued, "I even did that once."

"You nailed a deer with your car?" I asked.

"No, someone else did," he said. "I heard the crash all the way up here at the house and went running to see what happened, and there was this poor deer lying there on the road. So I ran back to the house, grabbed a knife, went out and jumped on the animal's back, and cut its throat. Otherwise who knew how long it would be on the side of the road, suffering?"

Brendan and I sat there, shocked at what Paul was telling us, less at the fact that he'd killed an animal—we'd gotten used to that concept by now, what with Ernie skinned and hanging from a tree outside as we ate—than at the idea that he leapt upon the back of a dying animal and slashed its throat like a crazed mountain man. I certainly wouldn't have had the temerity to try something like that, especially considering that a dying deer is a dangerous thing—one strong, panicked kick could put you out of commission, easily. No matter how much he ostensibly appeared to be about as square as the guy from tech support, I remember thinking, "That . . . is . . . bad . . . *ass*." And, of course, he took the deer back home and butchered it. After all, wouldn't anything less be wasteful?

Soon enough, conversation naturally turned to Ernie. Paul and Marilyn weren't the only ones to have become attached to the now late calf. A couple of teenage girls, on a visit to the farm, became positively smitten with him and were devastated by the idea that, come winter, the couple was going to slaughter him for meat. They pleaded with Paul via e-mail to spare Ernie's life—they'd found a farm where he could live and, well aware how much food the calf would inevitably provide, were willing to trade a quantity of venison for his release. Paul considered their proposition, and responded in the fashion of a true Shameless Carnivore:

We understand [how you feel] about Ernie. However, this is where meat comes from. If we don't slaughter Ernie, we will still need meat, and thus effectively sentence another calf to a much less pleasant life in a commercial beef factory. At the end of this dismal life he instead WILL be killed and fed into the commercial meat industry from which we (meat eaters) so casually purchase our meat.

I hope this cycle is obvious to you, although the meat industry hopes you won't see anything but the pretty packaged meat on your store shelves. Finally, Ernie now weighs almost 700 lbs, of which 300 pounds is our veal for 2007. Even at $5/pound, Ernie is worth over $1,500 at this point. If you were to purchase him, he will then require over $100 a month in food alone to keep. That's $1,200 per year, or $24,000 for the next 20 years, and he will probably live even longer than that.

Would you really want to spend $24,000 to keep a single cow alive, while at the same time sentencing another cow to a horrible life in a commercial beef farm? I think your efforts would be better spent convincing people not to eat meat, nor to feed it to their carnivorous pets. Alternately, you might want to become a scientist involved in In-Vitro Meat research.

Think this through completely . . . Ernie won't suffer at all, and we will be purchasing another baby calf in a few months, to begin the cycle again, the same way it's been done for tens of thousands of years.

Paul.

It wasn't hard to see that Paul had a number of valid points (and it was a little surprising that he knew all about in vitro meat, too). In the end, the girls basically agreed that freeing Ernie would solve fewer problems than they'd imagined, and would require them to pay over a thousand dollars a year for at least the next couple of decades, a prospect that they hadn't anticipated and weren't fully prepared to commit to. So they relented, though not before expressing the hope that Paul might still see Ernie as they did, as a pet, rather than ultimately a source of nourishment. As you might imagine, Paul was less than persuaded, no matter how much he cared for Ernie. I suppose it's easy to be idealistic, so long as it doesn't make its way too far into one's pocketbook.

Once lunch was finished, it was time to return to butchering—the afternoon was getting on, and it was important to get at least all of the primal cuts divided (and preferably subdivided into steaks, roasts, and ground beef) and either packaged or hung by the end of the day. We took off the front limbs, removed them to hang in the makeshift meat locker (simply a dry space connected to the exterior of the house where the meat would be kept above freezing and out of the elements), and then went back inside to plan our next step. This would be the tricky part, as none of us was an expert at butchering the massive primal cuts to make those picture-perfect steaks we're used to seeing on display in the meat case at the store—Paul's poor, cancer-stricken neighbor used to take care of that as well as the slaughtering. "Look at the book," said Marilyn, a capable, hardworking woman who was becoming increasingly exasperated by our stalling and lack of manly know-how. She was referring to one of several important reference volumes the couple kept on hand for such purposes, in this case John J. Mettler's *Basic Butchering of Livestock and Game.* (One of the other titles I noticed in the stack was called *Tan Your Hide!*) The Mettler book was a concise, practical, unsentimental guide to doing exactly what we were up to that day without totally screwing up three hundred pounds of meat. Helpful drawings showed the entire process, illustrating everything from the bovine anatomy (lines drawn to point out the crucial organs, with labels such as "brain," beside which was the helpful note "spot to shoot") to painless slaughtering, then the butchering of every section of the animal. We pored over the diagrams and descriptions, strategizing.

"The fun thing is," said Paul, "you don't even have to follow these instructions if you don't want to. You can butcher the cow any way you want, really. You know, most beef ribs you'll get in a restaurant are only half the ribs. When you have a whole animal like this, you don't have to do that. We can take the entire left or right rib rack, roast it up whole, and have giant, three-foot Fred Flinstone ribs. Isn't that cool?" I had to agree, it was. Three-foot ribs! This struck me as wonderfully primitive, like sitting down to a plate of woolly mammoth or brontosaurus. As our excitement grew, Marilyn brought us back to earth. "No way," she decreed. "How will we cook them? They won't fit in our oven, or even on the grill."

Thus deflated, we went back outside to start taking Ernie apart, beginning with the ribs. Now, you may be able to get through certain bones with a sharp knife, but beef ribs are terrifically sturdy, and require a bit more power. In this case, Paul employed a radial saw to cut the two rib sections—one on either side—in half. I've seen butchers go to town on sections of beef and lamb before, but it's quite a sight to witness a farmer sawing off whole, huge chunks of cow with a power saw, all the while trying not to take an arm off the guy helpfully holding the hanging carcass in place (Brendan, in this case). Once that was completed, the rear third of the cow was still hanging from the killing tree, and the front two-thirds was ready to be sectioned—this would be the chuck, brisket, rib, short loin, plate, and flank—and further butchered into large roasts and individual steaks. This proved to be more difficult than I had thought. Sure, I've trimmed my fair share of steaks and tenderloins (my mother cooks an entire tenderloin once a year, when we go on vacation to the Gulf Coast), but I'd never done so with fresh meat. And this meat was really, really fresh. About as fresh as meat can get, actually—it was a rich, glistening crimson red, and still releasing gases that caused the fat and connective tissue to form small bubbles on the surface. This meat was so fresh, some of it, I swear, was still actually *twitching*. Not to mention that it was warm, and the fat had a stickiness to it I'd never dealt with before, clinging stubbornly to the meat as I tried, with varied degrees of success, to remove it.

For the next couple of hours, we had a big butchering party inside Paul and Marilyn's kitchen, which suited me fine—I was tired of being out in the cold, standing around in the blood and mud. To tell the truth, at this point things became kind of fun. Now that the carcass was duly sectioned and indoors, not only was it easy to forget that just hours ago this meat had belonged to a living, handsome young calf—it even looked delicious. I now saw what Paul was talking about, and I was once more reminded of what happened when Leroy Nuckolls cleaned the squirrels we'd bagged: I was looking at this as food, rather than a dead animal. No matter what conflicting emotions coursed through my mind at the moment, there was no denying that the sight of all this meat had me hungry, even excited. I worked as hard as I could to trim as much meat as possible as other friends and helpers, including a neighbor and his girlfriend, variously rinsed fresh cuts, put scraps through the electric meat grinder to produce bowls of ground beef, packaged the meat into plastic, vacuum-sealed bags and labeled them with the name of the cut and the date, a very important thing to do when you're anticipating having a freezer or two filled with bag after bag of frozen meat.

As it turns out, I am not a brilliant butcher. While the others, particularly Marilyn, worked their way through steak after steak, rib rack after rib rack with ease and seeming effortlessness, I found myself falling further and further behind—"in the weeds," as they say in the restaurant business. Although I made a half-assed attempt to justify my slothful kitchen skills, telling myself that it wasn't me, it was the warm meat ("a few hours of chilling in the refrigerator, or even outside, would make it much easier," I rationalized), or the relative dullness of my knife (could everyone else's be sharper than mine?), I wasn't really fooling myself. I may be a true meat lover, a carnivore extraordinaire ready and willing to dig into this meat even though—or perhaps even because—I knew precisely from whence it came, but it was plain to see that I wouldn't be taking Frank Ottomanelli's place anytime soon. Granted, I wasn't terrible. I didn't completely annihilate any of the meat I trimmed, but I definitely needed improvement, to say the least. Luckily, this was a terrific way to learn. There were lessons in removing fats and silverskin—that white, almost metallic-looking tissue attached to the muscle that needs to be cut away, lest your meat shrink as it cooks—as well as identifying different cuts and choosing among various butchering options. When I worried that the rib section I was trimming still had too much fat on it, Paul told me not to worry. "Oh, that's fine," he said. "Actually, you want to leave at least some of the fat on there for flavor, and most of what's left will cook away, so it's not a big deal. Don't think about it too much—just keep working."

By late afternoon, with the sun going down and fat flakes of the season's first snow spinning through the air, Brendan and I decided to call it day. We wanted to get on the road soon, just in case it started snowing heavily, and besides, we were bushed. Paul was right: butchering a cow *is* a tremendous amount of work. So we gathered up our dirty, blood-smeared clothing and other belongings, called Bode the golden retriever in from outside (he was totally beat, too, having frolicked himself silly with the other dogs all day), and prepared to return to New York. "This is for you," said Marilyn, indicating a small stack of packaged meat on the kitchen counter. Looking more closely at it, I realized that everything in that pile was the exact same meat I'd cleaned and trimmed over the past few hours, plus a little extra for lagniappe. "That's how we do it here," said Paul, smiling. "You worked for it, you get to keep it. Plus there's some more tenderloin in there, too—we thought you might enjoy some." I thanked the two of them as graciously as I could while I placed the packages in my cooler, and after we had exchanged a few last pleasantries and promises to keep in touch, Brendan and I packed up his truck and headed south, to the city.

The ride back to Brooklyn was surreal, if anything. It had been a long day, a day packed with insights and lessons about the nature of meat—and life, and death—as well as one filled with good companion- ship and hard work. Still, it seemed hard to believe that, just that morn- ing, Ernie was alive and well, and now he was a collection of steaks, chops, and roasts chilling in dozens of plastic bags. If there was ever a concrete lesson about the fleeting, impermanent nature of life, this was it. And as much as I didn't want to witness the end of Ernie's short stay in this world, I was ultimately glad that I did. After reveling in meat for so long, extolling its joys and the pleasures of enjoying and embracing it, I was reminded just how solemn this business of carnivorism can be—my hands were literally stained with the blood of my efforts. I'd never had more respect for beef in my entire life. Never again would I be able to look at a rosy rump roast or a beautiful display of T-bones and strip steaks in the butcher's case without thinking, however briefly, of Ernie. It's a lesson I wish I could impart to all carnivores, the grave importance of taking meat seriously, because death is never pretty, no matter how attractive and enticing the end result might be. So then and there, in the car, contemplating the day's events as I looked at the pass- ing countryside, I considered the late Ernie, and then thought of every animal I'd ever eaten over the course of my life, all the chickens and pigs and sheep, the turtles and snails and frogs, snakes, guinea pigs, nu- tria, and everything else I'd enjoyed. These animals died, and as a re- sult, I continued to live. I vowed to be as respectful and cognizant of that fact as I could, to never forget where my meat comes from.

Ernie deserves no less.

CHAPTER 13

Primal Cuts

As eager as I was to dig into Ernie, the meat needed to age. This process is something that most people, even carnivores, don't regularly consider. All beef, not just the fancy dry-aged kind (more on that in a moment), should age somewhat before it's really suitable to be consumed. The reason for this is simple: fresh meat, just after slaughter and butchering, is almost always going to be tough and chewy if you cook it right away. Meat is muscle, remember, and muscles from fresh meat have been very recently exercised. So, unless you add meat tenderizer or grind your meat, a tenderizing process in itself, you need to wait a while before you can throw it on the grill, allowing the muscle to begin breaking down and rendering it more supple—and, in many cases, more flavorful. Many people say that unaged steak, aside from giving your mandibles a hearty workout from all the chewing, tastes semimetallic and not very "beefy," in spite of its freshness. Aged meat, conversely, tastes much better, more like the red meat we're used to.

How long should your beef age? That depends. Most meat we get commercially at the supermarket goes through what's known as "wet aging," meaning that it stays in its vacuum-sealed and hence oxygen-free bag at a temperature just above freezing (should the temperature rise above 40 degrees Fahrenheit, you run the risk of spoiling) for anywhere between seven and twelve days, slowly absorbing its own juices and being broken down by naturally occurring microorganisms. Generally speaking, beef producers plan this process to occur between the time that the animal was processed and its arrival at the grocery store or other retailer, so that by the time you buy it, you won't have to worry about aging it any further. It's simple, economical, and not particularly difficult. All you really need is a reliable refrigerator and the knowledge that your meat is well sealed. The advent of wet aging was a massive boon to the meat industry when it was adopted as standard practice in the early 1960s, since it allowed the meat to age enough to be tender for consumers, while at the same time not losing any net weight.

Then there's dry-aged beef, a much more delicate, precise, and costly operation, one that almost every steak enthusiast will agree results in significantly more flavorful meat. It's not very appetizing to admit, but any aging of beef is essentially "controlled rotting." During the dry-aging procedure, once the only way to age beef, the meat—usually from the rib or short loin, as they have the best intramuscular fat (aka marbling) and hence take well to the process—is kept at a temperature between 35 and 38 degrees in a clean area in which the humidity level must be tightly controlled and monitored, and is generally regulated at between 50 and 60 percent. A slight miscalculation of air moisture or temperature could destroy thousands of dollars in prime beef, a crime against carnivorism that, in my opinion, should warrant immediate jail time. As it ages in the cool, slightly moist air, the meat develops a thick dark crust on its exterior that, while admittedly disgusting looking, seals in the meat beneath it, protecting it from the elements. When all is said and done, a number of weeks will have passed. Exactly how much time is often debated by enthusiastic carnivores, though it's never less than fifteen days. You can find six-, eight-, or even ten-week dry-aged beef in certain butcher shops and steakhouses, though the longer a piece of meat ages, the more expensive it becomes, since a critical part of the aging process involves the evaporation of moisture from the meat. This liquid loss shrinks the size of the steak, but as a result the flavors of the beef are intensely concentrated, making a rich, earthier flavored strip, rib eye, or porterhouse. By the time it's ready for cooking and eating, a dry-aged steak will have lost up to half of its original weight, both in moisture evaporation and in its outer crust, which needs to be removed. (You weren't actually going to eat that, were you?) Ultimately, a dry-aged cut of cow is going to have a deep, musty beefiness to it you simply cannot get in a standard wet-aged steak, which is why it commands such steep prices, and why it's so highly prized among discerning carnivores.

In the case of Ernie, Paul advised me not to dig into any of mine for at least a week, and I made sure to give it a solid twelve days, for good measure. I was happy to wait, to be frank. For some reason, throwing Ernie steaks and ribs into the oven or broiler right away didn't feel right. I felt as though it wasn't just the meat that needed a week to rest—I did, too. Your first butchering day is a hell of an experience, and I felt it best to let everything I'd been through and witnessed sink in before I was really ready to put this meat on the table.

Now, there are eight primal cuts of beef, and I needed to decide where to start. Thanks to Ernie, I had that small section of tenderloin, a small rack of ribs, some short ribs, a rib steak, and a flank steak. Ultimately I felt that I should let my tummy do the talking—which of these was I really hungry for? The consultation between my brain and my belly was a short one: it was beef ribs all the way.

Primal Cut #1: Rib

The rib section of a side of beef contains some of the most tender, flavorful, and expensive cuts, everything from your basic rib rack to all kinds of steaks and roasts, including rib eye, rib steak, the magestic crown roast, rib chops, and standing rib roasts. For me, though, I loves me some barbequed ribs. If you're from the American South, especially Texas or states close by, you'd be a rare person indeed if you didn't adore a big, hot, tender rack of BBQ beef ribs. And that's what I decided to cook first.

The problem was, as popular as beef ribs are, I had trouble selecting a recipe. Looking online and in my meager selection of cookbooks, there were hundreds of different preparations, many of which gave conflicting instructions. Covered or uncovered? High heat for a short time, or low heat for longer? Braised in liquid or cooked alone? Dry rubbed or slathered in sauce? I didn't want to leave my Ernie ribs to chance—after all, I would be devastated if I managed to screw it up, and I felt that would be a disgrace to the poor, late calf—so I carefully consulted my preferred sources, gave my mother a call for her input, and devised a strategy of my own: First, a nice sprinking of salt and pepper on the outside before anything got going—seasoning is always a must. I wanted the ribs to be nice and tender but didn't feel like cooking them for hours and hours. This meant that I'd have to bake them covered in a roasting pan with a little liquid (about a cup of water and, for flavor, a cup of beer). I'd had some decent success with 350 degrees in the past, most notably with my leg of wild boar, so I felt that'd be a good place to begin. If I let the ribs roast like that for an hour and a half or so, I could check their progress and see how my little babies were coming along, and how much longer I felt they might need to continue in the oven. If they were looking nice and a jab with a fork didn't meet any real resistance, I'd mop a little BBQ sauce on the top and finish them, uncovered, for another half hour to give them that beautiful deep red color you'd expect out of this dish. Technically speaking, of course, these were baked ribs, not barbeque, seeing that the definition of barbeque is slowly cooking your meat over indirect heat on a grill for a very long period of time. But, technicalities aside, I hoped this plan would do the trick.

When all was said and done, the ribs turned out to be magnificent, just as good if not better than I might find at a real BBQ restaurant. My dinner guests enjoyed their ribs—accompanied by my friend Sam's pan-fried potatoes with onions and Hillary's asparagus wrapped in phylo dough and a butter-and-cheese sauce (this was not an especially healthy meal)—but for me, it was a truly special experience. Not only did I have direct knowledge of whence my meat came but I'd worked for it, spent a whole afternoon on a farm and a fair bit of effort, not to mention emotional energy, to get these ribs, and I felt as though there was a special connection between me and this meal. By comparison, the cooking process was simple, a joy.

The meat was tender, falling perfectly off the bone with each bite, as well as deeply beefy. Ernie was almost at the border of being a young beef steer instead of veal, and given his diet (mostly grass, until near the end), this meat indeed had a richer, more pronounced beef flavor than many of the ribs I'd had before it, which now, in comparison, seemed too fatty and greasy, and usually overseasoned to disguise the inherent shortcomings of the meat itself. This made me think again about how the diet of an animal directly affects the flavor of its meat.

GRASS VERSUS GRAIN— A CATTLE-FEED DILEMMA

In the same way a wild animal (like my boar and squirrel) has a distinctly more developed taste to its meat as a result of its living conditions, the same applies to beef. While there's really no such thing as "wild beef"—cows are, by definition, domestic animals, and even if they aren't living on a farm I doubt you could ever refer to them as being "feral"—how a beef cow is raised and fed makes a big difference. Historically, up until the industrial age, all cows were grass fed. That's what cows do: eat grass. Like all ruminants, they have a digestive system that evolved specifically to be able to digest cellulose (which we humans, of course, cannot digest), and their natural waste serves to fertilize the ground, ensuring a continually renewable food source. It's a perfect arrangement of nature.

Grass, however, does not make a cow big, and it does not make a cow fat. With time, effort, and developments in modern agriculture, farmers learned that if you fed a cow grains instead of grass, even though that's not what they're designed to eat, it was possible to raise animals that grow much larger much faster, producing significantly more milk and meat in less time, and hence making more dough for the farmers and ranchers. Not only that, the meat itself had substantially more intramuscular fat, an attribute that steak enthusiasts look for when selecting a stellar piece of beef, and that also affects the meat's grading by the USDA— better marbling results in a higher rating. Though it caused large increases in cattle diseases, requiring more widespread use of antibiotics than ever before to ensure healthy cows, this process proved to be so effective that grain-fed beef has become the norm in the United States, and unless you want to shell out for a special, organically raised steak, you're stuck with the grain-fed variety. Another downside of pumping cattle full of corn, other than the health issue mentioned above, is the fact that doing so has the unfortunate effect of leaching out much of the meat's natural flavor. Many older Americans who were raised in the time before the standardization of grain feeding swear that the meat today just doesn't taste as good, as rich, as the meat they enjoyed in their youth.

"Where's the beef?" indeed.

It also seems that grass-fed beef isn't just tastier, it's actually better for you, too. According to a number of studies, grass-fed beef contains certain beneficial omega-3 fatty acids and vitamin E, as well as higher concentrations of conjugated linoleic acid. (Remember this from the kangaroo? It's said to have positive implications for cancer risk, heart disease, the immune system, even weight loss!) Perhaps this is why, in places like Argentina, world renowned for the quality of its beef, people can eat two steaks a day and get along just fine. I'm not rushing to blame grain-fed beef, but I know that if I tried the two-steak-a-day diet on conventional American beef, I'd be reaching for the Rolaids pretty fast, not to mention freaking out the doctor at my annual physical. Also, if you eat only grass-fed beef, you're pretty much guaranteed to never run afoul of mad cow disease, since BSE is caused by animals eating proteins from other animals (bone meal and fragments of the brains and spinal columns of other cows, in this case—and boy, doesn't *that* sound yummy), which only tend to sneak into the feed of CAFO cattle.

So here's the deal: with grain-fed, you get bigger, juicier steaks that cost less but are milder in flavor; with grass-fed, you have cuts of meat that are smaller, leaner, somewhat tougher, and more expensive, but that also have a deeper beef flavor and better health implications. Personally, I'd love to eat mostly grass-fed beef, because I appreciate the idea of letting an animal live and eat as nature intended, and Lord knows how I love a deeply flavored steak, but I'm surely not opposed to digging into a ten-ounce, corn-fed Black Angus *filet au poivre*, either. Six in one hand, a half dozen in the other. But for both, I'm adamantly against my beef being pumped full of unnecessary antibiotics and, even worse, growth hormones. I have enough of my own hormones to deal with, thank you very much; I don't need to be dealing with cow hormones as well.

Fortunately, there has been a recent resurgence in grass-fed beef, and both supply and demand have shown a significant in-

crease in the past few years. Many discerning carnivores who decry the practices of modern CAFOs as unnatural are thrilled with
the prospect of eating a cow that's been eating grass and roaming
around pastures its whole life, like Ernie. They're willing to pay
more for that privilege as well, which of course is a boon to the
rising number of grass-fed beef producers, according to the
American Grassfed Association. Not that everyone is hopping on
the grass bandwagon—according to a 2006 *New York Times* article examining the growing call for grass-fed steaks, a number of
restaurateurs claimed that many of their patrons disliked the
"greener" meat. This makes perfect sense, when you consider
that people who've grown up loving huge, soft, intensely juicy
steaks probably won't be as keen on a smaller, chewier cut of
meat, even if it is possessed of a more robust flavor. Some of those
diners even preferred the flavor of the corn-fed beef. But at least
now, as opposed to, say, ten years ago, people have the option of
grass-fed versus grain-fed beef, and isn't the freedom to choose
one of the hallmarks of our great nation?

On the other hand, there have been problems with labeling,
specifically regarding the question of what, exactly, should be required to label beef "grass-fed." As with the term *veal*, there is still
no definitive set of regulations for that designation, so it's become
a murky gray area of agricultural practice and protocol. Big industrial farms might keep their animals indoors or packed together in
pens, but if the cows are fed grass for a certain portion of their
lives, doesn't that make them eligible for the grass-fed label?
The American Grassfed Association was terribly irked by this
prospect, insisting that the grass-fed designation should be applied only to pasture-raised cattle who eat nothing but grass and
who forage from the time they are weaned until the day they're
slaughtered. But can a beef steer that eats grass for only most of its

life still acquire the label? Many farmers, like Paul and Marilyn, fatten up their animals on grains for the last few weeks of their lives, a process, known as "finishing," that helps to make the meat juicer and more pliable. It's a tricky situation, and the debate still continues today. So, if you're a consumer interested in comparing grass-fed and corn-fed steaks, make sure to do a little research into the producers to find out exactly how they raise and treat their cattle. Try out 100 percent grass-fed, then taste some corn-finished beef. You are a carnivore: Be discerning! Care about your meat!

Primal Cut #2: Short Loin

If there is a single food item that springs to people's minds when you begin discussing the subject of carnivorism, it is almost always steak. Okay, bacon, too, I've noticed, but more often than not steak reigns supreme. There's a reason for this, as in all things: steak is largely viewed as one of the ultimate luxury foods, an expensive, special-occasion dish, and nothing signals "meat lover" in the minds of most people more than a big, bloody cut of prime beef. Inspect the image on the cover of this book for further evidence of this phenomenon.

We didn't eat a ton of steak in my family when I was growing up. There were plenty of meat dishes, of course. I would generally have some sort of meat at two of the day's three meals, usually cereal for breakfast; a turkey, ham, or roast beef sandwich in my school lunch; then meat at a big family dinner in the evening, my mother's opportunity to trot out whatever new recipe caught her fancy that week or to serve up one of our favorites that she'd perfected over the years. Dinner is where meat really shined at the Gold family table: lamb patties with couscous; spaghetti with meat sauce; chicken marsala; rosemary chicken; jambalaya with chicken and sausage; spicy chicken pasta with tasso (we ate a lot of chicken); and dozens of entrées employing fish, shrimp, crawfish, and all the other Gulf seafood so popular and freshly available in New Orleans. But only occasionally steak, which was reserved on those rare summer weekend evenings when the weather basically commands you to fire up the grill, or during our annual vacation to the beach, when we'd grill up an entire marinated beef tenderloin, a meal I would look forward to every year with bated breath and giddy anticipation bordering on night-before-birthday levels.

The same was the case on those rare and wonderful occasions when I got to eat at Ruth's Chris. A large part of what made the Ruth's experience so wonderful, naturally, was the meat itself. While it surely wasn't pasture-raised or grass-fed, it was USDA prime, the highest level of meat quality, assigned only to the steaks with the very best marbling, color, and age, as generally judged in rib-eye steaks. Also, they served the most desirable cuts, mostly coming from the lauded short loin, the primal section that lies between the rib and sirloin, and that meat-thusiasts and agricultural scientists alike agree yields the steaks with the best balance of tenderness and fat. This is a crucially important ratio to consider when thinking about beef—some cuts, like the chuck, have a fantastic amount of marbling, but the lean part of the meat is considerably tougher. Conversely, cuts such as the sirloin, also very desirable, are about as tender as the short loin but comparatively lacking in precious fat, and therefore not quite as juicy when cooked, though still delicious.

Of the most sought-after steaks, more often than not people gravitate toward filet mignon, which comes from the tenderloin. Known as the backstraps in game animals, the tenderloin, or anatomically speaking the *Psoas major* muscle, which splits the top and bottom sirloin and runs through the back section of the short loin, is prized for its softness, hence the name *tenderloin*. When cut into steaks, this is where filet mignon and Chateaubriand (a large-portioned cut of middle filet prepared to serve two people—*not*, as is commonly believed, another name for a whole tenderloin) come from. Because they make up a very small portion of a cow's retail beef yield, and due to their popularity in restaurants, these steaks usually command a high price, and people are willing to pay it. On the other hand, many avid steak aficionados consider the filet good but often too supple, bordering on mushy, and much prefer alternative cuts from the short loin that have a more robust flavor. Personally, I love a nice filet, especially when it's been prepared with The Best Meat Marinade in the World (see recipe, page 93) or in one of those magical Ruth's Chris ovens, although I certainly concede that they can sometimes be a little too soft. But that's only in grain-fed cattle, I've noticed. When it came time to cook up the small section of Ernie tenderloin Paul and Marilyn had so generously given me, a seven-inch-long cut about two inches in diameter (small tenderloin for a small cow), mushiness would definitely not be a problem. Knowing how a grass-fed cow raised on a small farm might tend toward the tough side, even for a young animal's most tender part, I marinated it to ensure that it would be both appropriately pliable and tasty. I also marinated my rib steak and the small section of flank, but more on that later. It was a good call—Ernie filet was easily the least tender tenderloin I'd ever eaten. Conversely, it did have more of a pronounced beefy essence that was easy to make out even through the various flavors of the marinade. Okay, maybe it was a little on the chewy side; what mattered is that it tasted swell, a distinctly different kind of meat than anything I'd be able to buy at any supermarket. Once again, thank you, Ernie.

Indeed, tenderloin is good and mostly worth the price you pay for your *filet au poivre* at that nice French bistro. But when it comes to the king of steaks, nothing trumps the porterhouse, largely considered to represent the apex of beef flavor, especially if dry-aged. What makes it so great? Basically, a porterhouse is two steaks in one—as it's cut from the larger, rear end of the short loin, this big-ass hunk of beef contains a strip steak on one side of the bone,* and a filet on the other, combin-

* New York or Kansas City, take your pick, or even "Delmonico steak." They're all the same, since they refer to exactly the same cut of meat. The different names are little more than regional branding.

ing the tenderness of the filet and the hearty beef taste of the strip in a single, humongous serving. This distinguishes it from a T-bone, a steak that has the same general properties as the porterhouse, but since it's cut from the front end of the short loin, it's smaller and lacks that critical section of tenderloin. (A note on steak culture and nomenclature: In the UK, a strip steak is known as a porterhouse—having been popularized there in the same bars and pubs that served "porter" ales and stout beer—and the American porterhouse is known as a T-bone. Good to know if you're traveling across the pond for a steak dinner.)

Dry- or wet-aged, preparation for a porterhouse is the same. Season simply and cook over dry heat until no more than medium rare. This is a hard-and-fast law, and anyone out of their gourd enough to order such a marvelous piece of meat medium well or, God forbid, well done, should be forced by the Carnivore Cops to surrender their steak knife and given only the option of ordering a chicken breast. In this case, meat really is murder: the murder of a great steak by overcooking it. If you order well done because you're worried about the bacteria content of a medium-rare cut of meat, don't, since accumulated bacteria on the outside of the steak (if any) will be killed in the searing process. And really, do you know what cooks do when they get an order for well done? According to a number of accounts from restaurant industry insiders, they'll take the worst piece of meat they have—no point wasting a primo cut on someone who clearly has no sense of taste—and broil it until all that's left is a charred block of carcinogenic carbon. They might even throw it in the microwave or the deep fryer because clearly whoever ordered it isn't going to be one to notice. I don't care how you like your steak, do *not* order it well done when you're dining out. If you really have to destroy an expensive cut of beef, do it at home, and spare yourself and the cook some measure of humiliation.

WHAT'S DONE IS DONE— A GUIDE TO COOKING STEAK

Doneness	Color, Texture	Internal Temperature (degrees Fahrenheit)	To Note
Raw, i.e., "blue" or "Pittsburgh"	Deep blood-red throughout.	80°	Still likely to moo. Beware.
Very rare	A cursory outside sear, deep red and relatively cool throughout. Mushy.	110–115°	Basically still raw but with a browned exterior.
Rare	More cooked through, but still red/soft/cool inside.	120°	For those who want to satisfy both bloodlust and desire for flavor.
Medium rare	Good outside sear, a little graying just under the exterior. Warm, red, and soft in the middle.	125–130°	Perfect. Balances the meat's flavor (from the Maillard reaction) and texture.
Medium	Mostly pink throughout. More firm, but not hard.	135–140°	Good for burgers, less so for steak. Here you've lost that beautiful crimson at center.

Doneness	Color, Texture	Internal Temperature (degrees Fahrenheit)	To Note
Medium well	Gray, with a narrow band of pink though the middle and quite firm.	150°	Flirting with disaster. You are forewarned.
Well done	Hard, black, and gray. Cremated.	160°	The meat has died twice. Be ashamed of yourself.

Primal Cut #3: Sirloin

Second to the short loin for steak lovers is, naturally, the sirloin. Steaks from this primal cut between the short loin and the round (read: rump) tend to be on the leaner side with less marbling, richly flavored, and moderate in price, costing distinctly less than the premium neighbors in the short loin. These steaks include the culotte; the top, head, and hip sirloin steaks; and a number of others, all of which I love, but to be frankly honest, what I adore most about the sirloin is its use as ground beef. While ground beef can come from any part of a cow and has dozens of uses, from chili to tacos to spaghetti Bolognese, when I think ground sirloin, only one thing comes to mind: hamburgers. You were wondering when I'd get around to that particular subject, weren't you? Yes, as an American, it would be an impossible thing to write an entire book about the joys of eating meat without addressing the importance of the humble burger, since, as a food and a cultural phenomenon, burgers are an important part of America, both for good and ill.

There is much dispute as to the definitive origins of the hamburger, though it's pretty much agreed that the ground beef patty was initially served in Germany and other nearby places in Western Europe. One claim holds that some hungry German sailors, trading with Russians in the Baltic region, returned to their native land with the concept of eating raw, shredded beef (aka steak tartare), after which an enterprising chef in Hamburg decided to cook it up. Take it off the grill, and voilà: hamburger steak (or steak *haché*, as the French call it). This concept was, like many other cultural contributions that make America great, brought to the United States by German immigrants around the early 1800s, soon becoming a popular menu item and making its way to swanky Delmonico's restaurant in New York by 1834 as "Beefsteak à la Hamburg."

By the dawn of the twentieth century, the hamburger sandwich (its original name) had become quite a popular dish, though speculation as to who added that critical bun component continues unabated to this day. Alternate accounts have it being invented in a New Haven, Connecticut, restaurant, at a fair in Seymour, Wisconsin, and at the Summit County Fair in Ohio, but many agree that the burger as we know it today owes its origin—or at least its initial introduction to a wide American audience—to the 1904 World's Fair in St. Louis, Missouri, right alongside the waffle ice-cream cone and Dr Pepper. (Try all three in the same meal for a bit of early-twentieth-century nostalgia!)

It took some time for the burger to gain its massive foothold on the nation's culinary consciousness, however, since most people were distrustful about the quality of ground beef itself. And for good reason: at the time, many butchers ground up their least desirable meat, even meat that had begun to spoil. Add the horrors of the meat industry chronicled in Upton Sinclair's abattoir exposé *The Jungle* in 1906, and the reputation of what was to become an American classic was quite dubious. According to the *Oxford Encyclopedia of Food and Drink in America*, "Regardless of who was first, the early hamburger did not immediately gain a popular following, remaining either somewhat of a 'fair food,' or an inexpensive snack sold to workers from food carts at factory gates." And it stayed that way for a couple of decades. In one of the more surprising bits of hamburger trivia, it wasn't until the advent of White Castle restaurants in the 1920s that the humble burger's image began to shift. The chain's creators, two shrewd midwestern businessmen, decided that they could make oodles of cash by selling a sandwich that was easily and inexpensively manufactured, but they needed to overcome public concerns about sanitation and quality. Hence the name *White Castle*, specifically calculated to convey an image of cleanliness and wealth, paired with the founders' insistence that each of their restaurants be kept immaculately clean, and that they grind their fresh, quality beef within viewing range of hungry patrons. They even advocated the nutritional value of their burgers in order to reel in customers. It worked: White Castle was a smashing success.

My oh my, how things have changed. The fast-food hamburger has become, rather than the fresh, clean dish endorsed by the White Castle entrepreneurs, largely seen as one of the least healthy food items available, and the hamburger concept itself has even come under scrutiny. This is a tremendous shame. A hamburger does not have to be horrible for you. Sure, there are many healthier options, but grilled ground beef with a few vegetables (lettuce, onions, pickles, tomato) on a bun isn't really all that terrible for your body. When it's not high-quality meat to begin with—much of the hamburger used in fast-food burgers comes from broken-down old dairy cows, you might be alarmed to know—and it's further altered by the introduction of dozens of fats, chemicals, and preservatives, that's when you start to get into trouble. The key? Make burgers yourself, see the difference. When I'm having a grand old time grilling burgers in my yard for friends and using fresh ingredients, I never get that horrible, bloated, sickly feeling I do whenever I cave in and patronize a chain burger joint.

This is where our dear friend Sir Loin comes into play. Though more expensive than other ground beef you might buy, sirloin makes fantastically tasty burgers that are relatively lower in fat (patties made from pure sirloin tend to be a little on the looser side, so if you want a tighter consistency you might want to mix in a little ground chuck as well, though this will definitely make for a fattier burger). A seasoned, grilled sirloin patty on a fresh roll, cooked to order, is a thing of wondrous beauty and pleasure, especially done in the summertime in the yard with your family and friends, just before sunset. All burgers don't have to be the greasy, chemical-, hormone-, and antibiotic-laden abominations being hawked internationally by cartoon clowns and kings, the subpar foodstuffs that many cultures have tragically come to equate with American-ness.

As in all things to be held dear by the true carnivore, the keys are quality, freshness, and good preparation. It's a simple thing, really: get some good ground or chopped sirloin—the meat masters at Peter Luger use sirloin freshly chopped *that morning* for their famous Luger Burger, and you can do the same simply by purchasing some decent steaks and "grinding" them briefly in your food processor—mix it in a bowl with your seasonings of choice (I like soy and Worcestershire sauces, chopped garlic, and a tiny bit of parsley for color, Tony Chachere's Creole seasoning, and occasionally some finely chopped onion, but if the meat is nice and fresh, all you really need is salt and pepper), form it into a patty, grill it or fry it in a cast-iron skillet to your preferred doneness, and slap it on a bun with the condiments of your choice. *E basta*, as the Italians say—that's all you need. And that, dear friends, is a *real* burger. It takes barely any time at all, and what you get is galaxies better than the tragic, cheapened versions of this proud dish found in all those ubiquitous plastic "hamburger" restaurants. Doesn't that sound more appealing to you? Wouldn't the world be better off with house burgers instead?

My meat-loving brothers and sisters: Can I get an "amen"?

Primal Cut #4: Flank

When most people go shopping for steak, they're usually looking for the big names listed above: T-bone, porterhouse, rib eye, strip, and so forth. While these cuts are splendid, steak doesn't begin and end with these most expensive cuts. Enter the flank. As far as underappreciated steaks go, flank is the one flying under the radar that I appreciate the most. This long, flat, lean cut of the cow in the rear of the belly beneath the strip loin and sirloin is both inexpensive and healthful—both owing to the fact that it has little to no marbling whatsoever. Plus, given its firm but porous texture, it cooks quickly, takes very well to marinating, and never becomes mushy as a result. As opposed to the fattier, pricier steaks you might enjoy on special occasions, the flank is a great everyday kind of steak: nutritious, tasty, and quick to prepare. My mother marinated hers in a teriyaki sauce, grilled it, and served it alongside rice and vegetables, Japanese style. With a good marinade, you don't need all that fat to produce flavor.

Historically, marinated flank steak was the original London broil, which is a mode of preparation, not, as many believe, a specific cut of beef (you might see this label in the grocery store, and it can refer to a steak cut from the round or sirloin instead of the flank). Personally, I've never failed to impress with my own preparation, using The Best Meat Marinade in the World, a personal take on the classic London broil, but you can pretty much use any marinade you enjoy. The important thing is, first, to score the steak in a diamond pattern no deeper than one-eighth of an inch, to let the juices sink in and to prevent your steak from curling up as it cooks. Marinate for a few hours, then toss on the grill for only a few minutes, until about medium rare, though cooking to medium won't destroy it. If you have some aromatic wood chips to toss in the grill for further flavor, even better. Finally, after making sure to let the steak sit for about five minutes ("take five, Mr. Steak"), slice it into thin strips about a quarter of an inch thick, making sure to cut across the grain of the meat. As far as steak goes, it's easy, flavorful, and healthy as well as inexpensive, and even a kitchen imbecile could impress and satisfy a small crowd with it. What more could you ask?

Primal Cut #5: Short Plate

Like its neighbor the flank, the short plate—or simply "plate"—comes from the lower section of the cow, underneath the rib. The belly of the beast, if you will. While you can buy the whole, thirty-pound short plate relatively cheaply, there are two cuts that really stand out: short ribs and skirt steak. Short ribs are the bottom section of the steer's rib cage, extending from the chuck to the end of the plate, and are filled with fat and connective tissue, making them substantially tougher than the top ribs. On the other hand, this precious fat adds tremendous flavor to the meat when it's braised or slow-cooked for long periods over very low heat, which is why short ribs are a darling of BBQ enthusiasts. One of my absolute favorite preparations of this is *bulgalbi*, or Korean barbequed short ribs (also known as *galbi*, *kalbi*, *galbee-gui*), which I'm always happy to enjoy alongside some wicked spicy *kimchi* and a couple of OB beers. I love the Koreans for this, as well as for their fantastic use of offal, from beef gelatin to oxtails and all the delicious parts in between. I've never been audacious enough to attempt a *bulgalbi* recipe on my own, partly because of my own fears of culinary ineptitude, but mostly because it gives me a reason to head down to Little Korea.

Then there's skirt steak, an immensely enjoyable cut often passed over for more big-name fare, since it's both tough and fatty, though cheap. One word for anyone who might make that mistake: *fajitas*. Marinated, grilled, and sliced thin and across the grain (much like flank steak), the skirt—that smallish, fan-shaped piece of beef right on the belly of the cow—is actually considered to be "one of the most flavorful of all steaks," according to the *Field Guide to Meat*. If you separate the inside skirt from the less desirable outside skirt (more membrane), you get a kind of beltlike strip, which is actually where the name *fajita* comes from, meaning "little belt" in Spanish, and way more tasty than eating an actual belt. Don't ask how I know this, just trust me. Also, note that you should never cook this cut to any more than medium, after which it starts to get tough. Seriously, skirt steak is a bargain, even a steal, for those who care to take the time to marinate and cook it properly.

That delightful little cut also has a cousin, the hanger steak, known also as "hanging tender" or "butcher's steak." Now why, of every cut of beef, does this one carry the name of the butcher? Like the oysters of a chicken, the hanging tender is often secretly cut and kept by the one preparing the whole animal, because he knows that it's not often called for, not to mention how delicious it is. Hence, the butcher would traditionally keep this little guy for himself. It's kind of hard to locate, unless you know exactly what you're looking for—if you take a good gander at a cow's diaphragm, on the internal side of the carcass, you'll see a dark-colored, oddly shaped wedge of meat that literally "hangs" from it, attached to the last rib. That's the one. Grab it and run before someone else does, because there's only one of these per cow, and the powerful flavor pretty much ensures that someone who knows his meat well (like a butcher, for example) is eager to get to it. It's slightly chewy with a coarse grain, so either marinate it or cook it rare to medium rare, and you'll be a very, very happy carnivore. In fact, I was actually hesitating to tell you about this one, for fear that I'd cause the demand to spike and the price to go up, but ultimately, if you've purchased this book and have committed yourself to the cause of good meat, I think it's only fair you know.

Primal Cuts #6 and #7: Chuck and Brisket

These two are, technically, distinct cuts, but they share many of the same properties: high in flavor and fat, low in tenderness and cost.

Yup, they're tough, cheap, and fatty, which is why cuts from both the chuck (the large upper section of the cow from the neck to the rib, including the shoulder) and the brisket (the "breast" of the animal) are often slow-cooked, barbequed, or braised to ensure maximum tenderness. In the case of my friend Chuck, there are a number of steaks and other cuts that can be sectioned from the primal cut—especially the top blade, which has come to be known as the "flatiron steak" in a remarkable bit of clever marketing—as well as some of the juiciest ground beef to be found on the entire animal (ideal for chili), but my favorite thing to do is to braise a nice big pot roast and serve it family-style.

I love a good chuck roast—cut properly, it looks like a huge, square, thickly marbled brick of meat, a cinder block of pure beef. That fat comes in very handy when you cook it, since the meat is very flavorful but also very tough, hence the long cooking time and braising. My favorite recipe involves seasoning the raw slab of chuck with salt and pepper, then browning each of the sides in a little olive oil. After that, it's into a roasting pan with a broth, a concoction of beef stock, mushrooms, onions, crushed tomatoes, a little red wine, garlic, and whatever herbs I feel might be nice that night. Covered (or tented in foil), it should cook for at least three hours at 300 degrees Fahrenheit, turning halfway through. After that, all that's left is to remove the meat to a cutting board and cook down the remaining broth while you cut the roast into nice half-inch slices. Bingo—pot roast for the whole family.

The same basic principle applies to brisket, the primal cut lying just below the chuck. Brisket has long been praised by barbeque aficionados for the way it becomes incomparably juicy, tender, and flavorful when placed over low coals for, say, half a day. In Texas, BBQ brisket is practically the state dish. For me, however, this cut of beef means something else entirely. If you grew up Jewish in America, chances are high that you have a long-standing, nostalgic fondness for a nice brisket. Not only does it make the very best pastrami and corned beef, but it's often the centerpiece of every traditional religious meal. Lamb might play a crucial part in the Pesach story, but I have an extremely difficult time trying to remember a single Passover dinner throughout my entire life that didn't involve brisket—it seems almost as essentially Jewish as matzo, Manishewitz, and guilt. Again, like its cousin Chuck, brisket should be cured, slow-cooked, or braised to ensure proper tenderness. My cousin Kerry has a brilliant recipe that involves using pineapple juice as one of the braising components, which has the added benefit of using citric acid to further tenderize the meat. Whatever method you decide to use, the real secret behind making a perfect brisket is to cook it the day before you're planning to serve it, and let it sit in the refrigerator overnight to allow all the flavors to really sink in. The following day, simply heat it up in the oven, and you're good to go.

Just make sure to make a double recipe so you'll have some to spare—that leftover brisket makes for a brilliant sandwich.

Primal Cut #8: Round

One of the largest active muscle groups to be found in a cow's body, the round is the entire upper leg, extending from the top of the rump down to the knee, and it makes up about 20 percent of the total retail yield of beef. That means there's a lot of meat to be found there, but since it was primarily used to help the cow to stand and walk around, it's both lean and tough. Still, there's plenty to love. There are six major sections into which the round can be divided: the rump; the four main muscles (top round, sirloin tip, bottom round, and eye of round); and the heel. For the most part, you're not likely to find a lot of cuts from the round in fine dining restaurants, though that's not to say it doesn't have its lovable qualities. There are rump roasts, rump steaks, butterball steak, one version of a London broil (though officially speaking that should come from the flank, remember), top sirloin (the sirloin tip, technically), triangle, bottom round roast, eye of round steaks . . . The list goes on and on. Here's also where you get a lot of your beef for stews

and kebabs, which are always either braised or marinated. The tenderness of the entire round varies, going progressively from the very tough
meat down by the knee joint, to the slightly tender inner thigh, to the
relatively soft top round, which is often used in restaurants and delis to
make roast beef. You know that big, half-football-shaped hunk of meat
steaming at the carving station of a wedding reception buffet? It's likely
from the round, the toughest, leanest part of a steer.

So maybe the round isn't the top shelf of all the primal cuts—that
doesn't mean it should be ignored. I for one have a deep affection for
roast beef sandwiches, especially if the meat is rare, beautifully
browned on the outside and bloody inside, sliced paper thin the way
they serve it at a corner deli in New York. Heat that up and throw it on
a Portuguese roll with some lettuce, tomato, and a squirt of horseradish sauce—crucial when you're talking roast beef—and you have yourself a perfectly contained bit of beefy bliss.

Addendum: Shanks and Oxtails

There are a few parts of a cow that lie in a sort of classification limbo—
neither part of any primal cuts, nor considered offal, since they're still
technically skeletal meat. Most notably on this list are the shanks, or the
animal's shins, and oxtails, which, as you might guess, come from the
tail. Both flavorful and inexpensive, these cuts have long-standing traditions on the tables of the world, despite the fact that they are notoriously lean and tough. When those two attributes combine in the meat
world, you have few choices for preparation except for long, slow braising or stewing until all the tendons and connective tissue melt into gelatin. When prepared with diligence, shanks can provide some truly
sublime dishes. Take osso buco Milanese, for instance, one of the most
famous Italian dishes in the world (the words *osso buco* literally translate to "veal shank"). But you don't have to take it from me; here's what

former U.S. poet laureate Billy Collins had to say about this particular delicacy in his poem "Osso Buco," which appears in the collection *Sailing Alone Around the Room*:

> *I love the sound of the bone against the plate*
> *and the fortress-like look of it*
> *lying before me in a moat of risotto,*
> *the meat soft as the leg of an angel*
> *who has lived a purely airborne existence.*
> *And best of all, the secret marrow,*
> *the invaded privacy of the animal*
> *prized out with a knife and swallowed down*
> *With cold, exhilarating wine.*

In terms of exalting in the pure, simple joys of meat, Collins has accomplished something truly spectacular here: comparing what very well might be, in its raw state, the toughest part of the entire animal to the leg of an angel who's never actually walked upon the ground—that, friends, must have been one *hell* of an osso buco.

On the less formidably haute end of the culinary world, many praise the humble shank because it makes some of the best ground meat for chili, as well as, I was delighted to discover, beef jerky. Not wanting any of dear Ernie to go to waste, Paul used the meat from his shinbones to make what one of his friends fondly referred to as "meat crack," a thin, crispy, chewy, peppered jerky that was better than any dehydrated beef I'd had in my life. And indeed, it was addictive—Paul graciously sent along a generous helping of Ernie jerky several weeks after our butchering day, and it was all but gone in a couple of days, in spite of my every effort to hang on to as much of it as possible to share with friends, and not down it all by myself in a single afternoon, which would have been entirely feasible had I been unable to muster up the willpower to set the stuff aside (it took a lot of willpower). Dried meat has of course been a dietary staple for thousands of years, since dehydrating or curing meat was an essential process in the days before refrigeration. Though beef jerky is easily the most popular type of dried meat, you can make jerky from just about any kind of animal. In fact, the word *jerky* doesn't originate with beef at all but, surprisingly, llama: the Incas of South America referred to the animal, in their Quechua language, as *ch'arki*, and were fond of freeze-drying its meat in the cold, dry Andean air. Which is why it eventually adopted the English name *jerky*, despite the fact that no actual jerking occurs in the process of making it. You can still find charqui today in the same part of the world, though it's now generally made with beef or horsemeat.

Oxtails are often thought to be cousins of beef shanks, since they share a similar appearance, flavor, and texture when crosscut into small cylinders of meat and bone, which is how you'll usually find them at the butcher shop. Originally the term applied only to tails of oxen, but now it refers to those of beef cattle, and it's been used by many cultures as the basis for some truly splendiferous comfort food, usually in soups and stews, from the classic British oxtail soup to braised Korean oxtails, or the ancient Roman dish *coda alla vacchinara*. My favorite, though, comes by way of Jamaica—oxtail curry is a West Indian regional treasure. Like shanks, oxtails release a tremendous amount of gelatin when slowly braised, lending the broth a rich, silky-smooth consistency. So, once again, if you're one of those people laboring under the sad delusion that you'll get the best beef or veal from only the most expensive cuts, here's proof of your folly. Trust me: go to a Jamaican restaurant, preferably one run by the same family for several generations. Order the oxtail curry. I guarantee, when you take that first bite, you won't be lusting after a T-bone.

DOES YOUR MEAT MAKE THE GRADE?

When shopping for meat at the grocery store or at your favorite butcher's, you'll often see words like *prime*, *choice*, or *select* on the packaging. Most people know that these terms refer to the quality of the beef as determined by the USDA, and bear much weight not just on the taste but also on the price of your meat. But how do the inspectors make that call? What's the process? What is it about a steak (or a cow, for that matter) that makes it worthy of the finest steakhouses, and what condemns beef to the pet food plant?

First, unlike USDA inspection, grading isn't mandatory for the retail sale of meat. However, having that prime or choice stamp on your ranch's beef will help you get the best price when selling to retailers, so many farmers and producers voluntarily pony up to bring in an official, licensed inspector from the Food Safety and Inspection Service (FSIS), an agency in the USDA. Most cursory explanations of how the beef-grading system works will say a little about the most crucial factors—marbling and age— and that's about it. Fact is, the FSIS has rather extensive guidelines and regulations for how meat makes the grade, using its own system of complicated, algebra-like formulas, symbols, and variables. This is serious business. The process goes something like this: First, the inspectors take a look at a side of beef—specifically the surface of the rib-eye muscle after the carcass has been cut between the twelfth and thirteenth ribs—and evaluate it for the quality and abundance of the intramuscular fat, what we know as marbling. According to the beef-grading guide provided by the Texas A&M Meat Sciences Department, "Each degree of marbling is divided into 100 subunits. In general, however, marbling scores are discussed in tenths within each degree of marbling (e.g., Slight[90], Small[100], Small[110])." Using these subunits, the top four grades—prime, choice, select, and standard, respectively—are further subdivided into three categories to give them their total marbling score, represented by the symbols +, °, and –. So, for instance, prime beef can be graded as Prime[+] (abundant marbling); Prime° (moderately abundant); or Prime[-] (slightly abundant). The marbling score adjectives continue to decline from there, going from *moderate* to *modest*, *small*, *slight*, *traces*, and, finally, *practically devoid*. After the fat's been duly appraised, the inspector examines other qualities of the lean, looking for desirable color and texture. So say the A&M meat masters: "Desirable rib eyes will exhibit an adequate amount of finely dispersed marbling in a firm, fine textured, bright, cherry-red colored lean. As an animal matures, the characteristics of muscle change, and muscle color becomes darker and muscle texture becomes coarser."

Which brings us to the second key attribute determining USDA grade: maturity. The most desirable beef comes from cows between the ages of nine and thirty months, the younger the better, since this results in rosier, more supple steaks and chops. Because the inspectors rarely know the actual age of the animal, they rely on anatomical cues to determine the approximate age, and hence the maturity rating, on a scale of A to E (no, your steak can't get an F for being too old). First is color and texture—the youngest and hence most desirable beef will have a very fine texture and a light, cherry-red color to the lean (maturity grade A). As the texture goes from fine to moderately fine, slightly coarse, and coarse, the rating declines, and it does the same as the meat gets progressively older and its color becomes a darker red.

In addition to color and texture, other critical factors include the ossification of the cartilage in the vertebrae and the bone characteristics. As a cow matures, its vertebral cartilage begins to turn into bone (a process called "ossification"), so inspectors look for the fusion of certain parts of the spinal column, beginning with the sacral vertebrae, the first to ossify; then it's on to the lumbar and thoracic vertebrae. They also scrutinize the condition of the split chine bones (the top of the T in a T-bone steak), which go from "red, porous and extremely soft" (A), to "white, nonporous, extremely hard" (E), as well as the rib bones, which grow from narrow and oval (A) to wide and flat (E). All of these factors help determine the grade of the entire carcass, and when all is said and done, you get a bunch of equations that look like this:

$$B60 + A80 = B30 \ (>40; 10\% \text{ to bone})$$

Again, this is pretty complex stuff, and I haven't even discussed the intricacies of calculating a carcass's "yield." It takes a budding inspector at least two years of schooling and another two years of experience in the meat industry to even begin examining beef for the USDA. Much as you might be suspicious of our government, I think there's little doubt that they take meat seriously.

So what does this all mean to you, the discerning carnivore? Now that you have a basic understanding of the FSIS rating system, you can consider the same characteristics of a steer's meat when you go to buy your steak. Note that you'll rarely find prime beef in a store—most of it, as you might guess, will sell to restaurants to be marked up considerably further, which is why you end up paying about forty bucks for a prime porterhouse at a top-end steak joint. But just because it isn't prime doesn't mean that it's not good—choice beef is both tender and flavorful, and at a fraction of the cost. When looking for a nice cut at the store, try pretending you're one of those FSIS meat geeks. Take a look at the bones, the texture and color of the lean, the amount of marbling. Sometimes, if you're lucky, you can find a low-level prime steak that might have been graded upper-tier choice by mistake. Who knows, maybe when it came to grading that one, it was the end of the day, the inspector just wanted to get home to his family or have a couple of beers with the guys, and he made a very slight judgment error. No one's perfect. If you're keen enough to notice the difference, when you take that sucker off the grill or out of the pan you can pat yourself twice on the back for being such a discriminating, not to mention economical, carnivore.

At the minimum, you'll know not to choose "select" or "standard" grades if you're looking for a truly nice crown roast, and that "select" is great to grind for burgers, chili, and tacos. Just be sure to steer clear of the bottom four grades, which you won't even find stamped on meat in the grocery store: commercial, utility, cutter, and—worst of the bunch—canner. Think about the phrase *utility-grade meat* the next time you're at that fast-food restaurant drive-through and see if you don't start to have second thoughts. And what could cutter meat possibly include? How about those spiced beef sticks you pick up on a whim at the convenience store, for instance? They don't seem that appetizing now, do they? As for canner, the lowest of the low . . . well, consider those deplorable tinned items known as "potted meat." That or pet food, take your pick. If there's ever been a moment in your life when, for whatever maladjusted, irrational reason, you've considered sampling potted meat, I hope this little nugget of info will set you straight. Come on, you're above dog food, aren't you?

CHAPTER 14

This Is Going to Be Offal

Now for the real fun. Of all the tests I'd faced, I have to say that the coming challenge was one I'd most looked forward to: offal. Also known by the more pleasant euphemism *variety meats*, offal is what's left over after all the skeletal meats (including ribs, chops, roasts, steaks, and ground meat) have been duly butchered and portioned away. The term actually derives from the words *off* and *fall*, as in, "Hey Gus, check out all this weird stuff that fell off the cutting table while I was butchering this hog!" Yes, I'm talking about organs—brains, glands, tongue, headcheese, kidneys, livers, intestines—but also bone marrow, blood, and all the other wonderfully savory but rarely appreciated bits of the animal left hanging around after all the rosy roasts and supple steaks have been sold to the highest bidder. There's a universe of flavors and textures to be found in this stuff, but only for those with the constitution to seek it out, order it in a restaurant, or, the ultimate test, cook it for themselves. I would do all of it.

"But why?" many ask. "Why eat all those weird organs and scraps when you don't have to? Why not just have a nice prime rib to satisfy your meat lust and call it a day?" Because, my friends, a true carnivore is an explorer, a meat Magellan ready to discover every delicious wonder that animals provide. I love offal, and not because I'm trying to prove something or freak people out. It's not like I'm eating these things on a dare—I genuinely enjoy them. But it's not just a matter of taste. Like the Native Americans, who have long been known to use every part of an animal, it's critical for all carnivores to appreciate that a cow, pig, or sheep isn't simply a collection of fine prime beef, pork tenderloin, bacon, or lamb chops. If you're going to eat an animal, why not *eat an animal*? Wouldn't anything less seem wasteful? And did I mention that, properly prepared, offal tastes amazing? That alone should have you sold, unless you're one of those alien creatures, the "food as fuel" beings who view mealtime less as a source of profound pleasure than a trip to the filling station. I have no use for these people, who would probably be happy to get all their nourishment in pill form. They might as well live on the moon, for all I care—they don't deserve what the earth has to offer. Me, I want my organ meats. As James Joyce puts it in *Ulysses*, when we first encounter the novel's protagonist:

> Mr. Leopold Bloom ate with relish the inner organs of beasts and fowls. He liked thick giblet soup, nutty gizzards, a stuffed roast heart, liverslices fried with breadcrumbs, fried hencods' roes. Most of all he liked grilled mutton kidneys which gave to his palate a fine tang of faintly scented urine.

What a meal! Okay, I could probably do without the taste of urine (the French usually prepare their *rognon de veau* with a mustard sauce expressly to counterbalance that particular flavor), but I certainly love a good serving of kidneys.

Bearing all this in mind, I could scarcely wait to begin. Now, many "off-icionados" take the pig as their animal of choice when it comes to organs. The pioneering and much feted British chef Fergus Henderson comes to mind here—he literally wrote the book on the subject, a world-renowned cookbook entitled *The Whole Beast: Nose to Tail Eating*, which celebrates such recipes as "duck hearts on toast," "crispy pigs' tails," even "blood cake and fried eggs." That, friends, is really the breakfast of champions. Still, while I exalt in my porky delicacies, my challenge was limited to the cow, so I'd have to stick with that. Veal calves not only provide some of the most tender meat, they also offer up some of the best offal to be found. But where to begin?

Less Fries, More Balls

Let's face it: most people do not eat testicles. There are many reasons for this, chief among them the general squeamishness and seat shifting of men when confronted with the idea. Then again, some people love their bull testes, so much so, in fact, that there is a festival every year in Montana celebrating what are affectionately known as "Rocky Mountain oysters." As soon as I found this out, I knew I had to attend. If ever there was a true salute to the carnivorous cause, this had to be it. I checked my schedule, and seeing that the twenty-fourth annual Testicle Festival (aka "Testy Festy") was coming up soon, I made plans to check it out. I'd fly into Portland, Oregon, to meet up with my brother Eric, and we'd drive together to Missoula, Montana, fortunately the current home of a few of Eric's friends from New Orleans, who offered us a place to crash when we weren't eating testicles and doing God knows what else Testy Festy attendees do. It seemed like fun, a good opportunity to start my offal odyssey and visit a part of the country I'd never seen before, as well as a chance to spend time with my brother, which we didn't often have now that we lived on opposite coasts. Little did we know what we were about to experience.

Oh, Testicle Festival . . . where can one even begin? First, I suppose I have to say that if you've never been there, Montana is jaw-droppingly gorgeous. For a person who grew up in a part of the country so flat that the city manually constructs a hill so that local children can have the experience of, well, having a hill, getting an eyeful of those purple mountains' majesty is a truly spectacular thing. As Eric and I headed along the Columbia River valley in Oregon, briefly dipping into Idaho and then to Montana, I couldn't help but be agog, wide-eyed at the unfolding natural splendor around us, the massive peaks wreathed in clouds and just showing the first signs of snow at their tips, what mountain folk call termination dust, because it signals the end of summer. This, I thought, was true mountain country. There will be manly men here, burly dudes who ride horses and motorcycles, who ranch and have massive beards and eat meat and don't take shit from anyone. That stereotype, I quickly learned, didn't quite apply to the city of Missoula as a whole. Naturally, there was plenty of excellent meat available, but it's also a fairly progressive town, a college town. At one of the local restaurants, not only could you get a locally ranched buffalo burger, they offered tempeh sandwiches as well. This was not the Montana of my mind's eye, not really. We'd have to go out to Rock Creek for that.

When Damon, our host, told his roommates that we were in town to attend the Testicle Festival, they were genuinely surprised. None of them, in the years they'd lived there, had been to the fest. We extended an invitation, but they balked. "I dunno," said one, clearly apprehensive about the prospect. "I've heard stories . . ." Stories? What kind of stories, I wondered. Stories about testicles? How weird could it be?

Well, pretty weird, to put it mildly. After having lived through more than my fair share of carnival seasons in New Orleans, what with the French Quarter and all the sin and depravity that are its hallmarks, I thought little could astonish me as far as drunken revelry was concerned, but Testy Festy actually gave me something of a culture shock. And in my own country, no less! It was like a crazy, redneck mountain Mardi Gras—"Mountain Gras," if you will—replete with every possible debauchery imaginable. And I use the word *redneck* affectionately here, I hasten to add, employing Jeff Foxworthy's definition of the term as a "glorious absence of sophistication." There were many things to be found at Testy Festy, but sophistication was definitely not among them.

As we pulled off the highway and drove down into the canyon housing the Rock Creek Lodge, we passed a checkpoint with local and state police officers standing vigilant over the festival below. You know you're in for a ride when the presence of law enforcement is required— it was a clear signal that the sense of decorum and mutual respect of the people living it up down there were not to be trusted. Eric and I paid our admission (fifteen dollars for the whole weekend, plus free entry into a raffle for a refurbished 1984 Chevy pickup), parked, and walked down to the lodge itself. It was almost as though we'd entered a time warp. Aside from the prevalence of digital cameras and cell phones, all cultural cues indicated that we might as well be in the parking lot of a Dokken concert circa 1987: girls with teased hair and that poofed-out claw of bangs, dudes in mullets and acid-washed jeans, a veritable ocean of cigarettes, leather, mustaches, and tattoo ink. The music of choice, blaring from loudspeakers throughout the weekend, was all hair metal and classic rock: Judas Priest, Mötley Crüe, Black Sabbath, AC/DC. It became immediately apparent that this wasn't just Testicle Festival in the literal sense that people were eating prairie oysters; this was *testicle* festival, figuratively, an unabashed, unforgiving, and truly shameless celebration of American testosterone.

It was awesome.

We walked the grounds, taking a survey of the festival's offerings, transfixed by this brazen salute to redneck culture. It was like spring break for every person that had ever been on *The Jerry Springer Show*, crossed with the massive annual motorcycle rally in Sturgis, only without all those poseur dentists and accountants. A line of polished Harleys and Yamahas stood gleaming outside the bar as their owners, guys who all seemed to resemble Lemmy from Motörhead, awaited the "nice bike" contest. And if you had any difficulty guessing the basic demographic of Testy Festy-ites, you could easily tell by the brands giving away free promotional swag, most notably Swisher Sweets cigars and what appeared to be a three-foot-tall box filled with discount, off-brand chewing tobacco, which festival-goers took by the handful. Two representative samples of Testy Festy enthusiasts, one of each gender, included:

1. A late-middle-aged man with a silver beard, double-fisting cans of Bud and wearing a tinfoil-wrapped cardboard box on his head that bore two deep, semicircular cutaways and lettering announcing "Free Mammograms," as well as a shirt with "UNFUCKING-BELIEVABLE" plastered on it.
2. A woman, with easily more than fifty years of hard living behind her, clad in leather chaps, panties, and vest, clenching a smoking Lite 100 cigarette between her teeth as she flashed her sagging bosom to anyone willing to give her Mardi Gras beads, despite the fact that Mardi Gras was five months and several thousand miles away.

No two ways about it: this was America.

What happened during the two and half days of the festival was this—there were a number of special events, eagerly viewed by mobs of attendees, between which everyone would eat some testes and then go inside to the bar and continue getting plowed on whiskey and Kokanee beer, or into the gift shop to purchase merchandise from the seemingly endless array of Testy Festy T-shirts, hats, jackets, bumper stickers, aprons, beer cozies, belt buckles, hot sauce, key chains, post-cards, and—I swear—official Testicle Festival wind chimes. For a small fee, you could also have your photo taken riding Gunsmoke, a taxidermied former rodeo bull who now stood, battered and shabby, his hind legs kicking up in an eternal buck, set against a backdrop photograph of a cheering audience, or with Big Thunder, a similarly preserved buffalo. I couldn't help but be a little sad for poor Gunsmoke and Big

Thunder—whatever their offenses on this earth, surely they'd earned a better fate than this.

Among the scheduled events, there was the "Undy 500," a tricycle race between pants-less, mostly inebriated guys; a game of "Bullshit Bingo," wherein two cows were brought to stand on a floor of plotted squares, and the first person to have their purchased square duly crapped upon would win two hundred bucks; a "nut-eating contest"; a hairy chest contest; the above-mentioned motorcycle competition; oil wrestling; and, naturally, a tattoo contest. The main draw for the weekend, however—other than the general bacchanalia that would ensue in the evenings once everyone was good and blotto—was the wet T-shirt contest. Now, I'm not the type of person who avidly seeks out such banal presentations of flesh, but hey, if it's there, I'm not one to miss it. I'd paid my entrance fee, after all, so I might as well get myself an eyeful of nakedness, and besides, this was all in the name of research.

In the days following the festival, when my friends asked me to describe the "show" that Eric and I witnessed that afternoon in Montana, I was hard pressed to come up with adjectives that could adequately express my true feelings. "Basically," I told them, "my eyes have seen things that they will never, until the day I die, be able to unsee." The much-anticipated wet T-shirt competition was essentially a version of the kind you might see if you're on spring break in hot spots like South Padre Island or Daytona Beach (the titular concept of a shirt soaking being a flimsy way to advertise eventual, fully nude frolicking), but with one major distinction: unlike those spectacles, which are populated exclusively by lithe, comely coeds, here there seemed to be no restrictions whatsoever holding back potential contestants on the basis of their age, weight, or general attractiveness. This struck me as extraordinarily American and democratic—if you have the chutzpah to shake your wet, semiclad moneymaker onstage in the forty-five-degree mountain chill in front of a couple hundred jeering bikers, speed freaks, and assorted rednecks, then you have earned the right to compete for the brass ring, in this case five hundred bucks. On the other hand, there are some people who ought to get naked in public, and others who probably shouldn't. Most people I know fall into the latter category, even more so, it turned out, at Testicle Festival. Yes, there were two quite lovely contestants, bless their hearts, but for the most part the big event was a cavalcade of cellulite, stretch marks, Caesarian scars, faded tattoos, fat rolls, and ass pimples. The crowd alternately cheered on the more appealing women ("Jam out with your clam out!" a man beside me hollered repeatedly) and groaned in revulsion at the others. This latter group included a woman who, were it not for her breast implants and what appeared to be a wig, could easily have passed as somebody's drunken grandfather—a gnarled, leathery, half-nude, transsexual Rumpelstiltskin. It is an image that will forever haunt my dreams.

To counteract the effects of the show, and perhaps attempt to erase some of the images that had burned themselves into our brains, Eric and I headed back to the car to smoke a joint, drink a couple of beers in peace, and regroup. When we got there, we were happily greeted by our parking lot neighbors, who were quick to offer us up a couple of Jell-O shots and regale us, Skoal packed firmly in their bottom lips, with tales of Testy Festys past and all the raunchiness they'd either been party to or that simply occurred next to them, everything up to and including sex on the picnic tables in front of cheering fans. "My God," said Eric once they'd sauntered up the hill to the festival. "Where *are* we?"

With all of the extraordinary happenings around us, it was easy to forget the primary reason I'd come to the festival in the first place: *balls*. As with everything else at the Rock Creek Lodge that weekend, the testosterone theme prevailed. Not only were we availed of steam trays filled with deep-fried bull testicles, it seemed that every menu choice was what could be called "man food," everything from burgers and chicken strips to grilled whole turkey legs, and let me tell you, there are few things that communicate that you are a red-blooded male more than gnawing on the entire leg of an animal, Hägar the Horrible–style. Waiting in the food line ahead of us, one man asked for a menu substitution. "Less fries, more balls," he demanded, and instead of being served the standard pairing of Rocky Mountain oysters (RMOs) and French fries, he got an entire plate filled with deep-fried bull testicles. By the time it was my turn to order, the woman behind the steam trays informed me that they'd just run out of fries, and that if I wanted some I'd have to wait until they could cook up another batch. Eric and I shared a glance, and we both knew, without having to say it, what to do. "Less fries, more balls," I said.

As alarming as they sound as a menu choice, bull testicles turned out to be something less than exotic. Pounded flat, breaded, and deep-fried, they resembled nothing so much as circular pieces of fried chicken—Testicle McNuggets, if you will (although I doubt Ronald McDonald will be advertising them next to the Big Macs anytime soon). It was bar food, the kind of snack you'd dip into tartar sauce, ketchup, or ranch dressing and munch on as you watched the Sunday afternoon football game, and if no one expressly went out of their way to tell you what they were, you'd likely never know. This was all fine by me, because I love bar food. We deep-fry just about anything in the South— meat, seafood, pickles, Oreos, you name it. The humble fried oyster po-boy (genuine oysters, the ones from the water, not the prairie) has long been one of my favorite New Orleans specialties. The problem I encountered was that, as a carnivore and a fan of offal, I really wanted to find out what bull testicles taste like,* and all one can initially discern when biting into one of these nut nuggets is the fried breading and whatever you dipped it in, in my case ketchup and hot sauce. So I made my way slowly through one of the "oysters," without any sauce, doing my best to get the flavor core, the essential "testicleness" of the testicles. After a few moments, it came through: veal cutlets. Aside from a slightly chewy consistency, these balls were very much like the kind of breaded veal cutlet you'd order smothered in marinara and Parmesan cheese at any Southern Italian restaurant—tender, with a mild beefy flavor.

---

* Insert your own joke at my expense here.

Yes, they were tasty. I enjoyed my whole plate of testicular good-ness, and would order up two more by the time Eric and I headed back into Missoula at the end of the festival, but not befroe we'd observed a mind-exploding array of licentious human behavior. That Saturday night alone, at the height of the party, we would witness extreme intox-ication, drug abuse, fully naked tabletop dancing, lesbian sex acts be-tween two apparent strangers, a sexual impropriety resulting in a ferocious fistfight, and an even more ferocious response to that fight by the police, as well as a truck raffle . . . and all within the span of twelve minutes. Basically, it was what I imagined an average weekend evening in Gomorrah might have been like.

And how did this experience resonate with my brother and me? The next day, we started making plans to return the following year, for the twenty-fifth annual Testicle Festival. It would be the fest's silver an-niversary, after all. How could we miss that?

There's Nothing Like Really Good Head

There are some organ meats that carnivores with moderate kitchen skills can prepare on their own without any undue fuss. Sautéing a liver, for instance, is far from rocket science. With others, unless you've spent years apprenticing to a butcher or a master chef, you'd be daft to attempt them yourself. Which is to say I wasn't taking any chances when it came to headcheese.

It's always been a mystery to me why, with the varied range of non-scary euphemisms and foreign names for this dish—such as *souse, pres-sack,* and *salceson*—we Americans have to choose the absolutely most disgusting-sounding one. Even the British refer to it as *brawn*. The words *head* and *cheese* paired together do little to inspire gustatory en-thusiasm. In fact, for many they do the opposite. Truth be told, head-cheese is nowhere near as horrifying as its name implies—there is no cheese, per se, but there is certainly a head, usually from a veal calf, pig, or sheep, which is emptied of organs (eyes, brain, tongue, and so on), then boiled for a long time until the skull is completely clean. The next step is to mix all the delicate scraps of flesh with spices and a gelatinous broth in a loaf pan or other mold. When you allow the resulting matter to cool, it forms a delicious terrine, or "loaf," of gelatin and savory chunks of meat. Cross-sectioned, it appears similar to one of those Jell-O desserts your grandmother might make, only instead of fruit or marshmallows floating around inside, you get little hunks of head flesh. Perhaps headcheese could be rebranded as Meat-O to make it sound more appealing. Just a thought.

Hog headcheese is a many-splendored thing, if you're into pork, and not at all something you should avoid if you're a squeamish eater. It's just meat and gelatin, after all, and the fact that it came from an animal's head is nothing to get into a snit about. You probably don't want to think about it, but if you've eaten a regular American hot dog in your life, there's more than a solid chance you've eaten pig snouts (not to mention a variety of other piggy parts like ears and tails) anyway. So why be picky now? Served in bite-sized cubes as an appetizer or sliced thinly and used as a sandwich meat, hog headcheese is a soft, richly flavored treat. If you haven't had it yet, do yourself a favor and give it a try. You can usually find fresh headcheese in most butcher shops and even at the deli department of many upscale supermarkets.

To get some head, so to speak, I had a few friends join me at a Manhattan restaurant that's the perfect spot for adventurous meat lovers looking for offbeat delights but less than willing to take out a second mortgage for the privilege: David Chang's Momofuku Ssäm. Chang is from the new breed of cooks, spawned by Fergus Henderson's take-no-prisoners approach to animal parts, whose restaurants are safe havens for carnivores, guys like Mario Batali, whose signature dish at Babbo, his signature restaurant, is beef cheek ravioli, and at another, Otto, is pizza topped with pure hog lard. *New York* magazine referred to these chefs as part of the "refined meathead" school of cuisine. If that were an actual school rather than a figurative one, I'd be enrolled faster than you can say "fatback." Momofuku Ssäm is Chang's second restaurant, the first being a noodle bar; both are located in the very hip, very vegetarian-friendly East Village. That hasn't been without its problems and confrontations: when he was screamed at and threatened over the phone by a vegetarian who'd consumed one of his broths, little knowing that it was meat based ("None of our broths are vegetarian," he said), his immediate reaction was not to apologize and, duly chastised, cater to the whims of the cabbage-head set, but rather to yank every vegetarian option but one (ginger scallion noodles) and to put pork in almost everything else. Plus, his restaurants also tend to be filled not with the soft, dulcet tones of harps and string quartets, but rather with Jimi Hendrix, Pearl Jam, and the Who.

My kind of guy.

There are lots of tasty treats on Momofuku's menu, but I was particularly drawn to Chang's take on variety meats. In fact, it's the only menu I've yet seen with a section simply labeled "Offal." Even better, none of the offal selections were more than about fifteen bucks, meaning that my three friends and I would be able to taste almost everything—as well as a Birkshire pork ssäm (a Korean version of a burrito), pork buns, and a hanger steak special—without worrying about having to eat nothing but cup-of-noodles and PB and Js for the following week, until our bank accounts returned to normal. Up first, naturally, was headcheese, in this case long, thinly sliced strips of the house-made "veal head terrine," served with a selection of their signature pickles and a few grilled slices of ciabatta bread. To confess, I'd tasted this delicacy before, as part of a *bahn-mi*, or three-terrine Vietnamese sandwich (it also contained ham and chicken liver pâté), which was so delicious it very nearly made me cry. I didn't know what it was, precisely, that made it so good, whether it was a single ingredient or a combination of everything, so I was just dying to sample that headcheese on its own. One bite, and the secret was revealed: it was definitely the headcheese. As soft as a great carpaccio (only not raw), the unctuous gelatin mixed with the buttery meat and the Korean flavors to produce a singular explosion of textures and tastes. It nearly dissolved in my mouth, it was so delicate, leaving behind it all the flavor of tender veal without any of the chewing. Marvelous. Once more, I was bewildered at the squeamishness with which people approach this delicacy—if you enjoy meat, what does it matter what part of the animal it came from if it's so damned good?

It's a Glandular Thing

Headcheese appropriately devoured—even by Liz, who'd eschewed the *cuy* in favor of "steak in Ecuadorian steak"—it was time to move on to Momofuku's next offal choice: sweetbreads. Of the foods that are completely different from what they sound like, sweetbreads are easily the most confounding. Much to the horror and revulsion of clueless diners who might order this delicacy thinking that it might be some sort of sugary, starchy confection (and who may have been misled by a particularly spiteful waiter), in reality the sweetbreads are either the thymus or pancreas glands of an animal, usually a veal calf, but sometimes lamb, particularly in Turkish cuisine. It's almost as though someone thought about this stuff, then specifically gave it a name directly opposite to its nature just to mess with people, or maybe pull a fast one. Something like this, perhaps:

> BUTCHER FRED: Hey, Maurice, why can't we seem to sell all of this weird glandular meat Rancher Bob sold us on the cheap? I tried it, and it's really good.
>
> BUTCHER MAURICE: I don't know, man . . . People just seem to get freaked out when I try to sell them on it.
>
> FRED: Hmmm . . . what are you calling it?

MAURICE: "Weird glandular meat we got on the cheap."

FRED: Well, there's your problem! You can't tell people about strange cheap organs and expect to make them hungry. We need to market it better, maybe give it a new name, something, I dunno, lovely sounding. Like "sugarmeats" or "candy steak."

MAURICE: How about "sweetbreads"?

FRED: Perfect!

Apparently, the marketing gimmick worked, and the masses came to appreciate this strange dish, making sweetbreads some of the most sought-after, and hence highly priced, offal on the market, rich in both creamy flavor and texture. Then there's the butter—the classic French preparation includes dusting the organ in flour, sautéing it in butter, and then topping it with a *beurre noir*—which further adds to the organ's appeal. Once more, no matter how much people cringe at the idea of eating weird bits of an animal—especially glands—I have to say that these weird bits are, like Lucky Charms, magically delicious. I remember the first time I ordered sweetbreads, at Brigtsen's, one of my very favorite French-inspired New Orleans restaurants. "You know what that is, right?" the waitress asked with a raised eyebrow, concerned that I know what to expect. I replied that I did, and asked if it was a recommended dish. "Oh, honey," she said, in that endearing way that New Orleans folk do, "you're gonna *love* it." She was right, of course. One adventurous bite into my sautéed thymus gland and I was hooked; it was intensely rich and buttery, with a familiar consistency that reminded me of something soft and wonderful that I couldn't readily place. I'd ordered the dish a number of times in the ensuing years, usually to great satisfaction, but no matter how much I racked my brain, I'd never quite been able to put a mental finger on what exactly the texture reminded me of.

This was part of my quest when I ordered the sweetbreads at

Momofuku. As an added bonus, the preparation was a new one for me. Instead of the standard French butter preparation, Chang decided instead to simply grill the sweetbreads and serve the dish garnished with only a lime wedge, some coarse sea salt, and a side of pickled vegetables. It looked like nothing if not a char-grilled chicken breast, pale white with black lines where they'd been seared. But lo, if only chicken tasted like this. The smoky grill flavor was powerful at first, followed by the sea salt and the acid from the lime juice, but then, after careful chewing, there it was, that elusive texture. Like a cartoon flashbulb popping above my head, it came to me: oysters. Sweetbreads have the same luxurious suppleness to them as freshly grilled oysters, a quality I looked forward to enjoying at my favorite seafood haunts every time I visited my hometown, something that had provided me with evenings of pure gustatory joy for years. It was a brilliant surprise, and a relief to have finally discovered something that had eluded me for so long. So now I can freely say, if you like grilled oysters, which are not scary in the least, you'll appreciate sweetbreads.

On the other hand, as with headcheese and many other variety meats, this is a dish I will order only at restaurants I know to be trustworthy and conscientious with their food. It should go without saying that, as with any meat, low-quality offal, or that which has been poorly stored or prepared, should be avoided like a pail of plague. But if you happen to see sweetbreads or headcheese or similar organs on the menu of an establishment you or your trustworthy friends have long enjoyed, I say go forth and enjoy. I might also note that if you're an oenophile, you should think of wine pairings with sweetbreads the same way you think of foie gras—it's best to go with a crisp, dry wine to cut through the richness of the dish, which can be heavy, especially if it's been cooked with a tub of butter. Me, I'm severely impaired when it comes to wine knowledge, so a nice glass of beer did the trick at Momofuku. Not that we were done with our offal tour at this restaurant. Still one more to go . . .

You Expect Me to Swallow This Tripe?

There are some types of offal, such as headcheese, that require a long and careful preparation and others, like sweetbreads, that tend to be on the pricey side. Luckily enough for adventurous carnivores, there do exist several other organ meats that are both inexpensive and plentiful. Enter tripe. As noted previously, cows have evolved a sort of Rube Goldberg digestive system that involves a series of four different stomachs, all in the name of best digesting and extracting nutrition from grass, which most other nonruminant animals cannot do. As a result, those stomachs make up a large part of what you'll find on the inside of a cow. When cooked, they (or parts of them, most often the stomach lining) become tripe, of which there are several varieties: honeycomb and pocket tripe come from the reticulum; smooth, or blanket, tripe is derived from the rumen; and the stomach called the omasum provides us with book, or bible, tripe. The fourth stomach, the abomasum, is rarely used because of its glandular content, but when it is, it produces reed tripe. In beef-eating parts of the world, tripe is largely cheap, abundant, and nutritious, which explains its popularity across dozens of countries and cultures, from haute cuisine (*The Food Lover's Companion* lists the Norman dish *tripes à la mode de Caen* as one of the most famous French preparations) to more rustic, peasant-style dishes such as the Mexican tripe soup called *menudo*, which is beloved both as a national dish and as a hangover cure. (Forget aspirin and Pepto . . . get yourself some beef tripe after a long night on the town!) Pig intestines, or chitterlings, are another tripe many people enjoy, especially as a soul food staple (the string of "safe" venues for African-American performers throughout the East and South during the Jim Crow era was called the "chitlin circuit"). And yet, despite the widespread consumption and enjoyment of this food, its name is also synonymous with garbage, as in "I've never seen such a load of tripe put forth by a president in my life!" Go figure.

Now, saying that you're going out to enjoy a dish made from the stomach lining of a cow is going to actually turn stomachs in most circles. But thanks to meathead chefs like Batali and Chang, tripe is on its way back. As our last dish at Momofuku, when we already had ingested several organs so far and were beginning to slow down, I couldn't help but order the tripe soup, a Korean-influenced take on *menudo*. I'd be happy I did. Based in a hot, savory, and spicy tomato broth, this tripe was far, far from garbage. It was honeycomb tripe, the most popular variety, so called because of its pale color and texture of interlocking hexagons. Sure, it may look a little weird, but that has no bearing whatsoever on its taste or texture, which was slightly chewy with a very mild beef flavor. So the next time you see that strange, white, blanketlike object in your butcher's case, know that it is tripe, and know that it is good.

The Horror!

As you may have noticed, throughout the course of researching this manifesto I had the opportunity to eat some outrageous stuff, most of which was really quite good. Not all of it, though. Working my way through the cow piece by piece, I would in fact have one encounter with meat that was just plain horrifying. So I have to say, based on personal experience alone, I cannot in good conscience recommend that you eat a bull's penis.

That's right, bull penis. Or "pizzle," if you will. In many cultures, an animal's schlong is prepared—boiled, grilled, stewed, dried, and powdered—and ingested as a means of giving a man's virility a boost. From elk to tiger to water buffalo, downing a schwantz has long been considered the original Viagra. In certain parts of Malaysia, a bull's dong is stewed to make a dish called "torpedo soup," which likely entices wiseacre tourists to order it for the opportunity to test their manhood and, I'm sure, have a chance to cry out, "You sank my battleship!"

Unfortunately, I was unable to locate a good Malaysian restaurant in the city offering up this delicacy ("why is it so hard to find a good penis these days?" a female friend noted wryly), although I did discover a Japanese restaurant that claimed it as one of their specialties. When I finally mustered up the yang to eat wang and headed down to St. Mark's Place with a few of my buddies, there were a number of factors that should have set off big, loud warning sirens in my mind. First, I should note that the place was an izakaya, which in Japanese essentially translates to "place in which we guzzle beer and sake until we're positively pontooned." Izakayas are, first and foremost, drinking dens, establishments that hardworking, stressed-out salarymen can visit after work to blow off some steam, drink themselves stupid, and get a little food. Since everyone knows you should have some carbs and protein in your system if you plan on drinking your face off, most izakayas offer a range of cheap dishes, mostly yakitori and ramen, but in the case of Kenka, the place I patronized for my pizzle needs, the selection was more extensive. On sitting down to the table with our first of many pitchers of beer and giving the menu a once-over, we discovered dozens of intriguing (read: bizarre) offerings, everything from pan-fried beef intestines (tripe, per above) and liver sashimi to turkey testicles and, of course, bull penis. Now, I love a big, exotic menu, but there were a few things that were a little *off* . . .

Alarm bell #1: Menu design. For some reason—and I don't know whether this was a cultural disconnect between my Western design sensibilities and those of the Japanese—on the menu was a picture of an attractive Asian woman, clad in a bikini, who looked as though she'd just been released from the hospital after being run over by a dozen Yakuzas on crotch rockets: bruised, bloodied, and bandaged, her arm in a sling and her head mummified in gauze. This, we all noted, was really, really weird, and not particularly conducive to piquing one's appetite.

Alarm bell #2: All over the menu were stern, disconcerting warnings to Kenka's patrons, admonishing them not to behave poorly. And by "behaving poorly," I don't mean answering your cell phone in the middle of the restaurant. Prohibited activities, as spelled out in the menu, included fighting, breaking glasses and dishes, masturbating, doing drugs, having sex, and vomiting anywhere but inside the toilet, which would result in not only having to mop up the offending spew yourself, but also a twenty-dollar fine. "I was wondering what the going rate for blowing chunks in a restaurant was," said my friend Blake. I'd love to see these caveats on the menu at, say, Le Bernardin. Was a place where such behavior required an actual written warning to customers on the menu really a place I could count on for diligent preparation of a bull's stiffy? Multiply my concern by two.

Alarm bell #3: The price. According to the bashed-up-lady specials menu, my plate of beef tallywhacker cost only $5.50. Not that I was looking to spend a fortune, but just under six bucks is hardly a lot of money for an exotic specialty dish, and certainly an insult to the bull. ("They're selling my Johnson for *what?*" he might be screaming up in the great Green Acres in the sky.)

But it was not all wacky menus and alarm bells at Kenka. The beer was flowing freely, and as you might expect, the dish I was on a mission to eat that evening provided us mountains of material on which to humorously riff. For instance, knowing that in a culinary context penis is often known as "pizzle," it's all but impossible not to immediately start talking in Snoop Dogg's signature dialect: "I'm gonna eat that pizzle!" "Fa shizzle? Tha pizzle?" "Yeah, that pizzle *is* the shizzle, fa rizzle my mizzle!" Perhaps it loses something in the translation—or maybe you need at least one pitcher of cold Sapporo in you to truly appreciate it— but it was all we could do not to fall off our wooden stools, laughing. Plus, I think it's easy to understand that, by the end of the evening, the proportion of dick jokes to all other conversation topics had spiked clear through the top of the chart. All of a sudden, those warnings on the menu didn't seem so outlandish after all. Not that I'm proud of such loutish behavior, but I found it of vital importance to ensure my proper "lubrication," considering what I was about to eat. Then again, could it really be so bad? I'd seen Anthony Bourdain enjoying some torpedo soup on his television program, and there's a guy who clearly loves good meat. *I'm sure it won't be as terrible as I imagine it to be,* I reassured myself.

And then my dinner arrived.

First, I have to note that there was no attempt by the chef to disguise the nature of the dish, to serve it in a way that one could perhaps pretend to be eating something else, by, for example, chopping it into tiny chunks and braising it in a stew with lots of big vegetables. No chance of that here—my plate contained a helping of carrots, a helping of shredded cabbage, a tomato wedge, and a boiled, sliced bull penis with a sad dollop of orange sauce on top. Our jaws hit the floor in shock and disgust. We could make out everything—the glans, the urethra, *everything.* "Dude," said my pal Sam, "I'd rather suck a dick right now than eat a dick." All eyes turned to me. Would I do it?

"Well," I told my friends, "it was on my list, and now it's on my plate, so I don't see any other choice than to give it a try." I tentatively removed a pale hunk of penis from the plate with my chopsticks, dipped it in the orange mystery sauce, and popped it into my mouth with a courageous flourish as my friends applauded and observed with unbridled curiosity about what would happen next. I'd like to say that I chewed it up, thoughtfully considering its flavors, getting to the bottom of its pizzle-y essence, after which I swallowed the mouthful and pronounced it good. Tragically, such was not the case. Flavor-wise, I was safe—it basically tasted like boiled blandness with sauce. But the thing was hard. I mean really hard, like a ball of solid gristle. When I bit down, my teeth felt some resistance, and when I increased my jaw pressure to bite through it, still more resistance, my mouthful of food staging a defiant coup in opposition to being eaten. I could barely masticate the damned thing at all, forcing me to spit the half-gnawed, soggy clump of bull penis back onto my plate as my buddies alternately laughed and moaned in disgust. And for all I knew, the cooks in the back were doing the same, ridiculing the absurd *gaijin* for ordering something that they'd put on the menu as both a joke and a dare. Still, I was on a mission, and I wasn't looking to give up—I'd be buried in the cold, cold ground before I was bested by a mere bull's penis. It was time to cowboy up. Filling my glass to near overflowing, I shoved the semichewed object back into my mouth, clamped my teeth around it like a pissed-off crocodile, and forced myself to chew through the tough mass until it was broken up just enough to choke back with a glassful of beer. And then it was over. I'd done it.

Now, I have had some sour meals in my day, but this was an abomination, the single most repugnant piece of food I'd ever placed in my mouth, causing me to invent a new category of culinary description: unconscionably disgusting. Fortunately, I have yet to eat anything else that qualifies for the term, but if I ever do, it will definitely join boiled bull pizzle on the list of foods to avoid at all costs. Suffice it to say, I now know to trust my internal alarm system, especially when contemplating the pairing of words like *cheap* and *penis* when I'm scrutinizing a menu. But it was done, thank God, and time to move on.

Fo' shizzle.

Maybe Vampires Are On to Something

Of all the parts of an animal, all its meat and bones and various organs, nothing carries more of a cultural stigma or taboo than blood. Not even brains (and I'd get to those soon enough). In the Jewish, Islamic, and early Christian traditions, particularly, many felt that the blood housed the soul; hence, it was a disgraceful and unclean practice to consume blood in any way, or even to touch it. Even today, Orthodox and other highly observant Jews must cleanse themselves in a ritual bath, or mikvah, after coming into contact with it. That's some hard-core taboo. Other cultures did and do not share this belief. In fact, many Scandinavian people felt it would be not only a waste but an insult to an animal to leave the blood unused, and you can often find it in their cuisine.

Elsewhere in the world, blood itself has been used as a source of nutrition for thousands of years by many nomadic peoples, one of the best known being the Masai in Kenya and Tanzania, a people for whom cows are currency, and the very basis for their economic and class systems (no vegetarians *there*, boy howdy). They will pierce the cow's vein with an arrow at a close distance and collect a fair amount of the resulting blood in a bowl, after which they stanch the wound and let the cow heal, making the animal a renewable source of nutrients. With the blood on hand, they either consume it right then and there, or mix it with milk. Blood poured into boiling milk is considered an African delicacy—the two combine together and congeal to form a kind of scrambled egg consistency. This thickening property is actually one of the most desirable attributes of using blood in the kitchen, and many chefs throughout the world employ it in a wide range of soups, stews, and other dishes.

This, in fact, is where we get "black puddings" and "black sausage," which owe their color to the presence of blood as a thickener. Sounds kind of terrible and not a little bit gruesome, but if you've never had it, I highly recommend availing yourself of some quality blood sausage if you enjoy things that taste good. Although blood, technically speaking, is not meat, my mission to sample every culinary possibility afforded us by our bovine friends pretty much made it impossible for me to avoid. Plus, it's delicious. So, once again, I couldn't help but betray my religion's laws of kashrut in the name of carnivorism, especially when it came to *boudin noir*, the traditional French blood sausage. Boudin is a Cajun delicacy, one I've long had a love affair with, though most of the Cajun variety of this dish is *boudin blanc*, or white boudin, which has seasoned pork liver and rice, but no blood. Fortunately, the Poles share the French affinity for black sausage, and in my predominantly Polish neighborhood with all its tiny, smoky, family-owned butcher shops and meat markets (Emily's Pork Store comes to mind), footlong, wrist-thick links of blood sausage are a breeze to come by. Made with beef blood and buckwheat groats instead of white rice, the Polish variety of this dish, grilled until almost splitting apart, is an intensely rich thing to savor, as I did in my backyard during my Tour de Boeuf. A quick trip to the little Polski Meat Market on Manhattan Avenue in Greenpoint, and I came away with two gorgeous black beauties flecked through with bits of fat and buckwheat. While some sort of fruit pairing (a pear compote or caramelized apples, for instance) can help cut and counterbalance the deep opulence of the dish, it's perfectly amazing on its own. A single taste is all it should take to make you renounce the stigma about eating blood and conclude that maybe poor Nosferatu got a bad rap for the wrong reasons.

I should also use this boudin discussion to make a note about haggis and other sausagelike examples of the pleasures of offal. After all, haggis, for all of its strange ingredients (heart, liver, lungs, and so on), is really just a very large sausage, its contents stuffed into a sheep's stomach, which isn't all that different from a natural hot dog casing. These dishes were invented centuries ago, by thoughtful farmers and hunters who discovered that an animal's organs are quick to spoil and can easily be preserved if you chop them up, add some grain—usually oatmeal, in the case of haggis—and maybe a bit of onion and seasoning, smoke the thing out there in the field, and there you have it, a nice package of food waiting for a hungry afternoon up there in the highlands. But you don't have to take my word for it; much better things have been said about this delicacy by ole Robbie Burns, Scotland's late, beloved national poet, whose most famous songs and poems include, naturally, "Address to a Haggis." Scots take great pride in Burns's contribution to the arts of their nation, and every year on his birthday, January 25, they gather to read his songs and poems and, of course, eat a big, hot haggis. If you've ever read this poem (and you can get past the dialect), you'll know that it's a brilliant ode to the inherent splendor of this dish. As Burns writes, near the middle of the poem:

His knife see rustic Labour dight,
An' cut ye up wi' ready slight,
Trenching your gushing entrails bright
Like onie ditch;
And then, O what a glorious sight,
Warm-reekin, rich!

Hooray! Three cheers for warm-reekin, rich entrails! The Scots have every reason to treasure the poet as well as the dish, as this is truly a testament to the beautiful, poetic carnivorism of the eighteenth century. Later, Burns goes on to extol haggis's health benefits, not to mention actively disdaining those who mock the Scottish delicacy, particularly the French and Italians, whose own cuisine Burns attests would make a pig vomit:

Is there that owre his French ragout
Or olio that wad staw a sow,
Or fricassee wad mak her spew
Wi' perfect sconner,
Looks down wi' sneering, scornfu' view
On sic a dinner?

Poor devil! see him owre his trash,
As feckless as a wither'd rash,
His spindle shank, a guid whip-lash,
His nieve a nit;
Thro' bluidy flood or field to dash,
O how unfit!

But mark the Rustic, haggis-fed,
The trembling earth resounds his tread.
Clap in his walie nieve a blade,
He'll make it whissle;

An' legs, an' arms, an' heads will sned,
Like taps o' thrissle.

That "poor devil" Burns alludes to, the non-haggis-fed one, has tiny fists the size of a nut ("his nieve a nit") and spindly legs unfit to even carry him across a battlefield, whereas your average, haggis-eating Scotsman is deft and hearty enough to lop off people's arms and heads as though they were the tops of thistles—basically a big, defiant middle finger by the poet toward pretentious culinary snobs. Even if I didn't enjoy haggis for its own merits, Burns's assertion that doing so would make the trembling earth resound my tread (*nice*) is certainly an endorsement. Let's see some watery-skinned, anemic vegan produce an "Address to a Tofurkey" and have it be filled with such passion and resounding power. "Poor devil," indeed. Also, I can't help but wonder how many other famous poets are renowned for their odes to meat (like Billy Collins's "Osso Buco"). What a marvelous idea that is. Future carnivorous literary icons of the world, I implore you: Let the meat poetry continue!

Here in the United States, while haggis is sadly reviled (actor/comedian Mike Myers, in *So I Married an Axe Murderer*, though he plays a Scottish character, proclaims that most Scottish food is based on a dare), we do have several nice analogues. I don't know what it is about the Pennsylvania Dutch, but they have an affinity for offal rivaling that of even the most stout-hearted Scotsman. For centuries they've been known to partake in the glorious "waste nothing" school of culinary thought, especially when it comes to pigs. Two dishes in particular come to mind: hog maw, which is sausage, potatoes, onions, and seasonings stuffed into a pig's stomach and boiled (very much like haggis in that regard); and scrapple, literally the scraps of pork leftover after the rest of the hog is butchered—including snouts, jowls, tongues, livers, and hearts—which are boiled, then mixed with cornmeal to make a mash, and the whole thing cools into a large brick of porcine deliciousness. Scrapple is usually sliced, fried in butter, and served on a sandwich or as an accompaniment to eggs on the breakfast plate, and is recommended for those people who both love pork and have super-functional cyborg cardiovascular systems surgically implanted by government scientists, like the Six Million Dollar Man. Because really, delicious as it is, this stuff will kill you. I'd be surprised if there didn't exist a version of the board game Clue in Pennsylvania that had a block of scrapple alongside the revolver, the candlestick, and the length of rope as one of the murder weapons—as in "It was Miss Scarlet, in the study, with the scrapple!"

Unfortunately, there have yet to be any major additions to the field of poetry on the subjects of either hog maw or scrapple, but hey, the twenty-first century is yet young . . .

"Things Best Enjoyed with Fava Beans and Nice Chianti" for $500, Alex

While in many contexts eating an animal's liver is a special occasion, a luxury meal—foie gras, for instance—or maybe a nostalgic cultural one (a chopped-chicken-liver sandwich in a Jewish deli, say), dining on a cow's liver doesn't seem to conjure up the same sense of either gastronomic joy or old-world charm. I'd go so far as to say that the notion of eating a classic pairing of liver and onions is hardly ideal, maybe even disgusting, to most Americans. I know this, because I've done an informal survey, which resulted in a delightful array of gag faces, "yuck" sounds, and mimed strangulation and purging. These people, I have to say, clearly have no idea what's good for them.

I mean this both literally and figuratively. A calf's liver, in moderation, is extremely good for you, being so rich in protein and essential iron, which the body needs to be strong and healthy. This is why, in the days before Flintstones multivitamins and iron-enriched foods, American mothers were told to feed calves' livers to their children, who, more often than not, immediately developed an instinctive, lifetime loathing of the dish. I won't blame it on the children, though—liver is certainly an acquired taste. What kid would choose foie gras over, say, Cocoa Puffs?

As an organ, liver is one of the largest and most nutritionally dense a cow has to offer, assuming that it comes from a very young cow or a calf. As *The Food Lover's Companion* puts it, "Because liver acts as a clearinghouse for substances that enter the body, it tends to store and absorb unwanted chemicals, medicines and hormones that an animal might be fed. Naturally, the older the animal the greater accumulation of these unwanted substances, which, according to some, offset liver's nutritional value."

I never had liver growing up, for the same reason I was never forced to eat tongue: my mother had been fed those dishes, they appalled her, and she had no desire to cook them for herself, her husband, or her children. Not that my father would have permitted it had she tried. "She knows better than to serve me liver," he told me, shuddering in pure disgust. "I would have vomited it up right there at the table." And yet as an adult, I eventually learned to adore that characteristic iron-y flavor of all kinds of livers, from lesser expensive chickens to insanely priced foie gras. But I'd never ordered calf's liver in a restaurant, been served it by friends, or cooked it myself. It was about time, I thought, to check out one of the classics, a simple *fegato alla Veneziana* (Venetian liver), or, put more plainly, "sautéed liver and onions."

As difficult as I imagine making a wonderful headcheese must be, that's precisely how easy cooking veal liver is, and it's wonderfully flavorful, provided of course that your ingredients are good. First, I have to say that I derive a certain macabre joy out of any recipe that begins with the words "wash thoroughly to remove any membranes, blood and veins . . ." I also love this recipe because it's time tested, reliable, appealing to the palate, and, most important, simple. Other than a nice piece of liver (no more than a pound, depending on how many people you're planning to feed), an onion, and a whole lot of butter, you're good to go with whatever simple side dish you or your cooking companion enjoys. In this case I was going for a classic, 1950s comfort food kind of vibe, so I made this one the way I imagined families enjoyed it while watching Donna Reed and Jackie Gleason on their tiny black-and-white television sets—which is to say accompanied by mashed potatoes and simple steamed vegetables.

The key to this dish, other than using plenty of butter, of course, is to make sure you slice both the pieces of liver and the onions very, very thin. Browned and reduced in butter until soft and golden, the onions go on the side as you place the seasoned liver slices (a little salt and pepper is all it takes) into the same skillet, again with more butter. Brown them quickly on both sides and place them on top of your onions, and you'll begin to note the wonderful aroma filling your kitchen with meaty, oniony goodness. Deglaze the pan with a little red wine, pour the pan gravy over the meat and onions (as well as the potatoes, depending on how much of it you have), give them a quick toss, and there you go: a classic made simple, wonderful from the sweetness of the onion—I love the Vidalia or Spanish varieties—balanced by the rich meatiness of the liver. It shouldn't take you more than thirty minutes to make a savory, nutritious, wholesome meal.

Just be wary about feeding it to your kids, unless you know for certain that they enjoy liver. Hey, anything can happen, right?

Hot Tongue Action on the Lower East Side

While many people have an aversion to liver, it's usually because of the flavor more than anything else. When cooked, it really just looks like another piece of meat, not very scary at all, though the flavor is of course markedly different. Not so with tongue. This is yet another of the meats my grandmother fed my mother in her childhood, and another one she always despised, mostly because, frankly, it looks like a big honking tongue cut out of an animal's mouth. It's easy to disassociate ourselves from a lot of different meats because they don't really look like much we can see as parts of our own bodies when we look in the mirror; we may know what muscle tissue or a liver looks like from seeing them in medical books, but there's a disconnect when we go to eat them. It's too easy to forget that we humans are also made of meat, much of which is scarcely different from that of other animals. The exceptions to this phenomenon are the organs that look like exactly what they are. Heart comes to mind, here, and maybe eyeballs. Many people also have trouble eating "trotters," or feet, usually from lambs or pigs. Taking a look at the deli case or the butcher's display cabinet and seeing a huge beef or veal tongue is enough to send these fussy folks screaming for the door, because it's very obviously a tongue. No way of deluding yourself: all told, it looks like Gene Simmons had an extremely bad day, and the result ended up there.

Again, as with liver, I'm a fan of tongue. It's a true delicacy, one that's served proudly in the best kosher delicatessens in the country, which is why I decided to go to the famous Katz's deli for a nice tongue sandwich instead of making my own. The textural antithesis to tenderloin, the tongue is one of an animal's most used muscles and hence is very strong, lean, and dense, so if you're going to cook it, you'd best either cure it somehow by soaking it in brine for a long period, or just boil the hell out of it, neither of which I was really up for, especially because Katz's tongue is one of their famous house specialties—theirs was going to be tastier than anything I could possibly come up with even on my most brilliant day in the kitchen, so I thought it best to leave it to the experts.

Located on Houston Street on the Lower East Side, which before it became a haven for hipster artists and musicians was filled with Eastern European Jewish immigrants, Katz's is one of the few remaining classic Jewish delis in New York, a stupendous testament to the shameless carnivorism of my forebears. Gigantic salamis hang proudly in the window, announcing to the world, "Come in! Come in! We have MEAT in here!" And oh boy, do they ever: chopped liver, bologna, pastrami, salami, corned beef, chicken, turkey, knobblewurst, knock-wurst, frankfurters, you name it (so long as it didn't come from a pig, of course). A simple pastrami sandwich (you have to pay extra if you want it lean or extra-lean, though I don't know any sane person who would go to a restaurant like this for a healthy meal) comes piled so high with spicy, salty, wondrously fatty meat that the place should probably have its own cardiac defibrillation machines on the premises, just in case one of their patrons keels over from a heart attack right there in the restaurant.

My two hungry friends and I ordered our sandwiches, along with a few pints of the brown ale the Brooklyn Brewing Company makes specifically for Katz's, and girded our bellies for the long haul ahead. Dan opted for the corned beef—and a quick note about that: As a meat, it has nothing to do whatsoever with corn, not counting the animal's diet. *Corning* is just an old English word for the curing process, as *corn* referred to a grain of salt used to brine the beef, which generally comes from tougher parts of the cow such as brisket, plate, or round. Pastrami is similar to corned beef but takes the process one step further. After brining, the meat is rubbed with spices (particularly black pepper, then everything else according to taste, including garlic, basil, allspice, red pepper, and cloves), then smoked. Done right, pastrami is a spicy, smoky, fatty, beautiful thing. And, in the immortal words of George Costanza, pastrami is "the most sensual of the smoked, cured meats."

For me, though, it was all tongue that night. Compared to the corned beef or pastrami, my sandwich—which was composed of only meat and mustard on rye bread, no need for vegetables other than the plate of homemade pickles served to each lucky diner—was remarkably lean and had the kind of grainy, spongy consistency you might expect from a processed lunchmeat, only I knew for certain that it wasn't. Let's see Oscar Mayer try to market sliced tongue to their consumer base—good luck with *that*. Since I didn't see the actual tongue from which my sandwich meat had been sliced, it might have been easy for me to forget what I was eating, so long as I didn't take a good, hard look at the meat itself. No doubt about it—given its singular texture, it was definitely tongue, and it was definitely good. Salty, smoky, with a nice beef flavor, it was a pleasant alternative to its fattier relatives behind the sandwich counter. I devoured the entire thing, a feat I can rarely accomplish when it comes to one of those towering pastrami master-pieces I usually order. And I felt great afterward, with none of that cement-in-my-stomach feeling that's often a sad side effect of ingesting huge quantities of the more lipid-licious cured meats. Aside from a higher-than-normal sodium content (given the curing), as well as the fact that my portion was well above the amount a normal person should eat in a single meal, beef or veal tongue is actually a fairly healthy choice when it comes to eating parts of a cow.

Again, if this is something you have yet to experience, go to the butcher shop and order up some nice sliced tongue. Better yet, make a picnic lunch for your friends with a basket filled with tongue sand-wiches, and don't tell them what they're eating until they've pro-nounced judgment. I'd be willing to bet dollars to doughnuts that until they find out, they'll fully enjoy their meal. Sometimes it takes a little artful subterfuge to get people to enjoy certain delicacies they'd never try on their own. Sure, you might get punched ("Son of a bitch! You made me eat *tongue*?"), but you also might get thanked for introducing someone to the long-treasured joys of a cured meat few people have the temerity to order. In the end, isn't it worth the risk?

Putting a Foot in Your Mouth

If all the various edible parts of an animal were ranked by their desir-ability on a scale of one to ten, ten being the most sought after and zero being the most abhorred, feet would probably score in the low ones, somewhere above brains but well below, say, tongue. That revulsion against feet on the supper plate exists mostly in the English-speaking world, however; in other parts of the globe, this cut conjures up little disgust. We're quick to disguise the dish, like other offal, by slapping it with an adorable euphemism ("trotters") or one with a historical vibe to it ("cow's heel"). Trotters, particularly of sheep and pigs, do have a storied history in Britain, although the *Oxford Dictionary of Food* is quick to note that "generally, the treatment of feet in Britain reflected a desire to use up all of an animal, rather than gastronomic aspirations."

On the other hand, there are many cultures that adore feet—although there's little meat to be found on them, they're filled with cartilage, tendons, and gristle that, when cooked appropriately, provide a wealth of wonderful gelatin. This is why some people are keen to note that when you take a bite of Jell-O, you're eating hooves. While that might once have been the case, today's gelatin, though it does still come from animals (there's no real vegetable source of gelatin), is not usually made from hooves and horns.

So, when it came time for me to eat some feet, picking up a package of gummy bears or marshmallow Peeps at the corner store wouldn't quite cut it. I'd have to get the real thing, though as you can imagine, I wasn't leaping at the opportunity to cook it myself. There are a few restaurants in New York that serve fancy preparations of pigs' trotters (a couple of classic French dishes include *pieds et paquets*—kind of like a French haggis—as well as *à la Sainte-Menehould*, which incorporates a mustard sauce), but I was on the prowl for cow parts, not pork. One noted dish is calf's-foot jelly, long considered a potent restorative for invalids, especially in Jewish culture, in which you can find recipes for a savory version called *petcha* (simply add sugar for a sweeter variety). But I'm still not jumping out of my chair for recipes including the words *foot* and *jelly*. I don't care if it *is* part of my culinary heritage—that combination of terms makes me think only of unspeakably foul things discovered on a locker room carpet.

As with many other types of offal, I'd look to Mexico for help. In true Mexican cuisine (not Tex-Mex) you'll find almost every part of the cow used as a filling for tacos, everything from tripe to tongue and, yes, feet, known here as *pata*. One of my favorite neighborhood haunts, and

in fact the place where I bought my first meal as a New York City resident, is a tiny Mexican grocery store with a kitchen in back. Again, this
isn't the type of "Mexican" restaurant where you might find slushy
machines filled with prefab frozen margaritas, heaping platters of chili
nachos, or deep-fried, cruise-missile-sized chimichangas, you know,
the kinds of places with names like Señor Sombrero's or La Casa Loco!
No, this is about as authentic as you can get this far away from Mexico,
which is why I so adore it. The price for my simple order of *dos tacos
de pata con salsa verde, para llevar, por favor* amounted to all of four
bucks, the warm, soft corn tortillas spilling over not just with bits of
slowly boiled, seasoned meat from a cow's foot, but also a gorgeous
green salsa, chopped fresh cilantro, diced onions, a few lime wedges,
and a generous helping of crunchy sliced radishes on the side. It was
cheap, filling, and staggeringly flavorful, and I made a note to myself to
express my appreciation for our neighbors to the south more often, or
at least hit them up more frequently for some delicious *pata*. Say what
you will about the immigration debate—if, in the end, opening up our
borders a wee bit results in more food like this, I'm all for it.

Eat Your Heart Out

Aside from brains, the heart is probably the one organ that turns people off the most, and it's not difficult to understand why—whole, the
organ does not look appetizing. It's a big, tough hunk of muscle filled
with all sorts of tubes and valves, and covered with weirdly textured
fats on the outside. It's a utilitarian organ, a pumping station made out
of meat. It's also quite tasty, if you're willing to cook it properly.

Like most other offal from cows, the veal variety of this organ is often recommended, on account of its relative tenderness, although some
people do prefer the more robust beef taste of an older animal's heart.
I picked up my two lovely-looking veal hearts at Ottomanelli's when
Frank called to let me know that he'd gotten some good ones in. This

is a double benefit of befriending your butcher—not only will he contact you personally when he acquires a product he knows you'll like, he'll make certain that it's of the highest quality. This was actually the second order of hearts Frank had received in the past week—he had turned down the first one because they didn't look good enough to his well-trained butcher's eyes. And if you're going to eat an animal's heart out, you want it to be very, very fresh.

Because the muscle fiber in a heart has been so thoroughly worked—no way to prevent that, short of killing the animal—you're best off marinating your heart. I used a recipe recommended by a brilliant California chef named Chris Cosentino, of the San Francisco restaurant Incanto. Like Momofuku's David Chang, Cosentino is a man of many meats, with an abiding passion for offal. He even runs a website, www.offalgood.com, devoted to the pleasures of eating organs, with recipes including everything from pig's head to tripe to duck "fries" (that's testicles, of course). His preparation for beef heart was a little intense for me—it involves a rather complicated-sounding beet salad—so I simply stuck with the heart itself, which I would marinate in a special mixture of herbs, a little oil, and orange juice (the acid helps break down the tough muscle tissue, remember) and then grill, slice, and serve on top of a nice bed of field greens.

I was a little tentative about throwing a couple of whole hearts onto the grill for fear of overcooking them, since hearts are quick to dry out and turn leathery if left on the heat for too long, but I was relieved to discover that it was really quite easy. Just a few minutes on each side over medium-high heat, one turn, and that was that. Sliced very thinly, like flank steak, the meat made a stoutly beefy addition to my lunchtime salad, and a healthy one at that, since it was so lean. The orange juice in the marinade gave the heart an exquisite zing, and there was no risk of apprehension about its appearance, either, since it didn't look at all like a heart anymore, now that it was sliced and beautifully medium rare. I had a feeling I'd be returning to this recipe sometime in the near future, should Frank give me that fateful call that he had some more fresh veal hearts in stock. I could even enjoy it if I decided to go on a health kick. After all, what could be better as a heart-healthy recipe than heart?

The Lovely Bones

It's a devastating shame that most Americans—at least most Americans I know—have little or no experience with the divine joys of simple, elegant roasted marrow. Among all carnivorous delights, it's perhaps the most basic. Maybe people are scared by the fact that you have to scoop the stuff out of an animal's severed shinbone, or maybe they're just in the dark. Who knows? Something, I'm not sure what, has gone terribly awry here—at one point in history, marrow was one of the most prized of delicacies, requiring its own special silver spoon. (How's *that* for a relevant metaphor!) Back in the day, despite the fact that marrow was seen as a wholly masculine food, Queen Victoria herself was known to enjoy marrow toast every day. Truly, this is a regal food if ever there was one. Today, though, you can find it only at the most schmancy of steakhouses, or in restaurants with chefs who've realized that a few dollars of veal bones can be the basis for an appetizer so good it might well turn your heart into molten jelly.

Fact is, all it takes is a good butcher, a very hot oven, and a little sea salt, and you're in store for some of the purest gastronomic bliss to be derived from a cow. It's stupidly uncomplicated, and not even very expensive. Just ask your loyal butcher—whom I'm sure, at this point, you're very good friends with—for a few pounds of veal marrow bones, making sure he cuts them into one- to two-inch segments, though he'll likely know exactly what to do if he's worth his salt. They should be nice and white, with a meaty red center and maybe a little blood in the bag. Usually they'll be frozen, but that's nothing to worry about; that's done for the sake of freshness, since most retail butchers don't normally get much call for the things. Now here's the tricky part—you need to soak them to leach out the blood. Put your lovely bones in a pot with a couple of tablespoons of salt and enough ice water to cover them for at least twelve hours, up to a whole day, before you get cooking. Keep the pot in the fridge and change the water every six hours or so, making sure to add another couple of tablespoons of salt when you do.

After that, all you need to do is drain them, and the hard part's all done with. Place your bones straight up on an oiled baking sheet (very important—you don't want your bones to bake straight onto the tin), and roast them in a preheated 450-degree oven for fifteen to twenty-five minutes, until you start to see the marrow puff out over the top. If you can stick a metal skewer straight down all the way through the bone without meeting any resistance, you're done. Serve on a platter with some toast points, a little coarse sea salt, and some small spoons for proper scooping—espresso spoons are remarkably good for these purposes, as are escargot forks, if you happen to have any of those lying around—and you've just made your friends the perfect carnivorous appetizer. I know it seems silly the way people get all poetic about bone marrow, but you'll only think that until you've tried it. First, the presentation of bones on a stark plate with a little toast and salt is arrestingly beautiful, not the sort of thing that most people see every day, and something that doesn't require any work. The bones speak for themselves. And as for the taste, well . . . the hot, white nutritious goo that you scoop out of those bones is, as one person put it, "butter from God." It's almost like eating pure, hot fat, only more delicate, airier, not as sinfully greasy. The Italians have long known the rich sensuality of bone marrow, which is what makes osso bucco such a notable dish. But for me, roasting is the only way to go, and my friends who enjoyed this treat with me were more than happy to dig into these bones once they'd come out of the oven, hot and soft and ready to be attacked with eager spoons.

Moans and swooning ensued, with the taste of rich, hot marrow exactly enough to get my friends into the appropriate carnivorous mood without spoiling their appetite. Which was good, because I was about to feed them something really special.

Kidney Punch

While my friends had no trouble merrily poking at bones to scrape out every last bit of the marrow therein, the thought of eating a kidney had most of them going all pallid and squishy-willed. Apparently, they're not alone. We all know what kidneys do, after all: excrete liquid waste. Okay, so maybe Americans are a little apprehensive about having their food taste like piss, I can understand that. But it doesn't have to, not if prepared properly, so why not go out on a limb and find out what the rest of the world is enjoying? We're lagging behind, here, American carnivores—let's get our heads in the game.

There are plenty of French recipes for veal kidneys—as I mentioned, *rognon de veau* with a mustard sauce is a classic—but I decided to abandon frog cuisine for a bit and go with something a little heartier: veal kidneys in Madeira sauce, Russian-style. The first step, as in any preparation of this particular organ, should be to remove the outer covering of fat and membrane (Frank Ottomanelli had conveniently already done this for me, thank goodness), then slice the thing in twain to remove the tough white core running down the middle. Once that's done, I cut the kidney up into small, quarter-inch-wide chunks, noticing that while the organ looked very much like liver—it had that same pale burgundy color of the calf's *fegato* I'd made earlier—the consistency was much more plump and firm. Yet another reason why people who cook kidneys tend to braise them in a sauce to let them tenderize, which is precisely what I was doing. With a little help from my friend Emily, some chopped onion and sliced mushrooms, a roux of flour and chicken stock, and of course a whole lot of butter, my kidneys were soon simmering away atop the stove and looking pretty tasty. Problem was, even after being simmered for half an hour, the kidney slices didn't seem to be getting much less firm. Ultimately, not wanting to let the sauce cook down too far, I had to just go ahead and serve the dish and hope for the best. It turned out to be very much something you would expect from Russian cuisine: dark, rich, fragrant, and filling, the kind of hearty meal you'd want if you had to live through a long, cold Moscow winter.

The reaction was mixed. Some of my friends—shamefully timid carnivores, I'm sad to report—wouldn't even get near the dish, despite its enticing aroma. They'd had no problem with bones, but the mere idea of eating an organ devoted to processing pee was just too much for them to bear, and they chickened out. My friend Martin, however, went in the opposite direction. Maybe it's the fact that he's Swedish, and the Scandinavian culture has a long, proud tradition of eating foods that would make even the sturdiest sailor lose his lunch, but dear Marty took to the recipe with relish. "It's got a great mushroomy flavor to it, very rich, like a good stroganoff," he noted. And the kidneys? "Pretty good, actually. I was hesitant at first, but the sauce really makes it." The consensus in the end, was, first, that the kidneys had absolutely no urine or ammonia taste to them at all, but rather a rich iron flavor akin to liver, though not quite as strong. We also agreed on the texture. The kidney slices, for all their stewing, still had a firmness to them at first bite, which soon dissipated, almost like biting into a plump grape, but meaty. It was wholly new, and surprisingly good, for most of us who were unafraid to indulge. On the other hand, Nina nearly gagged on the dish. "It tasted like bloody rubber," she claimed, adding "Blech!" Oh well, you know what they say: one man's meat is another's poison. Fact is, if you don't give it a shot, how will you know your meat from your poison?

Using Your Brains

I thought that the final dish of the evening, my big carnivorous coup de grâce—and indeed, the last of all the offal I would eat on my adventure in organ meats—would prove to be the most difficult for people to eat, but oddly enough this was not to be the case at all. Turns out, if you want Americans to step up and taste something new, all you need to do is serve it fried.

Even calf's brains.

I saved the brains for last, not because of the "ick factor," or because even I was apprehensive. Rather, I wanted to finish my tour of the inner workings of a calf with its brain because, first, I had absolutely no clue how to prepare it, and second, I was dying to try it, so it gave me something to look forward to. The first time I asked Frank Ottomanelli about getting me the ingredient, I was terrifically excited. How often do you really get to tell someone that you're looking for brains and have them act like you're deadly serious, without any snappy comebacks (i.e., "Yeah, I heard you could really use some!"). All Frank said when I called him up with the order was "Thursday. We usually get them in on Thursday." Apparently, I wasn't the only one looking forward to a nice dinner of calf's brains.

Believe it or not, brains are eaten throughout much of the world, and have been for centuries. The French prepare them poached with browned butter and capers (of course), and they have a notable history of being enjoyed in many other cultures as well. According to the *Oxford Companion to Food*, "in most countries they are marketed and eaten without any special inhibitions, although (one might add) without overpowering enthusiasm." It's easy to note that people value brains for their creamy consistency, but just as easy to see why they also might be disgusted by the things—they're *brains*, after all.

Case in point: When I picked up my veal brains at the butcher shop, all squishy and bloody in a clear plastic bag, it was easily the most gruesome and disgusting raw ingredient I'd ever purchased or planned to cook in my entire life. A bag of brains! It was like something straight out of a horror film, and in fact, it's difficult if not downright impossible for a person to buy, cook, or eat brains without lapsing into the monotonous droning of the undead in all those zombie movies we grew up on ("Braaaaaiiinnnnsss . . . *braaiinnnnnsssss!*"), followed by cheerful, childlike giggling. A person like me, anyhow. At the very least, there's a good chance you'll get the Scarecrow's song from *The Wizard of Oz* stuck in your head, causing you to absentmindedly whistle that refrain for a couple of days, minimum: "I would dance and be merry / Life would be a ding-a-derry / If I only had a brain!"

When I went to pick up my order, I spoke with Frank briefly about eating brains, and he was candid as always. "I've had them, sure, but they're not my favorite." I was about to be disappointed in my butcher—perhaps he wasn't as carnivorous as I'd thought—until he continued. "When I was a kid, my dad would get us a whole lamb's head as a special treat. My brother loved the brains, loved them, way more than me. You know what I loved? The eyeballs. I used to ask him, 'Hey, I'll trade you my brains for your eyeball,' and he'd always do it. We'd both win." Oh my, I thought. Growing up in the Ottomanelli household must have been *something*. My immediate reaction of course was to ask if I could get some eyeballs for myself. "Nope," said Frank. "Not unless you buy the whole head."

"Let's just start with the brain," I told him. "We can work our way up to the whole head eventually."

When it came to preparation, there were a few options. "Scrambled eggs with brains" is, I was interested to learn, a fairly popular dish in certain parts of the country, though I wasn't really sure if I'd be able to stomach some brains first thing in the morning. Thinking about all the dishes I'd explored during the course of my research, and their different preparations, I was aghast to realize that I had not deep-fried a single thing. In fact, the only deep-fried meat I'd enjoyed were the RMOs at Testy Festy, and those had been prepackaged, flash-frozen, and quickly reheated in some hot oil. Some kind of New Orleans native I was! The decision was made for me right then and there—I had no choice but to fry me up some brains.

The frying process itself was pretty simple, as frying generally is, but preparing the brains was a little more tricky. First, you have to be very careful with your main ingredient, since raw brains are mushy, delicate, and prone to falling to pieces. This seems simple, but not when you realize that you have to somehow remove that sticky, icky membrane that covers the entire organ, as well as any blood clots (*yech*). Don't want to be eating that, for certain. Then, according to Frank, one should poach the brains for about ten to fifteen minutes to firm them up enough to cook—it would be pretty much impossible to batter and fry them without doing so. After cautiously removing the brains from the boiling water and allowing them to cool, I had to delicately pick out any remaining membrane. Then you're into the home stretch. Break your brains up into bite-size pieces (how many times do you really get to say things like *that*); dip them in some seasoned, lightly beaten eggs; and coat them in flour. Shake off any excess, then pop them into some very hot oil. I like peanut oil for frying—it's more expensive than olive or vegetable oil, but it has a higher smoke point, which means that you can get it wicked hot before it begins to burn. Leave your brains to fry until golden brown on both sides, then remove and drain on a paper towel. Serve nice and hot with a few lemon wedges and perhaps some sauce for dipping, and there you go: fried brain tenders.

They were a hit. I was flabbergasted by this—who would've known that calf's brains would be the most popular dish of the night? The visual appeal was certainly a draw—on the outside the tenders looked like just about any other deep-fried foodstuff, so I was pretty sure people were eager to try them simply because of a shared association with other foods they've come to love. On the inside, though, it was a whole new ballgame. The brains were white and creamy. "Like a flan," one of my friends noted. I loved them, to tell you the truth, and found myself snacking on brain nuggets the rest of the evening as we drank beer and whisky and marveled at all the weird animal parts we'd consumed. The texture of fried veal brains is unlike anything else you're likely to have, though some of my guests were eager to note that they had to consciously try not to think about what they were eating in order to enjoy it. Others, like Brad (naturally) and myself, enjoyed them *because* we knew what we were eating.

Ultimately, I believe Martin probably put it best, when, with a smile and a mouth full of brains, he deemed them "crispy on the outside . . . *creepy* on the inside."

EPILOGUE

It's Monday, and for every native New Orleanian (even ones living in Brooklyn), that means it's red-beans-and-rice day. As I sit here writing away in my apartment, I have a nice big pot of red beans simmering away in the company of a truly splendid hock of ham, courtesy of a couple of friends whose brother—a vegetarian, if you'll believe it—gave them a twenty-five-pound whole country ham as a gift. I had to cut the thing off with a hacksaw, but that hock was my prize from Nina and Thea in exchange for helping them prepare and cook the gigantic ham, a process that included scrubbing the mold from its exterior, soaking it in cold water for two days, then slowly braising the thing in Dr Pepper. (It's an old southern recipe, I swear. You can also add a cup of pickle juice, if you want.) Eventually, the meat and fat will separate from the hock, mixing with the beans and adding to the dish an incomparable smoky, meaty richness. But that takes time. As I wait for the dish to simmer to perfect thickness and flavor, my kitchen gradually filling with the familiar, heady aroma from my childhood, I can't help but reflect on the fact that it's been one whole year since I began my exploration into the world of meat.

And what a year it's been.

After concluding all my research, all of the history and philosophy, the spirituality and ethics, the anthropology and biology and nutrition, after consuming every conceivable animal I could find and every part of the cow, I know, now more than ever, that being a carnivore is a truly wonderful thing. Meat is good for you, and so long as you're discerning and shy away from gluttony, know that you can eat the meat you love, be healthy, savor some splendid new taste sensations—and feel *great* about it. And while we might be taking fire from the go-veg militants on all sides, consider this: steakhouses are on the rise. It's true. In the hospitality industry, restaurants catering to carnivores are among the fastest-growing sectors, and the demand for high-quality meat continues to rise. Although this may mean that the prices of prime-grade cuts of steak will also inevitably increase, take this as your opportunity, as someone dedicated to the carnivorous cause, to seek out alternatives. Be adventurous!

Go out there and order the goat kebabs, feed your dinner guests a rack of llama or kangaroo tenderloin fillets, or even stew up some rattlesnake chili (just don't forget to wear gloves when you dice those peppers). Make friends with your butcher, for goodness' sake—it's a relationship that can be worth so much to both of you. Help out local farmers and buy their grass-fed, free-range beef or veal. Do yourself a huge favor and avoid the chicken nuggets made from reconstituted meat slurry—even if it means eating a few vegetarian meals, it's worth it to wait if the end result is a dinner of truly sublime, conscientiously raised pork, lamb, or beef, an evening out at your favorite restaurant, or a simple pot roast, prepared with love by a friend or relative. Just don't forget to be judicious, and to take your meat seriously. If you really want to put your carnivorism into perspective, go to the source yourself and take a hunting trip. See what it feels like to stalk and kill your dinner, the way our ancestors did for millions of years before we came along (a ritual that might just be the reason we humans—and our great big brains—came along at all). So long as you try to stay sensible and discriminating, feel free to speak out about your love of animals and their delicious flesh, carry the banner high and proudly, and remember that eating and loving meat is nothing to be ashamed of.

But enough of manifestos for now. My red beans are almost done, nearly ready to be enjoyed with my friends over an evening of good beer and bad jokes, in which we'll eat and pal around, blast some rock and roll, and tease each other mercilessly in my backyard as the sun descends in the late summer sky. And then, once everyone heads home, happy, slightly wobbly, with a bellyful of red beans and rice and ham and sausage, I'll reflect on what's to come next for the Shameless Carnivore.

You know what? I think I'll go fishing.

ACKNOWLEDGMENTS

When a writer publishes his first book, the sheer breadth of his grati-
tude is such that it generally results in the desire to engage in a sort of
infinite regression of thanks, to the point where he's tempted to go all
the way back to expressing his appreciation to the Universe for blowing itself up thirteen billion years ago to create life as we know it.
(Thank you, Universe, by the way.) But if I have to cap it somewhere,
I'll take it back to this point:

I'd like to thank the rabbit.

If it weren't for the fact that Katie McHugh—a dear friend and both
a brilliant editor and a carnivore—decided to order the rabbit during a
fateful lunch with a certain literary agent, this book would not exist.
That one dish spurred between Katie and this agent a spirited discussion about the nature of carnivorism, and hence the idea for the book
you hold right now. Katie, I don't think I could ever thank you enough

for suggesting (and truly believing) that I might be just the carnivore to pen a tome about carnivorism. You are the bee's knees wrapped in cat's pajamas. As for that agent, the incomparable Lisa Bankoff at ICM, I've always found it both puzzling and gratifying that you'd take such a whopping chance on an untested, unpublished, crazily exuberant person such as myself, and that no matter what insane ideas I'd come up with, you've afforded me nothing but your shrewd insight, considerate attention, and bulldoggish loyalty. Whatever good karma I drummed up in a previous lifetime that led me to you, it must've been a doozy. Thank you one million times over, and then some. And also thanks to Tina Dubois Wexler, for your excellent work and friendship, and for letting me into your home to cook you lamb chops.

I'd probably have to commit seppuku if I failed to thank my editor, Christine Pride, who not only believed in this project from the moment it landed on her desk, and who acquired it as though she were cast away on a desert island and my little proposal was the last scrap of roasted boar to be found, but whose savvy editorial direction and genuine faith never faltered once. Any writer would be truly blessed to have as his editor someone so damned *hungry*.

As for all of the wonderful people who were kind enough to submit their professional wisdom and opinions on the nature of meat and meat eating, your ranks are both legion and magnificent. Thanks to Dr. Craig Stanford for your insight on primate behavior and human evolution; to Kathleen Zelman for your fantastic contributions on diet and nutrition; to Dr. Rian Tannenbaum for medical advice (and many good laughs); to Mary Young and James "Bo" Reagan at the National Beef Cattleman's Association for the wonderfully comprehensive information on the benefits of beef and how to best prepare it; to Frank Ottomanelli and his brothers, the finest butchers I've known, for your geniality, sage advice, and, naturally, the very *best* meat; and to Eric Brown at my alma mater, Washington University in St. Louis, on philosophy. To the very venerable Lama Norlha Rinpoche, my warmest thanks not only for taking the time out of your formidable schedule to answer all my questions but also for the kindness, grace, and compassion you offered me at Kagyu Thubten Chöling during my visits. I pray for your long life and health. And the same appreciation applies to all the other extraordinary people at KTC who were kind enough to share their thoughts and meals with me, particularly Ani Jamdron, Tsultrim, Chonam, Lekshe Dorje, Ani Sonam, and Thubten.

It would be impossible to escape these acknowledgments without thanking Leroy, Peggy, and the magnificent "Mama" Nuckolls, as well as Vernon and Jimmy Crawford, for the kind of humble graciousness, humor, and neighborly generosity that you can only find in Louisiana, and that makes me pine terribly for home. The more time I spend with you, the more I reckon you might just make a good ole boy out of me yet. I can't wait.

To all of my friends, old and new, vegetarian and carnivorous, who both invited me into your homes so that I could make a horror show of your kitchens and joined in my various adventures, for your discriminating opinions on the food, for your excellent company, and for being kind enough not to spit the meat I cooked into napkins when I wasn't looking (or at least I assume): Dan Hewins; Hillary Hartman; Brad Bennett; Katie Hunt-Morr; Sam Morgan; Liz Schroeter; Nicole Johnson; Dan Backhaus; Julia Benedict; Marigny Lee; Kim Holmes; Tobias Rower; Loren Linder; Sarah Wefald; Jonathan Hanson; Martin Olson; Jessie Schwartz; Damon Metzner; Micaela Collins; Bobert Jenkins; Rudy Faust; Amy Fritch; Brendan Gilmartin; again to Tina and Doug Wexler; Ben and Margot Gibson (especially Ben, for contributing your intimidating artistic talent); Alys Kenny; The Fabulous Gunhouse Sisters, Nina and Thea; Brandon Bussinger; Liz Adele Allen; Hank Baker; Blake Johnson; Lyndon Roeller, for the excellent web support; Mahlon and Fiona Gross; Terri Hennessy; Emily Mahon; Wookosh Janik; and Jonathan Pastor, for the consistent and much needed positivity and support during the writing process. And all my heartiest bear hugs to everyone at South 4th Café—particularly Marshall, Aaron, Kim, Adam, and Jimmy (¡hermano!)—for giving me a home away from home in which to work, and for your outstanding coffee, free Internet, Goldfish crackers, and spirited encouragement.

A truly special thanks to Paul and Marilyn Jeanneney at Beaverwood Farm, not just for welcoming a total stranger into your home like an old friend, and not just for eagerly sharing your lives and thoughts on farming and food, not just for the steaks and ribs and jerky but also for the invaluable opportunity to experience and participate in the food chain firsthand, up close and very, very personal. Three bold cheers to you for being the kind of considerate, humane farmers that Americans can be proud of, and of which we should definitely have more. May you thrive in work and life.

Then there are my brothers, my two best friends in the world: Eric, who invited me to travel the entire breadth of the continental United States so that we could cook up some exotic meats in his home, play some music together, and, naturally, to have both of our minds exploded by the goings-on at Testicle Festival, I'll have you know that our adventures have only just begun, mon frère. Keep the grill ready for my return. And to Colin (or, I should say, Lama Tashi Namgyal), my big bubby, my very favorite vegetarian, thank you for your invigorating zeal in helping me understand some of the intricate complexities of Tibetan Buddhism, for your unwavering support, your patience, and, always, the inexhaustible bounty of your atrocious puns. When you attain nirvana, I'm fairly confident it will be to the sound of a vaudeville-era rim-shot.

And of course to my parents, Mel and Jacque Gold, who between them are, in my less-than-humble opinion, the most interesting, spirited, smart, caring, and talented couple on the face of the planet. Even on the best days, it takes a pair of fine, strong souls to believe in the power of familial love over all, that it is bigger than hurricanes and floods, stronger even than losing everything. You've always been there, my biggest cheerleaders, rooting me on no matter what ridiculous trouble I got into over the years, in the lean times and the fat ones, and no words in the back of a book could ever come close to capturing my appreciation for you. So I'll just leave it here with "Thank you" and "I love you."